The Law Commission
Consultation Paper No 195

CRIMINAL LIABILITY IN REGULATORY CONTEXTS

A Consultation Paper

ISBN: 9780118404938

Printed in the UK by The Stationery Office Limited
on behalf of the Controller of Her Majesty's Stationery Office

ID P002384581 08/10

Printed on paper containing 75% recycled fibre content minimum.

THE LAW COMMISSION – HOW WE CONSULT

About the Law Commission
The Law Commission was set up by section 1 of the Law Commissions Act 1965 for the purpose of promoting the reform of the law.

The Law Commissioners are: The Rt Hon Lord Justice Munby (*Chairman*), Professor Elizabeth Cooke, Mr David Hertzell, Professor Jeremy Horder and Miss Frances Patterson QC. The Chief Executive is: Mr Mark Ormerod CB.

Address for correspondence: Steel House, 11 Tothill Street, London SW1H 9LJ.

Topic of this consultation
This consultation paper deals with the use of the criminal law in regulatory contexts, and with some aspects of corporate criminal liability. A summary of the main points can be found in Part 1.

Scope of this consultation
The purpose of this consultation is to generate responses to our provisional proposals.

Geographical scope
The contents of this consultation paper refer to the law of England and Wales.

Impact assessment
An impact assessment is included.

Previous engagement N/A.

Duration of the consultation
We invite responses to our provisional proposals and questions from 25 August 2010 to 25 November 2010.

How to respond
Send your responses either –

By email to: criminal@lawcommission.gsi.gov.uk   OR   **By post to:**   address above.
                    Tel: 020-3334-0271 / Fax: 020-3334-0201

If you send your comments by post, it would be helpful if, whenever possible, you could send them to us electronically as well (for example, on CD or by email to the above address, in any commonly used format).

After the consultation
In the light of the responses we receive, we will decide our final recommendations and we will present them to Parliament. We hope to publish our report by Spring 2012. It will be for Parliament to decide whether to approve any changes to the law.

Code of Practice
We are a signatory to the Government's Code of Practice on Consultation and carry out our consultations in accordance with the Code criteria (set out on the next page).

Freedom of information
We will treat all responses as public documents in accordance with the Freedom of Information Act and we may attribute comments and include a list of all respondents' names in any final report we publish. If you wish to submit a confidential response, you should contact us before sending the response. PLEASE NOTE – We will disregard automatic confidentiality statements generated by an IT system.

Availability of this consultation paper
You can view/download it free of charge on our website at: **http://www.lawcom.gov.uk/docs/cp195.pdf**.

CODE OF PRACTICE ON CONSULTATION

○ **THE SEVEN CONSULTATION CRITERIA**

Criterion 1:   When to consult

Formal consultation should take place at a stage when there is scope to influence the policy outcome.

Criterion 2:   Duration of consultation exercise

Consultations should normally last for at least 12 weeks with consideration given to longer timescales where feasible and sensible

Criterion 3:   Clarity and scope of impact

Consultation documents should be clear about the consultation process, what is being proposed, the scope to influence and the expected costs and benefits of the proposals.

Criterion 4:   Accessibility of consultation exercises

Consultation exercises should be designed to be accessible to, and clearly targeted at, those people the exercise is intended to reach.

Criterion 5:   The burden of consultation

Keeping the burden of consultation to a minimum is essential if consultations are to be effective and if consultees' buy-in to the process is to be obtained.

Criterion 6:   Responsiveness of consultation exercises

Consultation responses should be analysed carefully and clear feedback should be provided to participants following the consultation.

Criterion 7:   Capacity to consult

Officials running consultations should seek guidance in how to run an effective consultation exercise and share what they have learned from the experience.

○ **CONSULTATION CO-ORDINATOR**

The Law Commission's Consultation Co-ordinator is Phil Hodgson.

○ You are invited to send comments to the Consultation Co-ordinator about the extent to which the criteria have been observed and any ways of improving the consultation process.

○ **Contact:**   Phil Hodgson, Consultation Co-ordinator, Law Commission, Steel House, 11 Tothill Street, London SW1H 9LJ – Email: phil.hodgson@lawcommission.gsi.gov.uk

Full details of the Government's Code of Practice on Consultation are available on the BIS website at http://www.bis.gov.uk/policies/better-regulation/consultation-guidance.

THE LAW COMMISSION

CRIMINAL LIABILITY IN REGULATORY CONTEXTS

CONTENTS

PART 1
REGULATION, BUSINESSES AND CRIMINAL LIABILITY[1]

OUR TERMS OF REFERENCE

1.1 In early 2009, it was agreed between the Ministry of Justice, the Department for Business, Innovation and Skills, and the Law Commission, that the Commission would undertake a project with the following broad aims:

> To introduce rationality and principle into the structure of the criminal law, especially when it is employed against business enterprises. In particular, this will involve the provision of non-statutory guidance to all Government departments on the grounds for creating criminal offences, and on what shape those offences should take.

> To consider whether there should be created a statutory power for the courts to apply a 'due diligence' defence (the burden of proof being on the accused) to a criminal offence.

1.2 It was agreed that the Law Commission would add to this project other issues arising out of its on-going work on corporate criminal liability, as a part of its 10th Programme of Law Reform. These issues were added because of their close connection to the project. These issues, which will be fully explained in due course, are:

> The scope of the consent and connivance doctrine. This doctrine imposes individual criminal liability on directors (or equivalent company officers) for crimes committed by their companies, if those individuals consented or connived at the commission of the offence.

> The status of the identification doctrine. This doctrine is used by courts to determine the basis on which corporate criminal liability arises under crimes requiring proof of fault created by statute. According to this doctrine, if a company is to be convicted of an offence, it must be possible to prove that the directors (or equivalent persons) themselves possessed the fault element in question.

> The status of the doctrine of delegation. According to this doctrine, if someone (X) delegates the running of the whole of their business to another person (Y), and Y then commits an offence in connection with the running of the business, it is not only Y who can be convicted of the offence. X can be convicted as well, even if X was in no way at fault respecting the commission of the offence by Y.

---

[1] The text of Part 1 is identical to the text of the Overview, "Criminal Liability in Regulatory Contexts", that we have published separately, with this CP.

1

WHAT OUR TERMS OF REFERENCE MEAN FOR THIS PROJECT

The origins of the project

1.3 The genesis of the main part of this project, establishing a principled basis for the creation of some kinds of criminal law,[2] lies in unfinished business arising out of Professor Richard Macrory's report, *Regulatory Justice: Making Sanctions Effective*.[3]

1.4 In his report Professor Macrory said this:

> I am not prescribing changes to the legal framework or status of current offences relating to regulatory non-compliance. Offences relating to regulatory non-compliance come in many forms: some impose strict liability, some allow for defences like taking reasonable precautions or similar wording, some require proof of knowledge or intent. The rationale for the differences is not always clear. This is a subject I believe will merit further investigation in the future ... . Some consultation responses have supported my view that there may be a case for decriminalising certain offences thereby reserving criminal sanctions for the most serious cases of regulatory non-compliance. It is however outside my terms of reference to consider this in great detail.[4]

1.5 We will explain shortly what is meant by 'regulatory' non-compliance;[5] but few are likely to disagree with the proposition that, in general terms, the criminal law can and should be used for the most serious cases of non-compliance with the law. The question is whether it is possible to develop some guidelines about the principles to be followed when considering the creation of criminal offences to support the regulation of the activities of individuals and businesses.

1.6 This is an important issue, not least because of the costs and uncertainty associated with use of criminal law and procedure in regulatory contexts. Giving evidence to Professor Macrory, the Environment Agency and the Health and Safety Executive said that many cases could take the best part of a year to bring from discovery of the offence to the point of prosecution, creating unacceptable delay for both prosecuting regulators and business or individual defendants.[6]

---

[2] We briefly consider the other part of this project, the doctrines of liability bearing on the liability of businesses, when setting out our provisional proposals and questions: see para 1.60 and following below.

[3] R Macrory, *Regulatory Justice: Making Sanctions Effective* (Better Regulation Executive), (Final Report, November 2006).

[4] R Macrory, *Regulatory Justice: Making Sanctions Effective* (Better Regulation Executive), (Final Report, November 2006) para 1.39.

[5] See para 1.9 and following below.

[6] R Macrory, *Regulatory Justice: Making Sanctions Effective* (Better Regulation Executive), (Final Report, November 2006) para 1.30.

1.7 In an analysis we commissioned from Professor Julia Black, she also points out that, from a regulator's point of view, the outcome of criminal proceedings may not bring much benefit in terms either of individual retribution or of general deterrence.[7] When a case eventually reaches the criminal courts, even supposing that prosecuting regulators can meet the standard of proof – beyond reasonable doubt – they may nonetheless find that sentencing judges do not have the specialised knowledge required to ensure that appropriate and proportionate sanctions are imposed. This was a point also emphasised by Professor Macrory,[8] and has been noted in other jurisdictions.[9]

1.8 What this shows is that, in regulated fields, reliance on the criminal law as the main means of deterring and punishing unwanted behaviour may prove to be an expensive, uncertain and ineffective strategy. That leaves open the question of when reliance should be placed on the criminal law in those fields.

Regulation and criminal liability

1.9 We will be almost solely concerned with the use of the criminal law in 'regulatory' contexts. Very broadly, a regulatory context is one in which a Government department or agency has (by law) been given the task of developing and enforcing standards of conduct in a specialised area of activity. For example, the Department for the Environment, Food and Rural Affairs describes as one of its Strategic Objectives:

> To enable society to adapt to the effects of climate change through a national programme of action to reduce greenhouse gas emissions by promoting and supporting the development of new technologies and initiatives to reduce UK energy consumption, and carbon intensity of energy production.[10]

1.10 Areas of activity subject to regulatory enforcement can be very varied. Examples are farming, animal welfare, food safety, waste disposal, health and safety at work, the dispensing of medication, retail sales, education, pensions' provision, the governance of many professions, banking and the giving of various kinds of financial advice. This means that the areas in which we will consider whether less reliance should be placed on the criminal law in principle cover a very wide range of activities, involving millions of people and thousands of businesses.

---

[7] See Appendix A.

[8] R Macrory, *Regulatory Justice: Making Sanctions Effective* (Better Regulation Executive), (Final Report, November 2006) paras 1.18 to 1.29.

[9] See, generally, Australian Law Reform Commission, *Principled Regulation: Federal Civil and Administrative Penalties in Australia*, ALRC 95 (2002) p 112 to 115.

[10] Department for Environment, Food and Rural Affairs, *Enforcement Policy Statement* (2010) p 3. In that regard, DEFRA is responsible for investigating and prosecuting offences under, for example, the Water Act 2003.

1.11 However, it follows that we are not concerned in this project with the question of whether less reliance should be placed on the criminal law, when what is sought is an improvement in standards of behaviour by the public at large. In other words, our terms of reference do not include consideration of whether less, or indeed more, use should be made of the criminal law to, say, encourage civilised behaviour in public and more tolerant attitudes, or to discourage the use of violence, sexual abuse, and so forth. Very important though these goals may be, they are not the responsibility of an expert regulatory agency with the power to develop standards, and to create and enforce laws directing at upholding those standards.[11]

1.12 So, to give a specific example, criminal offences supporting the regulation of the activities of chemists fall within the scope of this project. These offences apply to people already linked by licensed trade, and the offences support, amongst others, Chemist Inspection Officers in their work ensuring safe custody, disposal and record-keeping in relation to drugs. By contrast, offences aimed at punishing and deterring members of the public from using or dealing in illegal drugs fall outside the project's scope. This is because illegal drug users or dealers almost all identify themselves as such, in legal terms, only by committing the offences in question. They are not already linked (as by engaging in a licensed trade), and do not form part of a pre-determined group for regulatory purposes.

1.13 Accordingly, the most important task undertaken in this Consultation Paper ("CP") is the introduction of rationality and principle into the creation of criminal offences, when these are meant to support a regulatory strategy. We have understood this to mean the development of a set of proposals to reduce routine reliance on relatively trivial criminal offences, as a means of trying to secure adequate standards of behaviour. In particular, we will consider whether much more use should be made of other, more cost-effective, efficient and ultimately fairer ways of seeking to achieve that goal than the creation of ever more low-level criminal offences. Consequently, we will explore whether all relevant Government departments should make a concerted effort to use these alternatives far more than they have in the past.

1.14 We will also set out the circumstances in which there is a legitimate case for creating criminal offences to support a regulatory strategy. We consider the longstanding argument that criminal offences should be created to deter and punish only serious forms of wrongdoing, as we will explain in Parts 3 and 4. By serious wrongdoing is meant wrongdoing that involves principally deliberate, knowing, reckless or dishonest wrongdoing.

---

[11] Additionally, we will not be concerned with the merits of techniques of regulation, or of securing what is in the public interest, that do not involve using the criminal law, such as licensing, inspection, remedial notices, taxation, or public information campaigns.

1.15   In so far as enforcement measures are needed for less serious kinds of wrongdoing, it has already been accepted by Government that much more use should be made of civil measures, rather than criminal penalties.[12] Such measures include fixed penalties, but also warning, 'stop' or remediation notices (alongside powers of search and seizure where appropriate).

1.16   Our terms of reference do encompass special consideration of the position of businesses. Businesses are the most common target of regulatory initiatives. In addition to the issues just described, we will be addressing some questions about the criminal liability of businesses. We will consider a series of criminal law doctrines, described briefly above,[13] that have an impact on businesses. We will consider the extent to which these doctrines may be arbitrary, or unfair, perhaps especially where small businesses are concerned.

THE BACKGROUND TO THE MAIN PART OF THE PROJECT

Increasing numbers of criminal offences

1.17   Since 1997, more than 3000 criminal offences have come on to the statute book. That figure should be put in context, taking a longer perspective. Halsbury's Statutes of England and Wales[14] has four volumes devoted to criminal laws that (however old they may be) are still currently in force. Volume 1 covers the offences created in the 637 years between 1351 and 1988. Volume 1 is 1382 pages long. Volumes 2 to 4 cover the offences created in the 19 years between 1989 and 2008. Volumes 2 to 4 are no less than 3746 pages long. So, more than 2 and a half times as many pages were needed in Halsbury's Statutes to cover offences created in the 19 years between 1989 and 2008 than were needed to cover the offences created in the 637 years prior to that. Moreover, it is unlikely that the Halsbury volumes devoted to 'criminal law' capture all offences created in recent times.

1.18   These figures must be set alongside ways in which it has become more common for criminal offences to be created in regulatory contexts.

Bureaucratic bodies and criminal law-making

1.19   First, in such contexts, it is normal for primary legislation – a statute – to provide that criminal offences can be created by regulation or order (secondary legislation). Although the relevant government minister will be responsible for introducing secondary legislation creating an offence, the impetus will normally have come from the Government agency created by the statute in question. A statute will not usually itself set out all the criminal offences that might be needed to assist the agency to enforce appropriate standards of behaviour.

---

[12]   See the Regulatory Enforcement and Sanctions Act 2008, based on the recommendations of Professor Macrory: see his report, *Regulatory Justice: Making Sanctions Effective* (Better Regulation Executive), (Final Report, November 2006).

[13]   See para 1.2 above. For more detail, see Parts 5, 6 and 7 below.

[14]   A source book of law generally recognised as authoritative and comprehensive.

1.20   Secondary legislation is easier to create than primary legislation. This is because once laid before Parliament, secondary legislation normally becomes law simply if no one objects to it within a certain period. In recent times, each year has seen the creation of well over 3000 pieces of secondary legislation (whether or not creating a criminal offence). So, as the number of agencies asking Ministers for secondary legislation to create offences themselves multiply, ever more criminal offences come to be created through such legislation, as well as through primary legislation (the statute itself).

1.21   It is worth saying something about the increase in the number of regulatory agencies. Agencies to which Government has granted powers to create and regulate standards of behaviour in particular areas have become much more common. There are now over 60 national regulators with the power, subject to certain limitations or checks, to make (criminal) law. These powers sit alongside the law-making powers already possessed by trading standards authorities and by the 486 local authorities.[15] Correspondingly, the numbers of criminal offences have increased, with the creation of these new authorities and agencies, to provide the support thought necessary for them to carry out their duties.

1.22   Here is an illustrative example. The Department for the Environment, Food and Rural Affairs (DEFRA) is a Government department with very wide-ranging responsibilities for standards relating to food, the environment, and the countryside. DEFRA (or its constituent parts) has always had at its disposal very many criminal offences to support its strategic objectives. For instance, in 2008, DEFRA introduced the Transmissible Spongiform Encephalopathies (No 2) (Amendment) Regulations 2008.[16] These regulations created 103 criminal offences aimed at reducing the risk posed by the spread of bovine spongiform encephalopathy.[17] The Department for Business, Innovation and Skills (BIS) is likewise a Government department with major and widespread responsibilities. The department regularly plays a role in the creation of criminal offences relating to its core concerns. For instance, in 2008 it introduced 74 offences by way of regulation or order, or in schedules to pieces of primary legislation.[18]

---

[15]   See the discussion of the law-making powers of these and other agencies: J Kitching, "Better Regulation and the Small Enterprise", in S Weatherill (ed), *Better Regulation* (2007) p 157.

[16]   SI 2008 No 1180.

[17]   Some of these offences may be re-enactments of older offences.

[18]   These included, for example, offences under the Companies Act 2006, the Export Control (Burma) Order SI 2008 No 1098, the Consumer Protection from Unfair Trading Regulations SI 2008 No 1277, the Batteries and Accumulators (Placing on the Market) Regulations SI 2008 No 2164, and the Cat and Dog Fur (Control of Import, Export and Placing on the Market) Regulations SI 2008 No 2795. Some of these offences may be re-enactments of older offences.

1.23   Notwithstanding the width of these already existing responsibilities, in 2008, a further Government agency, the Department of Energy and Climate Change was created, as an offshoot of DEFRA and BIS. The new agency has responsibility for the former's role in relation to climate change mitigation and for the latter's role in relation to energy policy. The new agency has taken three pieces of legislation through Parliament: the Energy Act 2008, the Climate Change Act 2008, and the Energy Act 2010.[19] The Energy Act 2008 contains 22 criminal offences, and the Climate Change Act 2008 three criminal offences.[20]

1.24   This is not the only example of expansion of the criminal law being driven, at least in part, by the continuous creation of new Government agencies.[21] Another example involves the relatively new Independent Safeguarding Authority. The Authority was established under the Safeguarding Vulnerable Groups Act 2006 to seek to ensure that inappropriate people are not employed in positions where they may exploit or endanger children or vulnerable adults. The Authority is supported by 18 new criminal offences, and by a power, created by section 14, granted to the Secretary of State to create yet further offences.

Criminal laws created, but then little used

1.25   It is not for us to say whether any particular agency, along with the offences created to support its regulatory activities, are unnecessary. However, it is important to point out that the offences created to support the activities of regulatory agencies are often rarely used. For example, section 8 of the Asylum and Immigration Act 1996, which prohibits the employment of illegal migrant workers, was meant to assist Home Office agencies in their work in reducing and deterring illegal immigration. Yet, that provision saw on average only one prosecution a year between 1998 and 2004, prior to the setting up of the UK Border Agency in 2008. As we explain in Part 3, this new agency now has the power to impose fixed civil penalties, instead of taking prosecutions under section 8.

---

[19]   Department for Energy and Climate Change, "Legislation" http://www.decc.gov.uk/en/content/cms/legislation/legislation.aspx (last visited 12 July 2010).

[20]   It would be right to point out that some of these offences may be re-enactments of older offences.

[21]   See, for example, the law-creating powers given to appropriate national authorities by the Animal Welfare Act 2006.

1.26 More generally, a rough estimate is that only 1.5 to 2.0% of defendants tried in the Crown Court are tried for offences arising out of regulatory contexts (excluding motoring offences). In the magistrates' courts, perhaps around 10% of criminal cases arise out of regulatory contexts (excluding motoring offences[22]). Moreover, the steep increase in numbers of criminal offences since 1997 has not led to a corresponding increase in prosecutions and convictions. In 1997, 2 million defendants were proceeded against in magistrates' courts, but in 2008, only 1.6 million faced prosecution. In the Crown Court there was some increase from 80,000 defendants facing prosecution in 1997, to 89,000 in 2008, but that increase may be explained by a number of factors, such as a greater number of cases being transferred from the magistrates' courts. The total number of people found guilty in both kinds of courts put together was 1.49 million in 1997, but only 1.36 million in 2008.

1.27 If a very large number of offences are being created, but these offences are not being used, resources put into creating them are being wasted. Further, ordinary people and businesses are being subjected to ever increasing numbers of what, in all probability, will turn out to be illusory or empty threats of criminal prosecution.

OUR PROVISIONAL PROPOSALS AND QUESTIONS

General principles: the limits of criminalisation

1.28 **Proposal 1: The criminal law should only be employed to deal with wrongdoers who deserve the stigma associated with criminal conviction because they have engaged in seriously reprehensible conduct. It should not be used as the primary means of promoting regulatory objectives.**

1.29 **Proposal 2: Harm done or risked should be regarded as serious enough to warrant criminalisation only if,**

> **(a) in some circumstances (not just extreme circumstances), an individual could justifiably be sent to prison for a first offence, or**
>
> **(b) an unlimited fine is necessary to address the seriousness of the wrongdoing in issue, and its consequences.[23]**

1.30 **Proposal 3: Low-level criminal offences should be repealed in any instance where the introduction of a civil penalty (or equivalent measure) is likely to do as much to secure appropriate levels of punishment and deterrence.**

---

[22] If motoring offences are included in the magistrates' courts figures, then the figures rise to around 50% of cases. The reason for giving figures that exclude motoring offences is that these figures give a better picture of the limited extent to which the criminal courts feature across the entire spectrum of regulatory activity.

[23] Putting aside factors such as whether the individual has previous convictions for other offences, and so on.

1.31 We will not argue specifically for proposal 1, which is really in the nature of a conclusion that follows from our other recommendations. Nevertheless, we believe that it is important to have a proposal in the form of a general statement of principle. This can act as a way of setting the justificatory bar high when the question facing a Government department is whether a criminal offence should be created.

1.32 Proposal 2 follows our analysis of the current use of criminal law in regulatory contexts in Part 3 below. As indicated above,[24] we find that an important explanation for the rare use of low-level criminal offences is, quite simply, that the cost, uncertainty and delay involved in undertaking criminal proceedings are not worth bearing, if the outcome will be little more than a fine (the amount of which is at the court's discretion). The stakes must be higher, if the criminal law is rightly to be invoked, on grounds of fairness to accused persons and on grounds of economy, efficiency and effectiveness from the prosecution's perspective.

1.33 Proposal 3 follows from proposal 2, but is concerned specifically with the reduction of the number of criminal offences on the statute book, whether created by primary or by secondary legislation. If low-level criminal offences are rarely used, there is a compelling case for removing them from the statute book if civil (non-criminal) measures will do as good a job, in terms of punishment and deterrence. Whether or not that is true depends in part on the nature of the civil measures at issue. Until recently, there were relatively few such measures available for Government departments to employ instead of criminal sanctions. So, it is in a way perfectly understandable that reliance has been so frequently placed on the criminal law.

1.34 During the 20th century, an increasing number of areas of business – and, indeed, individual – life became subject to regulation, or to more intensive or wider-ranging regulation. So, for example, there is now more regulation of the way individuals and businesses dispose of waste, treat the environment, address health and safety concerns, produce and sell food or other products, care for their animals, and so on. Without an adequate range of civil measures to carry through the regulatory goals in these areas, the volume of criminal law thought necessary to help achieve those goals was almost bound to increase. That is what has happened, and happened quite dramatically over the last 20 years.[25]

1.35 Fortunately, following the enactment of the Regulatory Enforcement and Sanctions Act 2008, there is now a wider and more flexible range of non-criminal measures available to regulatory authorities, to help them to achieve their goals without relying in the first instance on criminal prosecution. For example, under section 39 of the 2008 Act, a fixed monetary penalty (like a parking fine) may be imposed by a regulatory authority in respect of an offence, whether or not that offence is also a low-level criminal offence.

---

[24] See paras 1.6 to 1.7 above.

[25] See para 1.17 above.

1.36 Further, under section 46 of that Act, a regulatory authority can issue a 'stop notice', requiring someone to stop carrying on a specified activity, unless and until certain steps (such as those designed to make the activity safer) have been taken. Similarly, under section 50 of the Act, a regulatory authority can negotiate an 'enforcement undertaking' with someone, according to which that person agrees to take action to prevent what would otherwise be offending behaviour, or to restore damage done. It is only if these measures are not complied with that criminal prosecution will be contemplated: breach of a stop notice is itself a criminal offence.[26]

1.37 The introduction of these civil measures creates a real opportunity for an achievable reduction in the number of criminal offences on which departments and regulators used to have to rely. It is important that a determined effort is made to secure that reduction.

General principles: avoiding pointless overlaps between offences

1.38 **Proposal 4: The criminal law should not be used to deal with inchoate offending when it is covered by the existing law governing conspiracy, attempt, and assisting or encouraging crime.**

1.39 **Proposal 5: The criminal law should not be used to deal with fraud when the conduct in question is covered by the Fraud Act 2006.**

1.40 So far as proposal 4 is concerned, there are specific statutes dealing with 'inchoate' offending in English law.[27] Very broadly, inchoate offending is a lawyer's term for conduct that is criminal when directed at, or posing a risk of, harm done, whether or not the harm in question is actually done. So, for example, when people conspire or attempt to commit offences, the acts in question (reaching the agreement to commit the offence; trying to commit the offence) are themselves prohibited by the criminal law. Someone can thus be prosecuted for conspiring or attempting to commit an offence, whether or not the offence actually took place.

---

[26] Regulatory Enforcement and Sanctions Act 2008, s 49.

[27] The main examples are the Criminal Law Act 1977 (conspiracy), the Criminal Attempts Act 1981 (attempts) and the Serious Crime Act 2007 (assisting and encouraging crime).

1.41   It is far too common for offences in regulatory contexts to make special provision for conspiracies or attempts to commit those offences, or for acts of encouragement or assistance to that end, when the general provisions in the specific statutes just referred to[28] already cover such conduct. For example, under section 8 of the Animal Welfare Act 2006, it is an indictable offence (an offence that may be tried in the Crown Court) not only to cause an animal fight to take place, but also to attempt to cause such a fight to take place. However, if causing an animal fight to take place is an indictable offence, then an attempt to commit it was already an offence in 2006, by virtue of section 1 of the Criminal Attempts Act 1981. So, the creation in section 8 of the offence of attempting to cause an animal fight was unnecessary. In Part 3, we will explain why this kind of duplication is not simply unnecessary but may lead to unanticipated expansion of the scope of the criminal law.

1.42   Turing to proposal 5, an objection to many fraud-based offences that are being created in regulatory contexts is similar to the objection just outlined in relation to inchoate offences. In other words, too many fraud-based offences are being created where the conduct in question is already covered by the Fraud Act 2006. For example, in 2008, around 30 fraud-based or fraud-related criminal offences were created.[29] It would have been perfectly acceptable, in a substantial proportion of these cases, to leave the conduct in question to be dealt with under the Fraud Act 2006.

1.43   Fraud under the Fraud Act 2006 is a serious offence, carrying a maximum sentence of ten years' imprisonment, following conviction in the Crown Court. It is questionable whether someone who commits a fraud-based offence created for a regulatory context should be exposed to what is commonly a much shorter maximum sentence for that offence, if the conduct in which they engaged would have amounted to fraud under the Fraud Act 2006. Quite simply, that looks unfair and may create anomalous differences in sentences handed down for similar kinds of acts. This is because a far higher maximum penalty is likely to face those who have engaged in almost identical kinds of fraudulent acts, but are charged with fraud under the Fraud Act 2006 because their conduct happens not to fall within the jurisdiction of a regulatory scheme that has a fraud-based offence with a much lower maximum penalty.

General principles: structure and process

1.44   **Proposal 6: Criminal offences should, along with the civil measures that accompany them, form a hierarchy of seriousness.**

1.45   In Part 3, we will examine a number of different areas subject to regulation and consider how appropriately criminal offences are used by regulatory authorities in those areas. Our discussion leads us to propose that the criminal law is best employed as a measure to target the worst examples of non-compliance, as when an offender has deliberately not complied with an obligation, or has made a fraudulent application for a grant, or the like.

---

[28]   See n 27 above.

[29]   It is hard to be very precise about numbers because some offences do not easily lend themselves to precise categorisation.

1.46 **Proposal 7: More use should be made of process fairness to increase confidence in the criminal justice system. Duties on regulators formally to warn potential offenders that they are subject to liability should be supplemented by granting the courts power to stay proceedings until non-criminal regulatory steps have been taken first, in appropriate cases.**

1.47 Following the passing of the Regulatory Enforcement and Sanctions Act 2008, there are now clearer duties on regulatory authorities to warn offenders or potential offenders that sanctions or other measures may be imposed on them. This is an aspect of what might be called 'process fairness'; in other words, fairness in the way that sanctioning procedures are undertaken. In that regard, we provisionally propose that process fairness in regulatory contexts should be central to the way that courts approach regulatory prosecutions. Courts should have the power to stay – that is to say, to stop – criminal proceedings if, in their view, the requirements of process fairness have not been met in an individual case. This can be through the use of warnings, enforcement undertakings or stop notices, or other analogous measures.

1.48 **Proposal 8: Criminal offences should be created and (other than in relation to minor details) amended only through primary legislation.**

1.49 As we suggested above,[30] and as we will argue in Part 3, it has become far too easy to create criminal offences through secondary legislation. The creation of a criminal offence should be regarded as a law-creating step of great (arguably, of something approaching constitutional) significance. That significance can only adequately be reflected in a commitment to create criminal offences in primary legislation (statutes). Should the criminal law have the reduced scope for operation in regulatory contexts that we propose, that ought not to be the radical step that it might otherwise appear to be. This is because the offence will be one concerned with serious wrongdoing.

1.50 **Proposal 9: A regulatory scheme that makes provision for the imposition of any civil penalty, or equivalent measure, must also provide for unfettered recourse to the courts to challenge the imposition of that measure, by way of re-hearing or appeal on a point of law.**

1.51 Only a tiny minority of convicted people challenge their convictions under regulatory legislation in the higher courts. However, as a matter of fair procedure (and of constitutional and European obligation), it is important to provide access to an independent tribunal, such as a Crown Court, when someone subject to a regulatory penalty, or equivalent measure, wishes to challenge that measure. In particular, we doubt whether it is in all instances likely to prove adequately fair or efficient for the regulatory authorities to seek to restrict appeals, in whole or in part, to bodies that the authority has itself set up for this purpose.

---

[30] See paras 1.20 to 1.21 above.

General principles: fault in offences supporting a regulatory structure

1.52 **Proposal 10: Fault elements in criminal offences that are concerned with unjustified risk-taking should be proportionate. This means that the more remote the conduct criminalised from harm done, and the less grave that harm, the more compelling the case for higher-level fault requirements such as dishonesty, intention, knowledge or recklessness.**

1.53 As a general rule, criminal offences created in regulatory contexts prohibit conduct that creates unnecessary and undesirable risks, although harm actually done is also targeted when it is not covered by the general law governing offences against the person or against property. Conduct that poses an unjustified risk of harm may in many instances be very remote from harm done. For example, the making of a misleading statement about safety procedures to be followed in manufacturing a product, submitted when an application is made for a licence to produce that product, may be an act very remote from any harm that might result from someone's reliance on that statement.

1.54 Just because an unjustified act, such as the making of a misleading statement about a product's safety features in a licence application, is remote from any harm to which it might lead, does not mean it is wrong to make the doing of that act a criminal offence. However, the remoteness of an act that creates risk from the harm that may result provides a reason to include stringent fault requirements – such as intention or dishonesty – in the relevant offence, to avoid over extension of the criminal law. That is the explanation for proposal 10. Proposal 11 below provides an example of how this works, in the key area of information provision.

1.55 **Proposal 11: In relation to wrongdoing bearing on the simple provision of (or failure to provide) information, individuals should not be subject to criminal proceedings – even if they may still face civil penalties – unless their wrongdoing was knowing or reckless.[31]**

1.56 In very many areas of regulation, the provision of the wrong or of misleading information, or a failure to provide the right information, to the regulatory authority, will involve the commission of a criminal offence. Of course, we understand that regulatory authorities could not do their job properly unless those subject to regulation had to provide the authority with the right information on many issues. However, it will rarely be right to make a simple failure to provide the right information, or even the provision of the wrong or of misleading information, a criminal offence. At best, such conduct should be subject to a civil measure of some kind. Businesses and others who faithfully seek to comply with regulatory requirements to provide information should not be penalised by the criminal law simply because they fall short of the precise requirements.

---

[31] It is important to emphasise that our concern here is with the simple provision of the wrong or incomplete information, and so forth, to a regulatory agency. Where false or misleading statements are knowingly or recklessly made in a dishonest way, with a view to gain or to imposing (the risk of) loss on another, they will fall foul of the Fraud Act 2006; and rightly so.

1.57 However, it is a different matter when information is deliberately or knowingly withheld, or when the wrong or inadequate information is knowingly or recklessly provided. Such conduct may not involve fraud, as understood by the criminal law. Even so, it does involve the deliberate or knowing adoption of an obstructive approach to defeat the regulatory objectives in relation to the individual's own business, when others may faithfully have sought to comply.

1.58 **Proposal 12: The Ministry of Justice, in collaboration with other departments and agencies, should seek to ensure not only that proportionate fault elements are an essential part of criminal offences created to support regulatory aims, but also that there is consistency and clarity in the use of such elements when the offence in question is to be used by departments and agencies for a similar purpose.**

1.59 We hope that this proposal needs little by way of further explanation. Naturally, the Ministry of Justice does not have the expertise in the regulatory fields that fall under the jurisdiction of other departments. Having said that, people are entitled to treat the Ministry of Justice as having the highest level of authority, short of Parliament itself, for the general standards observed in criminal law-making of all kinds in England and Wales. We know that the Ministry of Justice already takes its responsibilities in this regard very seriously. Even so, we believe that more could be done across departments, and publicly, to spell out the permissible limits of the criminal law.

Doctrines of criminal liability applicable to businesses

1.60 We now turn to the part of this project concerned with particular doctrines of criminal liability whose importance, in this context, is their application to businesses.

1.61 In practice, businesses – and especially small businesses – are in many fields the main targets for regulatory offences. This fact will have an impact on the shape of our proposals for the use of criminal offences in achieving regulatory objectives. Our specific concern is whether or not particular doctrines of liability applicable to businesses are unfair to such bodies, and in particular, whether or not they are unfair to small businesses.

The doctrine of identification

1.62 **Proposal 13: Legislation should include specific provisions in criminal offences to indicate the basis on which companies may be found liable, but in the absence of such provisions, the courts should treat the question of how corporate fault may be established as a matter of statutory interpretation. We encourage the courts not to presume that the identification doctrine applies when interpreting the scope of criminal offences applicable to companies.**

1.63 When companies are charged with criminal offences involving proof of fault, they are normally judged by reference to the so-called identification doctrine. This doctrine requires a controlling officer of the company him or herself to be proved to have had the fault element of the offence. We look at this issue in relation to the interpretation of statutory offences.

1.64   On the one hand, the identification doctrine can make it impossibly difficult for prosecutors to find companies guilty of some serious crimes, especially large companies with devolved business structures. For example, if bribery is committed by an employee of a company to win a contract for the company, it will only be possible to convict the company itself of bribery if, in some way, a company director (or equivalent person) him or herself had a hand in the decision to offer a bribe. If the employee was conducting business on the company's behalf as, say, a regional manager, that may be almost impossible to prove.

1.65   On the other hand, it follows that the identification doctrine can make it easier to convict small companies of offences committed by employees. This is because the smaller the company the more likely it is that the directors played some kind of active role in the commission of the offence, for example by explicitly or implicitly authorising it. In itself, that might not seem problematic, if the directors did play such a role. However, it gives a perverse incentive for companies to operate with devolved structures that insulate directors (or equivalent persons) to a certain extent from knowledge of what their managers or employees are doing, when that knowledge might involve awareness of offences being committed for the benefit of the company.[32]

1.66   It follows that the identification doctrine also provides an incentive for prosecutors to pursue small businesses in respect of offences committed to benefit the company, rather than larger companies in respect of the same kind of offences. This is because it will be faster, cheaper and easier to prove directorial involvement when small companies are being investigated (something referred to as the temptation of 'low-hanging fruit'). Such a policy development may undermine a statutory scheme of liability aimed at small and large companies alike.

1.67   By contrast, our provisional proposal involves the court in looking to the underlying purpose of the statutory scheme for guidance on the right basis on which to hold companies liable for offences committed relating to that scheme. This is something that the courts have already started to do.[33] It is an approach that is preferable to the application of the identification doctrine as the default doctrine of liability. Of course, it is always possible that, having considered the underlying purpose of the statutory scheme, a court could conclude that Parliament intended the identification doctrine to apply.

A general defence of due diligence

1.68   **Proposal 14: The courts should be given a power to apply a due diligence defence to any statutory offence that does not require proof that the defendant was at fault in engaging in the wrongful conduct. The burden of proof should be on the defendant to establish the defence.**

1.69   **Proposal 15: If proposal 14 is accepted, the defence of due diligence should take the form of showing that due diligence was exercised in all the circumstances to avoid the commission of the offence.**

---

[32]   For an illustrative example, see *Director-General of Fair Trading v Pioneer Concrete (UK) Ltd* [1995] 1 AC 456.

[33]   *Meridian Global Funds Management Asia Ltd v Securities Commission* [1995] 2 AC 500.

1.70   We also ask:

> **Question 1: Were it to be introduced, should the due diligence defence take the stricter form already found in some statutes, namely, did the defendant take all reasonable precautions and exercise all due diligence to avoid commission of the offence?**
>
> **Question 2: If the power to apply a due diligence defence is introduced, should Parliament prevent or restrict its application to certain statutes, and if so which statutes?**

1.71   Proposals 14 and 15 are linked to proposal 13. When considering criminal offences under statute that do not involve proof of fault, the courts sometimes apply a presumption of fault. In other words, they read in to the statutory wording a requirement of fault that the prosecution must prove, as a matter of fairness to persons accused of the crime in question.

1.72   As we will argue in Part 6, one difficulty with the approach is that it has never been clear when the presumption applies or what evidence will be sufficient to displace or overcome it. The presumption thus adds persistent uncertainty to the process of interpreting the scope of criminal offences.

1.73   We have no difficulty with the idea that courts should interpret criminal offences in such a way that they strike a fair balance between the interests of the prosecution and the interests of the defence. However, in our view, the presumption of fault is not the right way to strike that balance, especially in regulatory contexts when companies are most likely to be the defendants.

1.74   The presumption of fault commonly involves a presumption of 'subjective' fault, such as intention, knowledge or recklessness. That means that, when a company is charged with a criminal offence to which the presumption has been applied, the prosecution must satisfy the identification doctrine, described above. As we have seen,[34] satisfying that doctrine requires proof that a director (or equivalent person) him or herself possessed the fault element. This is not only something that may be an increasingly difficult task for the prosecution, the larger the company involved. It also poses almost insuperable difficulties for the prosecution, when looking at the activities of large firms, when what must be proved is that an individual director (or equivalent person) knew or was reckless as to whether the wrongdoing would take place.

1.75   Modern statutes imposing criminal liability on companies have circumvented this problem. Such statutes permit companies (or individuals) to escape conviction for offences under the statutes, only if the defendant can show that all due diligence was exercised and all reasonable precautions taken to avoid commission of the offence. A court will not apply the presumption that fault must be proven to an offence that has a 'due diligence' defence applicable to it.

---

[34]   See paras 1.62 to 1.67 above.

1.76 However, this leaves a difficulty with the large number of statutes, and possibly hundreds of offences of strict liability established by them, which were created before this policy of including a due diligence defence in the statute itself became more common. The presumption of fault is, sometimes, still being applied to these statutes when it would be fairer to apply a due diligence defence, with the burden of proof on the accused. The difficulty is that there is no due diligence defence at common law and so the courts have no alternative, when seeking to secure fairness to accused persons, to the employment of the presumption of fault.

1.77 Accordingly, we provisionally propose that the courts should be given the power to apply a 'due diligence in all the circumstances' defence (with the burden of proof on the accused) to statutes that are in whole or in part silent on the question of whether fault is required to be proved if the defendant is to be convicted. We are confident that the courts will use that power wisely, and will apply it only when it enhances the statutory scheme of liability.

1.78 Nonetheless, we also ask two questions (questions 1 and 2) about possible qualifications to our proposal.

1.79 Modern statutes that include a due diligence defence do not express it in the simple terms that form the basis of our provisional proposal: due diligence shown in all the circumstances. Instead, they commonly have a narrower version of it, less favourable to the defendant, a defence of having taken *all* reasonable precautions and having exercised *all* due diligence to avoid commission of the offence. We believe that this is somewhat stricter than is really necessary for a defence to a criminal charge, and is a kind of counsel of perfection. However, we ask consultees whether they would prefer the general defence that we propose to take this stricter form.

1.80 Finally, there may be some contexts – the road traffic context may be an example – in which, if our proposal becomes law, too much of the courts' time would be taken up by vain attempts to persuade the courts to apply a due diligence defence to offences under the relevant legislation. It might be better right from the outset to say that the defence simply has no application to offences created by road traffic legislation, and possibly other legislation. Do consultees think that is right, and if so, which statutes do they think should be exempted from the scope of the defence?

The consent and connivance doctrine

1.81 We will be making the following proposal about the basis on which directors can be made individually liable for offences committed by their businesses:

1.82 **Proposal 16: When it is appropriate to provide that individual directors (or equivalent officers) can themselves be liable for an offence committed by their company, on the basis that they consented or connived at the company's commission of that offence, the provision in question should not be extended to include instances in which the company's offence is attributable to neglect on the part of an individual director or equivalent person.**

1.83 We will be asking the following question in relation to this issue:

Question 3: When a company is proved to have committed an offence, might it be appropriate in some circumstances to provide that an individual director (or equivalent officer) can be liable for the separate offence of 'negligently failing to prevent' that offence?

1.84 Companies can commit a very wide range of offences, including, for example, corporate manslaughter and taking indecent photographs of children, as well as offences more commonly encountered in business contexts, such as false accounting. When a statute creates an offence that a business can commit, it usually provides that a director (or equivalent person) can also be found individually liable for committing that offence, if he or she consented or connived at the commission of the offence by the company. There is nothing especially controversial about this. It is a form of liability very similar to liability for an offence that arises when someone is found to have been complicit in another's crime (in this case, the other being the company).

1.85 However, in some statutes the basis on which a director (or equivalent person) can be found individually liable for an offence committed by his or her company is much wider. It extends beyond instances in which the individual in question has consented or connived at the commission of the offence, to cases in which the company's offence was attributable to neglect on the director's (or equivalent person's) part.

1.86 In our view, this broader basis for imposing individual liability on directors (or equivalent persons) for offences committed by their companies is unfair. For reasons that we will explain in Part 7, an individual (X) should not be exposed to conviction of a criminal offence committed by another person (Y), simply because the offence committed by Y was due to neglect on X's part. This is simply because in such circumstances, X him or herself has not engaged in any criminal act; only Y (his or her company) has. In such circumstances, only consent to or connivance at the offence committed by Y involves the kind of fault necessary to justify individual liability being imposed on X respecting Y's crime.

1.87 Clearly, some consultees may not agree that the criminal law should be so generous to individual directors. Accordingly, we go on to ask (question 3) whether, if an offence committed by a company is due to the neglect of a director (or equivalent person), a separate offence should be created to capture that individual's conduct. This would be an offence of negligently failing to prevent the offence being committed by the company.

The delegation doctrine

1.88 We will then turn our attention to what we regard as an antiquated doctrine: the so-called doctrine of delegation. According to this doctrine, where the running of a business is delegated from X to Y, X still remains liable to be convicted of an offence committed, in relation to the running of the business, by Y. We will ask:

Question 4: Should the doctrine of delegation be abolished, and replaced by an offence of failing to prevent an offence being committed by someone to whom the running of the business had been delegated?

1.89   Our objection to the delegation doctrine is similar to our objection to the extended version of the consent and connivance doctrine; that is to say, its imposition of individual liability for an offence committed by someone else may be wholly unfair and disproportionate, in the circumstances. To give a simple example, suppose X asks Y to run X's pub while X goes on a round-the-world cruise. In fact, Y turns the pub into an unlicensed lap dancing club and brothel. In this instance, Y can, of course, be convicted of running an unlicensed lap dancing club or brothel. However, the doctrine of delegation means that X can also be convicted of these offences, even if he or she had no reason whatsoever to think that Y would do as he or she did.[35]

1.90   We do not believe that this is right. There will always be a concern that business people may place the running of their businesses into the wrong hands. However, in order to penalise individuals for doing that, if it is necessary to penalise them at all, the criminal law should perhaps choose a different focus. It would be possible to focus on whether the original owner of the business (X) failed to prevent the offence being committed by the person to whom it was delegated (Y). A conviction for this separate offence would perhaps more fairly represent what X has done wrong than individual liability for the offence itself.

---

[35]   See *Allen v Whitehead* [1930] 1 KB 211.

PART 2
REGULATION AND PUBLIC INTEREST OFFENCES

CRIMINAL LAW AND REGULATION

2.1 This CP is about the use of the criminal law in regulatory contexts. It does not extend to the use of the criminal law in other contexts, even if some of the provisional proposals and questions may be just as relevant to other contexts in which the criminal law is employed. In that respect, there is a special danger of confusion between the use of the criminal law in regulatory contexts, and its use in the form of what can be called public interest offences (defined below). In this Part, our principal aim is to explain how our focus on regulatory contexts is distinct from a concern with public interest offences, in particular.

2.2 Consultees who are more interested in our main provisional proposals and questions than in how we have defined the scope of our project, may feel warranted in skipping this Part and moving straight to Part 3.

THE ROLE OF PUBLIC INTEREST OFFENCES

Regulation and public interest offences

2.3 The criminal law is used in many contexts to punish and deter harmful or risky behaviour. Although we are concerned with its use in regulatory contexts, contexts in which the criminal law comes to be used may overlap. Let us briefly consider offences designed to prohibit behaviour connected with actual or possible damage to the environment.

2.4 In some instances, such offences cannot be understood outside of their regulatory context. An example is obstructing a person inspecting a waste reduction account detailing payments received under a waste reduction scheme, an offence under the Climate Change Act 2008.[1] The specificity of this offence reflects the fact that it cannot be properly understood if detached from the regulatory structures in which it is meant to play a supporting role.

---

[1] Climate Change Act 2008, Sch 5, para 9.

20

2.5   However, there are also offences that make perfect sense in terms of environmental protection irrespective of any given regulatory context. Examples might be offences concerned with casual littering in public places, or (in some of its manifestations) the common law offence of public nuisance.[2] The latter kinds of offence may, for convenience sake, be called public interest offences. Such offences tend to be focussed on direct damage or threat to the environment. The directness of the damage or threat is in these instances in itself enough to justify the existence of the offence. By way of contrast with the offence just mentioned, contrary to the Climate Change Act 2008, with public interest offences there is no need for an additional justification in the form of support provided for a regulatory scheme of environmental protection.

2.6   Why choose a more holistic regulatory approach to a problem in society (including supporting offences), rather than simply employing public interest (or other forms of) offences to deter and punish the relevant kind of behaviour? This is not the place for a theoretical analysis of proper regulatory objectives and how to achieve them.[3] However, in broad terms, if there is a relatively clearly defined target group of persons liable to engage in the undesirable behaviour, it may be much easier and possibly cheaper, as well as fairer and more efficient, to adopt a carrot-and-stick approach to influencing the behaviour of that subject group. Such an approach will usually require regulatory oversight and policy delivery. This is because somebody – normally experts operating under delegated powers – must be responsible for developing standards, rewarding examples of good practice and seeking to engage the subject group in self-improvement by reference to those standards, or tackling departures from the standards through less crude forms of pressure and persuasion than are offered by the criminal law. Examples of non-criminal pressure applied, to that end, include the use of warnings, 'stop' notices or civil penalties for conduct prohibited by the relevant regulator.

2.7   By way of contrast, in some instances – casual street littering may be one example – whilst there may possibly be a small number of clearly defined groups who can be identified as prone to offend, and who can be appropriate subjects of regulation,[4] this may not be true in general.[5] There may quite conceivably be no way of identifying (and hence targeting) in advance those who tend casually to litter in public places other than through their engagement in the activity itself.

---

[2]   See Simplification of the Criminal Law: Public Nuisance and Outraging Public Decency (2010) Law Commission Consultation Paper No 193.

[3]   See R Macrory, *Regulatory Justice: Making Sanctions Effective* (Better Regulation Executive) (Final Report, November 2006).

[4]   For example, companies in certain kinds of business, such as street vending.

[5]   We omit from consideration issues of waste disposal, either commercial or domestic, which are largely if not wholly distinct from street littering. These areas of activity are, of course, regulated.

2.8   In such cases, the Government must seek to communicate with the public at large in order to convey its anti-littering message and to deter littering. However, it may be difficult to do this simply through information campaigns and the like. Any given message may become lost in the welter of other messages the Government is seeking to convey on other issues, and the costs of sustaining a high-impact message over a long period may be prohibitive. So, putting aside the possible use of non-legal measures such as public information campaigns, there may be no alternative in such cases to the use of the criminal law to deter and punish.

2.9   Alternatively, it may be the case that although a regulatory approach could easily be employed, it is for some reason likely to produce unwanted side-effects. Consequently, a criminal offence-led strategy (explained below) may be positively preferred, rather than being the only available option. Moving away from a specific concern with the environment, we will now give an example of such a case.

Comparing driving and car ownership, and cycling and bicycle ownership

2.10   A comparison between cycling and bicycle ownership, and driving and car ownership, provides an example of a case in which a criminal offence-led strategy has been preferred with respect to cycling and bicycle ownership. This strategy needs to be compared with the approach to car ownership and driving, where a mixed offence-and-regulation approach has been adopted.

2.11   The law, and delegated agencies, have a large number of means by which car owners and drivers can be cajoled and threatened into observing better safety or environmental standards, to supplement the use of the criminal law to prohibit harm done or threatened. Would-be car drivers must pass a test of driving competence if they are to obtain a licence, higher taxes can be imposed on very powerful or gas-guzzling models, and so on.[6] Car manufacturers can also be given incentives to fit safety or environmentally friendly features to cars, which individual car buyers might not themselves insist on.

---

[6]   Additionally, of course, there are informal, public means by which observance of better standards can be promoted, as when insurance companies offer cheaper car insurance to drivers with long records of accident-free driving.

2.12　The use of such regulatory devices is justified in virtue of the threat that motorised vehicles pose to life and limb on public roads, and the environmental impact (in a very broad sense) that they may have.[7] However, what makes Governments disposed to accept that justification is the fact that the incentives people have to own and run motorised vehicles are sufficiently great that they will be willing, by and large, to seek to comply with the regulations in order to stay on the road legally.[8] If the incentives to do these things were much lower, more intensive regulation might lead simply to a culture of evasion, undermining respect for the law and leading to higher costs being incurred in (possibly fruitless) attempts to enforce it.

2.13　By way of contrast, the law takes a very different, less dirigiste approach to cycling and bicycle ownership. Putting aside public information campaigns (which are also targeted at car owners and drivers) or children's education measures, it is left largely to the criminal law to deal with misconduct.[9] Even securing the *means* to regulate, as by insisting that every bicycle has some kind of registration number or other form of identification, has never been a public policy priority. Most importantly, though, this is not necessarily a matter for criticism.

2.14　It has become Government policy to regard it as desirable that people should switch from a variety of other forms of transport to cycling. There are, however, a variety of reasons why, for the individual, the incentives of switching to cycling may not be all that strong. Consequently, the introduction of 'bureaucratic' impediments to switching (for example, regulatory schemes to set and improve standards of cycling) may easily tip the balance against switching for would-be cyclists, and hence may not be welcomed by Government. It follows that any regulatory intervention that diminishes the marginal utility of cycle use and ownership, such as a requirement that cyclists take safer cycling tests before using public roads, will have to deliver very substantial benefits for it to be regarded as justified.

2.15　Public authorities like to emphasise the substantial benefits of cycling, and it generally poses less harm than driving even though it can be risky. It is, therefore, perhaps understandable, that there has been little political pressure on Governments to introduce a regulatory approach to this field.

2.16　Consequently, there may, ironically, be sound reasons to treat bicycle ownership and cycling as an area appropriate for a largely criminal offence-led rather than regulatory approach. This is for the following reasons.

---

[7]　Also coming into the equation is the cost to local and national authorities of maintaining the infrastructure necessary to sustain a road system that must accommodate millions of journeys.

[8]　The strong incentives for drivers and owners to stay legally on the road may possibly also lead them more readily to internalise the regulations as a good thing, keeping enforcement costs down and the degree of compliance relatively high. This is, of course, a matter of speculation.

[9]　For example, dangerous cycling (an offence under s 28 of the Road Traffic Act 1988); careless, and inconsiderate, cycling (an offence under s 29 of the Road Traffic Act 1988); and cycling when under influence of drink or drugs (an offence under s 30 of the Road Traffic Act 1988).

2.17   Although we have been speaking about a criminal offence-led strategy, it is important not to suppose that this means the same thing as the use of the term "strategy" does when people speak about a regulatory strategy. Regulatory strategies are usually pro-active and managed, with more or less clear policy goals set for or by the agency responsible for delivering the strategy. A criminal offence-led strategy may involve no such things. A criminal offence-led strategy may consist in nothing more than leaving to the police or local authorities the discretion to take occasional legal action in certain (bad) cases, or to conduct higher intensity operations from time to time to remind people of their obligations. The law's approach to cycling may be an example of this relatively unstructured, low intensity approach to offending and to deterrence.[10]

2.18   Such a relatively relaxed strategy may be no bad thing (although we take no view one way or the other); it is not an indication of failure or indifference, pure and simple. This is because, in terms of costs and benefits, tolerating a certain measure of offending by cyclists does not lead to anything like the kind and degree of harm (or the risk thereof) that such toleration would produce were the same non-interventionist strategy taken to the use of motorised vehicles. Police and prosecution resources may simply be better deployed against offenders other than cyclists.

2.19   In the example we have just given, the need to avoid reducing incentives to switching to cycling from other modes of transport means not only that a criminal offence-led strategy is preferred to a regulatory strategy, but that the criminal offence-led strategy goes hand in hand with a selective and (broadly speaking) low–intensity prosecution policy. Even so, it will not always be right that these go together.

2.20   Sometimes a criminal offence-led strategy will be accompanied by a high intensity prosecution policy. The modern approach to knife crime provides an example. In such cases, a criminal offence-led strategy may take on some of the characteristics of a regulatory strategy, although there is likely still to be no subject group identifiable apart from their engagement in offending behaviour.

---

[10]   In 2008, there was only one trial for a pedal cycle offence under the Highways Act 1980 in the Crown Court, and that resulted in an acquittal. There were only 133 convictions for pedal cycle offences in the magistrates' courts. As a reminder, we are not concerned in this project with the propriety or effectiveness of public information campaigns as a means of deterrence or of improving standards.

The example of knife crime

2.21   A criminal offence-led strategy may take on the higher intensity, targeted and managed characteristics typical of a regulatory strategy, if and when it is given a high priority. An example might be the Government's initiatives relating to knife-carrying by young people. These have involved the development and implementation, since June 2008, of the Tackling Knives Action Programme,[11] that, across its three phases, takes a holistic approach. Its latter phases have been aimed at engaging communities, schools, charities and local authorities, as well as the police, in an effort to broaden preventative effects and educational benefits. However, the initial phase, as well as some later developments, included the development of a higher intensity offence-led strategy. This strategy involved measures such as those that have:

- funded police forces to step up enforcement operations;[12]

- targeted the most dangerous people in an area;[13]

- doubled the maximum sentence for carrying a knife in public from two to four years;[14]

- raised the age at which someone can buy a knife from 16 to 18;[15]

- widened the powers of stop and search to give school teachers power to search pupils;[16]

- increased the number of test purchasing operations for knives;[17]

- raised the minimum term to be served of a life sentence for someone over 18 years of age who committed murder with a knife that was being carried to 25 years.[18]

---

[11]   Home Office, *Tackling Knives, Saving Lives – increased action to tackle knife crime* Home Office Press Release (18 August 2008): http://webarchive.nationalarchives.gov.uk/20100413151441/press.homeoffice.gov.uk/press-releases/tackling-knives.html (last visited 19 July 2010).

[12]   'Operation Blunt': http://www.itsnotagame.org/working-together.php (last visited 19 July 2010).

[13]   See for example Metropolitan Police Authority, *Knife Crime* (Report 13) (26 October 2006): http://www.mpa.gov.uk/committees/mpa/2006/061026/13/ (last visited 8 June 2010).

[14]   Violent Crime Reduction Act 2006, s 42.

[15]   Above, s 43.

[16]   Above, s 45.

[17]   Local Authorities Coordinators of Regulatory Services (LACORS), *Monitoring Underage Knife Sales Gives Cause for Concern* (14 June 2006): http://www.lacors.gov.uk/lacors/PressReleaseDetails.aspx?id=6 (last visited 8 June 2010).

[18]   Ministry of Justice, 25 Year Starting Point for Knife Killers (3 March 2010) http://www.justice.gov.uk/news/newsrelease030310c.htm (last visited 8 June 2010).

2.22 In legal terms, there may be little alternative to an offence-led strategy for knife-carrying so far as the carriers are concerned. Nothing links knife carriers together such as to make them an appropriate target for a regulatory strategy, apart from their pre-disposition to commit knife crime.[19] That point should, of course, be understood to take nothing away from the importance of preventative action and education of a non-regulatory kind, such as the measures involved in the Tackling Knives Action Programme. As we suggested earlier, though, such non-legal strategies can be expensive (just like their legal counterparts), and hard to sustain in the long term.[20]

2.23 So, there is an inherent flexibility in the purposes for which offence-led strategies may be employed. An offence-led strategy may be employed, in preference to a regulatory strategy, because a relatively low priority is given to the setting and maintenance of good standards through legal intervention. It may be enough that serious wrongdoing is targeted, and that offensives are occasionally conducted to prevent people forgetting their obligations. By way of contrast, the public interest may sometimes demand that an offence-led strategy is pursued with a high degree of intensity. In such cases, there may be new offences created, and new resources to secure a higher degree of enforcement, as well as, on the non-legal side, the engagement of local bodies in, for example, public information campaigns.

Conclusion on public interest offences

2.24 Public interest offences are not our main concern in this CP. However, it should be obvious that many of the issues we discuss are of equal relevance to such offences. That is important, given the overlap in many areas between such offences and a regulatory domain. For example, there may be just as strong a reason to have fault elements, or a due diligence defence, in a public interest offence as there is to have such elements in an offence that directly supports a regulatory scheme. Similarly, there may be just as much reason to adopt a civil penalty approach to wrongdoing in the public interest sphere as in the regulatory sphere. Even so, we will not be asking consultation questions, nor making proposals, in relation to public interest offences. This is for the simple reason that the issues are likely to become too quickly merged with controversial issues we have not been asked to address, such as the effectiveness of Anti-Social Behaviour Orders ("ASBOs").

---

[19] It may be different where knife sellers are concerned, although the measures taken by the Government respecting this group (see para 2.21 above) focus on offence-led initiatives.

[20] The Tackling Knives Actions Plan, focused on engaging community and local groups in the effort to educate about and prevent knife crime, has cost a sum well into eight figures. That is not to suggest that this money should have been spent in any other way. Still less are we suggesting that purely criminal offence-led strategies are cheaper (they may well not be). The point is that seeking to educate and persuade the public at large, necessary and desirable though it may be, is an expensive business.

PART 3
CRIMINAL WRONGDOING AND REGULATION

INTRODUCTION: IS THERE SIMPLY TOO MUCH CRIMINAL LAW?

3.1 The simple answer to this question is 'yes', but a simple answer does not necessarily entail a simple solution.

Our approach in brief

3.2 In this Part, we make proposals and ask questions about the use of the criminal law in regulatory contexts. Our overarching theme is that the criminal law is too often used in instances where a non-criminal civil penalty, or other non-criminal measure, would better fit the regulatory context and would be fairer to those subject to regulation. Our proposals and questions relate to ways in which the criminal law should be used in future when Government departments are seeking to deter and punish certain kinds of conduct.

3.3 To illustrate our theme, we will briefly examine three very different areas in which criminal law is used, to varying degrees, to support or to implement a regulatory strategy. These areas involve: (a) targeting parents to reduce truancy by their children, (b) targeting employers to reduce the employment of workers not entitled to work in the UK, and (c) targeting businesses to improve the safety of consumers.

3.4 In each case, we will assess some of the strengths and weaknesses of the use of the criminal law as part of the targeting strategy. That assessment will provide the basis for our proposals and questions. As will be seen, there are a variety of considerations and factors at stake when conduct falls to be deterred or punished, bearing on whether or not criminalisation is appropriate. It is not a simple matter.

3.5 The choice between civil sanction or criminal penalty is determined in part by questions of degree. For example, in relation to implementing an EU obligation, the guidance currently issued by the Ministry of Justice and the Department for Business, Enterprise and Regulatory Reform[1] requires departments to ask the question:

> Does the obligation require "dissuasive and proportionate" sanctions? (In appropriate circumstances this could mean the creation of criminal sanctions).[2]

---

[1] Now the Department for Business, Innovation and Skills.

[2] Ministry of Justice and the Department for Business, Enterprise and Regulatory Reform, *Guidance on Creating New Regulatory Penalties* (26 January 2009), p 3.

3.6   In broad terms, this is the right approach. That is to say, the guidance does not seek to rely on an intrinsic distinction in kind (producing a bright line) between conduct appropriately targeted through the criminal law, and conduct better targeted through civil sanctions or private remedies. Instead, the guidance treats that distinction as one of degree. The right question is whether, for example, the nature and degree of unacceptable risk posed by conduct together point towards a need for the deterrent and retributive effect of a criminal sanction, as opposed to a civil penalty, even though that will mean having to prove beyond reasonable doubt that the risk was posed.

3.7   All laws that create offences, whether criminal offences or civil penalties, should be as clear and specific in nature as possible, with fault elements and sentencing options that reflect the nature or gravity of the wrongdoing.

3.8   What sets criminal laws apart from civil penalties (and from other non-criminal steps that a regulator may take to deter or encourage conduct), is that either the intention or one of the important effects of criminal conviction is to create significant stigma.[3]

3.9   There are two dimensions to the latter proposition. The first is restrictive: when a criminal offence is created, its function should be to stigmatise the offender as a reprehensible wrongdoer. It should not be used merely (although it may be used in a supporting role) as a way of regulating conduct. The second dimension is interpretive: when an offence is created, it should be regarded as criminal in nature if conviction would have the effect of stigmatising both the offence and the offender.

3.10   One way in which our overall approach to regulatory legislation can be exemplified is by the use of a hierarchy of offences, to capture an adequate range of wrongdoing. For example, purely civil penalties, that can be committed without a substantially stigmatising fault element, can be underpinned by a more serious offence involving dishonesty, intention, knowledge or recklessness.[4] In such a scheme, it will be clear that the latter offence is meant to be the criminal offence. Cases involving the most serious forms of such wrongdoing may be met, if this is really necessary for adequate retribution and deterrence, with a sentence of imprisonment.

3.11   As we said in Part 1, in his report on regulatory justice, which led to the passing of the Regulatory Enforcement and Sanctions Act 2008, Professor Macrory said:

---

[3]   For a helpful discussion, see A Ashworth, "Is the Criminal Law a Lost Cause?" [2000] 116 *Law Quarterly Review* 225.

[4]   That is not to endorse a proposition to the effect that civil penalties should be unconcerned with fault. It will commonly be right to involve some fault element in a civil penalty, although this may take a number of forms. A fault element such as without reasonable excuse may be expressly included in a regulatory penalty, and rightly so.

> Some consultation responses have supported my view that there may be a case for decriminalising certain offences thereby reserving criminal sanctions for the most serious cases of regulatory non-compliance.[5]

3.12 We believe Professor Macrory's wish to see a substantial amount of de-criminalisation will only be fulfilled through adopting this kind of approach.

3.13 Finally, when the criminal law is employed in regulatory contexts, a question is always liable to arise over the extent to which there should be duplication of certain kinds of offence. Here are two examples. An agency involved in making grants to support a certain type of business may, as part of its regulatory structure, have offences designed to deter the misleading inflation of claims for grants. To what extent should such offences overlap with the offences of fraud under the Fraud Act 2006? An agency may wish to prohibit not only the causing of harm, but attempts or agreements to cause it, or conduct that may assist and encourage harm-causing conduct. To what extent should these offences duplicate the offences in the general law of attempt, conspiracy, and assisting and encouraging crime?

3.14 Closely related to this issue is that of the placement of offences in legislation. To give a simple example, it is perfectly legitimate to use special criminal offences in farming legislation to deter conduct that may result in the spread of Bovine Spongiform Encephalopathy (BSE).[6] However, the criminal law already prohibits acts that unlawfully and maliciously (intentionally or recklessly) cause someone to take a noxious thing, thereby endangering their lives, for which there is a ten year maximum sentence.[7] So, there is an argument that, whatever else they cover, special criminal offences in farming legislation should not cover cases in which it can be proved that someone's intentional or reckless conduct actually led to an infection of another person with human BSE. Such cases are already covered by the existing law.

3.15 These issues are addressed below.

Two quick fixes assessed

Is it simply a question of numbers?

3.16 It would be perfectly possible for a Government to insist that every relevant Government department reduce its stockpile of criminal offences by 25% over (say) five years. That is not the kind of law reform proposal that can be put forward by the Law Commission, whatever might be said about its merits. This is because it would be a policy decision, and in that sense a political response to having given an affirmative answer to the question posed at the start of this Part.

---

[5] R Macrory, *Regulatory Justice: Making Sanctions Effective* (Better Regulation Executive) (Final Report, November 2006) para 1.39.

[6] See, for example, the offences created by The Transmissible Spongiform Encephalopathies (England) Regulations SI 2008 No 1881.

[7] Offences Against the Person Act 1861, s 23.

3.17   In taking such an approach, though, it would be important to bear in mind some difficulties with the commonly heard proposition that there are too many criminal offences, and so the policy priority must be to address the sheer number of such offences.

3.18   In evaluating this proposition, it can be hard to make sense of the notion of 'too many', in this context. For example, in comparing England and Wales with other jurisdictions one may not be comparing like with like. Further, in counting simple numbers one may overlook sound reasons for breaking up what was a single offence (say, murder) into two offences (say, first degree murder and second degree murder[8]) or similar reasons for extending an offence by analogy (say, rape[9]) by creating an additional offence (such as assault by penetration[10]). More fundamentally, the notion of too many offences lacks a theoretically or practically defensible reference point. Exactly how many is an ideal number? How many would be, by way of contrast, too few?

3.19   Not the least of the difficulties in seeking to answer these kinds of questions is that, by focusing on numbers alone, there is the risk that one will wrongly fail to take into account vital qualitative considerations. For example, it is always possible to seek to rely on only one very broadly defined offence (such as public nuisance) to govern a given area to be regulated.[11] Pursuing such a strategy, one simply trusts the judiciary to apply the offence, with the exercise of some ingenuity in the exercise of their law-application discretion, in a way that both supports regulatory aims satisfactorily but also respects the need for predictability.[12] Appealing though such a solution may still be to some, it seems to us to be a relic of a bygone era. Such a solution must almost inevitably reduce the quality of regulatory impact in the area in question.[13]

3.20   More important than a concern about the simple numbers of offences is a concern about the law-creation processes that lead to the numbers. For example, we will suggest later in this Part that there is too much reliance on direct criminalisation to implement European law. We will explore other strategies that may be employed to secure regulatory compliance without the need for direct criminalisation.[14]

---

[8]   See, for example, Murder, Manslaughter and Infanticide (2006) Law Com No 304.

[9]   Sexual Offences Act 2003, s 1.

[10]   Sexual Offences Act 2003, s 2.

[11]   See the discussion in Simplification of the Criminal Law: Public Nuisance and Outraging Public Decency (2010) Law Commission Consultation Paper No 193.

[12]   Thereby doing something to safeguard people's human rights in the process. The House of Lords had to address this kind of problem in *R v Rimmington and Goldstein* [2005] UKHL 63; [2006] 1 AC 549.

[13]   See the analysis of Professor Black, Appendix A.

[14]   See paras 3.50 to 3.95 below. The meaning of direct, as opposed to indirect, criminalisation will become clear in the later discussion.

A general category of administrative offence?

3.21 Some jurisdictions have sought to carve out a formal distinction between crimes and other offences through the creation of a different procedure for each type of crime.

3.22 In Germany, following the passing of the Regulatory Offences Act 1968, there is a distinction between crimes (*Straftaten*), and breaches of regulations (*Ordnungswidrigkeiten*). A distinction along very broadly similar lines exists in France.[15]

3.23 The characteristic feature of an administrative offence is that a legally authorised person – who may him or herself be employed in the private sector – determines whether a regulatory offence has been committed, and imposes a penalty, or in some cases, a preventative measure, on the offender, or reports the offender to a higher authority to this end. The offender may then appeal, either to a court or to some other body, by virtue of a specially created appeal procedure.

3.24 In England and Wales, there is no general administrative offence regime. However, there are individual schemes for the employment of such offences in specific contexts. So, both parking offences, and civil penalty offences created by the Financial Services Authority (FSA), are subject to specially created appeals systems whose function is to keep the matters in question outside the traditional court system, so far as appeal (rather than judicial review) is concerned.

3.25 Should these kinds of individual examples be drawn together into a coherent and comprehensive scheme of administrative offences? In theory, there could be process benefits from the introduction of such a scheme. First, if employed generally, it could free the criminal courts from a very high volume of cases that may involve relatively trivial or technical breaches of the law.[16] Secondly, it could free these courts from cases where specialised knowledge outside that of an ordinary criminal court is really needed to assess the nature of the wrong done, in context, and the appropriate penalty. By way of contrast with the problem of high volume, the problem in the latter cases may be that so few will be dealt with by any individual court each year that the wrong approach is taken to those cases that are encountered. This is clear from the illustrative examples provided by Professor Black of how such cases, in the environmental field, have been dealt with by the ordinary criminal courts.[17]

---

[15] See J R Spencer QC and Antje du Bois-Pedain, "Approaches to Strict and Constructive Liability in Continental Criminal Law", in A P Simester (ed) *Appraising Strict Liability* (2005) p 237.

[16] On the importance of this factor, see Rt Hon LJ Auld, *A Review of the Criminal Courts of England and Wales* (September 2001), part 9.

[17] See Appendix A.

3.26   However, the practical question is whether it will be the introduction of a general administrative offence that itself delivers these benefits. There is the distinct possibility that the benefits are in fact delivered by the greater involvement of experts in specific regulated fields, in determining in the first instance whether particular risks have been posed, whether breaches of the law have taken place, and what the appropriate sanctions are. If that is right, it would be better to retain the current, emerging system in England and Wales under which regimes involving civil penalties and analogous measures are to a considerable degree tailor-made for each enforcement authority, and do not form part of a more general scheme. Such a context-specific approach to the greater use of civil measures does not, of course, diminish the importance of having general guidelines and a 'good practice' manual on the creation and use of such measures.

3.27   Nonetheless, it has been suggested by some commentators that a much more general system of administrative offence should be created, lodged between criminal proceedings and private civil law remedial actions. For example, Mr Kiron Reid[18] has argued that:

> Non-criminal 'offences' should be specified as regulatory or administrative to ensure fair labelling … . It would obviously be difficult to create a code of administrative offences quickly, but it could be done if a Criminal Code itself is adopted or, failing that, by placing new minor offences in an administrative code and incorporating such existing offences in the code over time.[19]

AGAINST A GENERAL ADMINISTRATIVE OFFENCE REGIME

3.28   The creation of such a regime is not a panacea for all ills. In our view, it would in fact be capable of generating as many problems as it solves.

---

[18]   University of Liverpool.

[19]   K Reid, "Strict Liability: Some Principles for Parliament" (2008) 29 *Statute Law Review* 173, 194.

3.29 First, complex and sophisticated systems have had to be created for administrative regimes, to try to ensure that, in appropriate cases, they meet the requirements for criminal proceedings of article 6(3) of the European Convention on Human Rights.[20] These requirements may need to be met, for example, where the defendant has, through carelessness, collided with a parked car, if the European Court decides that the offence is a criminal one.[21] In that regard, the European Court said that, in deciding whether an offence was criminal and thus subject to article 6(3), the following considerations are relevant:

(1) a member state's own classification of the offence would not be dispositive;

(2) the nature of the offence was a relevant factor;

(3) the severity of any available penalty was a relevant factor.[22]

3.30 As these considerations may operate independently, the fact that, for example, an offence can be met only with a fine (consideration (3)) does not mean that it can be classified as other than criminal. Similarly, it follows that Mr Reid's view that minor offences could simply be transferred to a code of administrative offences[23] might prove to be a mistake, if any article 6(3) protections are thereby abandoned, because the minor nature of an offence does not conclusively determine whether or not it is truly criminal. The same point could be made about the protection under article 6(2) concerning the presumption of innocence. For example, Professor Spencer and Dr du Bois-Pedain have indicated that under the French system of *contraventions* (administrative offences):

---

[20] Article 6(3) establishes that "Everyone charged with a criminal offence has the following minimum rights: (a) to be informed promptly, in a language which he understands and in detail, of the nature and cause of the accusation against him; (b) to have adequate time and the facilities for the preparation of his defence; (c) to defend himself in person or through legal assistance of his own choosing or, if he has not sufficient means to pay for legal assistance, to be given it free when the interests of justice so require; (d) to examine or have examined witnesses against him and to obtain the attendance and examination of witnesses on his behalf under the same conditions as witnesses against him; (e) to have the free assistance of an interpreter if he cannot understand or speak the language used in court". See the discussion in B Emmerson et al, *Human Rights and Criminal Justice* (2nd ed 2007) pp 192 to 198; A Pinto QC and M Evans, *Corporate Criminal Liability* (2nd ed 2008) pp 164 to 166.

[21] *Öztürk v Germany* (1984) 6 EHRR 409. The issue under consideration in this case was whether the defendant could legitimately be charged an interpreter's fee to assist him during the proceedings. The court's answer was that he could not legitimately be charged a fee for this service, because the charge was criminal and thus required free provision of such a service.

[22] *Engel v Netherlands* (1979-80) 1 EHRR 647.

[23] See the passage cited at para 3.27 above.

The simplified rules of criminal procedure ... ensure that they [contraventions] also carry something like a reverse burden of proof. Article 537(2) of the Code of Criminal Procedure provides that, for the purpose of establishing contraventions, official written reports from competent officials are taken to be true unless the contrary is proved.[24]

3.31 Further, it must be kept in mind that the European Court of Human Rights considers individual cases on their merits, and does not pass judgment on systems. So, no offence (or the procedure governing its prosecution) under a purportedly civil penalty or administrative regime is ever completely safe from classification in Strasbourg as a criminal offence. It is, for example, unclear whether an insider dealing case dealt with through market abuse proceedings undertaken by the Financial Services Authority would be validly treated as a civil case.[25] We simply do not know, until the European Court rules on the matter. This problem is especially damaging for a regime which seeks to treat all financial penalty regimes as part of a single 'administrative offence' regime, because the integrity of the entire system may be cast into doubt by the striking down of any one set of penalties within its ambit.

3.32 Secondly, any attempt to divide all offences in England and Wales into truly criminal and merely administrative is likely to result in long and sometimes inconclusive argument in many cases over which category is the most appropriate, both respecting old offences and proposed ones. Problems of parity, or of incommensurability, as between offences will quickly surface and will not be easy to dispel. Many people worry that it is already too difficult in some instances to secure sufficient Parliamentary scrutiny of Bills that include provisions creating criminal offences. Adding in this way to the number of issues that must be considered in that regard will make adequate scrutiny an even more difficult goal to attain.

3.33 Moreover, there is no guarantee that, once an offence has been classified in a particular way it will be left to remain undisturbed in its category. It is not fanciful to suppose that re-classification could develop into a whole new basis for seeking amendments to existing legislation. It is hard to see what merit there would be in such a development.

3.34 Thirdly, there is a risk that, for reasons of political or bureaucratic expediency, conduct which ought to be regarded as truly criminal will be classified as merely administrative. Examples under the German Criminal Code include reproducing banknotes and coins (for a long time, an offence that attracted the death penalty in England), and money laundering.

---

[24] J R Spencer QC and Antje du Bois-Pedain, "Approaches to Strict and Constructive Liability in Continental Criminal Law", in A P Simester (ed) *Appraising Strict Liability* (2005) p 262, cited by K Reid, "Strict Liability: Some Principles for Parliament" (2008) 29 *Statute Law Review* 173, 189.

[25] A Pinto QC and M Evans, *Corporate Criminal Liability* (2nd ed 2008) p 282.

3.35 Conversely, it will become easier, respecting conduct which ought not to be prohibited at all, to draw it into the net by making it a merely administrative offence rather than a criminal offence. It may seem to some that the mid-way course of making conduct they believe to be wrong an administrative offence will allow society to get past deadlock on or ceaseless controversy over whether or not to subject conduct to legal intervention. In many instances, it is hard to see this as anything other than a troubling prospect. It may be just as objectionable that one may be called to account for one's conduct by an administrative tribunal, even if the stigma of criminal conviction will not follow a finding of guilt.[26]

3.36 Finally, a point made earlier,[27] a unified concept of an administrative offence may, depending on the form it takes, deprive regulators of the specialised forms of offence or procedure that they genuinely need to tackle wrongdoing in their field.

3.37 In this CP, we will assume that regimes that introduce civil penalties or other analogous measures, to suit very different contexts, will not be improved by having to place those penalties in a more general administrative offence regime. Having said that, a more uniform approach may be appropriate where appeals against those penalties are concerned, a matter tackled later in this Part.[28]

CRIMINAL PROCEEDINGS AND REGULATORY LAW

A procedural understanding of criminal offences

3.38 It is important to say more about what we understand by a 'regulatory' context, and what we mean when speaking of, for example, 'non-criminal' civil penalties, and the like. In that respect, a rigid distinction between criminal or regulatory law and criminal or regulatory procedure may confuse rather more than it illuminates, even though one of our central concerns is the question of what conduct may be treated as criminal wrongdoing. Very broadly, the identification of criminal procedure provides an important foundation on which an understanding of criminal conduct can then be constructed.

3.39 The most helpful way to decide whether conduct is 'criminal' conduct in law is to examine it in terms of the kinds of legal procedures that are employed against it, rather than in terms of whether it has some intrinsic quality (of wickedness or harmfulness, and so) that makes it worthy of condemnation through criminal procedures.[29] Put shortly, conduct will be a criminal offence if, in a contested case, the allegation that it has occurred:

(1) must be pursued through the Crown Court or magistrates' courts;

(2) must be proved in such a court beyond reasonable doubt to have occurred; and

[26] For an analogous discussion, briefly considering administrative bodies constituted to assess the genuineness of, for example, conscientious objection, see J Raz, *The Authority of Law* (1979) pp 287 to 288.

[27] See paras 3.25 to 3.26 above.

[28] See para 3.159 and following below.

[29] See, for example, Glanville Williams, "The Definition of Crime" (1955) 8 *Current Legal Problems* 107.

(3)   when it has been proved to have occurred, the court may (although it need not) impose a detrimental, punitive measure on the offender simply because he or she is responsible for the occurrence of the conduct: the courts are, in other words, not confined to imposing preventative, compensatory or rehabilitative measures.

3.40   We do not put this forward as a definitive understanding of crime and criminal procedure. Some of the conditions imposed may not in some circumstances be necessary, if conduct is to be properly regarded as subject to criminal proceedings, and we may have omitted other conditions. What we have just described is more of a central case species of analysis than one of definition. The important function it is meant to perform is to accommodate and emphasise the fact that the same piece of conduct (such as damage to property) may be regarded as a civil wrong, or as a criminal offence, depending on the nature of the proceedings against it. Having said that, there are, of course, some kinds of wrongdoing that it would be unfair and disproportionate to subject to criminalisation and to criminal proceedings. This is an issue considered in Part 4 below.

3.41   Our understanding of crime and of criminal proceedings must be kept in mind when we turn our attention below to the examination of the kinds of conduct that it would be acceptable to make subject to such proceedings.

3.42   Traditional forms of civil procedure could be described using the same organising distinctions, with the relevant factors changed as appropriate: County Courts instead of Crown Courts, a balance of probabilities standard of proof instead of a beyond reasonable doubt standard, and remedies including those in the form of injunction, compensation, or restitution, instead of punishment. However, our concern in this CP is not with traditional civil procedure but with procedures to secure compliance adopted by regulators, procedures that may include criminal procedure.

Should criminal offences and regulatory offences be distinguished?

3.43   We will not be employing the familiar but misleading distinction between criminal offences and penalties, and regulatory offences and penalties. The distinction is unhelpful because criminal offences and criminal prosecution are, for better or worse, sometimes central to the way in which regulators must pursue their regulatory aims, and may have been designed for that purpose. Not uncommon examples are offences of pretending to be an authorised person under a regulatory scheme,[30] offences of obstructing a regulatory official in his or her legitimate attempt to gain access to premises or to documents,[31] and offences of dishonestly or recklessly providing false information in applications for licences or to have one's name placed on an approved register, or the like.[32]

---

[30]   The REACH Enforcement Regulations SI 2008 No 2852, 13(4).

[31]   See, for example, s 75(7) of the Education and Skills Act 2008 and s 63(7) of the Health and Social Care Act 2008.

[32]   See, for example, s 58(3) of the Planning Act 2008 and s 36(1) of the Health and Social Care Act 2008.

3.44 Moreover, a proper jurisprudential analysis of regulatory offences reveals them to be just a kind of subordinate rule created under powers conferred by primary legislation. It follows that such offences may include criminal offences of all kinds. Jurisprudentially, what marks such offences out is not their content or consequences, but how they were made.

3.45 That being so, it is not surprising to find that the courts have run into difficulties when they have tried to distinguish criminal offences and so-called regulatory offences. In that regard, Peter Glazebrook has gone so far as to say that, in seeking to make the distinction, there is now no more than "an all too familiar litany of vague, overlapping criteria".[33] The courts have been called on to give guidance on the basis for the distinction, when the distinction touches on the question whether to interpret a statutory offence as involving an implicit requirement of fault.

3.46 In *Sweet v Parsley*, Lord Diplock described so-called regulatory offences as involving "regulation of a particular activity involving potential danger".[34] The immediate difficulty with this definition is that many criminal offences aimed at the public at large also have, as a significant part of their rationale, the potential danger involved in a particular activity. Examples might be arranging or facilitating commission of a child sex offence,[35] possession of a firearm without a valid certificate,[36] or being a member of a proscribed organisation.[37]

3.47 In discussing the desirability of implying fault requirements, Lord Diplock once sought to contrast regulatory crime (which he regarded as in general highly context-specific) with "penal provisions ... of general application to the conduct of ordinary citizens in the course of their everyday life".[38] However, many true crimes have a bearing only in specific contexts (such as bribery), and may be far removed from the course of everyday life (such as treason or terrorism). On the other hand, many so-called regulatory offences have a very direct bearing on ordinary people in everyday life, because – like health and safety at work offences – they have an impact on the way that millions of people go about their daily work.

3.48 The lack of a practically workable distinction between truly criminal and so-called regulatory offences has led to categorisations that might bemuse the lay person, as well as the lawyer, seeking clarification on the point. For example, because they involve issues of 'social concern',[39] the following have been held to be offences that are truly criminal in character:

---

[33] P Glazebrook, "How old did you think she was?" (2001) 60(1) *Cambridge Law Journal* 26.

[34] *Sweet v Parsley* [1970] AC 132, 163.

[35] Sexual Offences Act 2003, s 4.

[36] Firearms Act 1968, s 1.

[37] Terrorism Act 2000, s 11.

[38] *Sweet v Parsley* [1970] AC 132, 163.

[39] The phrase of Lord Scarman in *Gammon v Attorney-General for Hong Kong* [1985] AC 1, 14. This phrase is especially unhelpful, in that it would appear neither to provide a basis for distinguishing regulatory from true crime, nor to provide a sufficient condition for making conduct either a regulatory or a truly criminal offence.

(1)   deviating from the approved plan for construction work, thus contravening local construction regulations;[40]

(2)   using a station for wireless telegraphy without a licence.[41]

3.49   By way of contrast, the following have be found *not* to be truly criminal in character:

(1)   selling a lottery ticket to someone under the age of 16;[42]

(2)   breach of the Water Resources Act 1991;[43]

(3)   offences of false description under the Trade Descriptions Act 1968.[44]

3.50   We suggest that there is in fact nothing in principle to distinguish these cases. It does not seem likely that what drives the distinctions the courts have drawn between 'true' crime and 'regulatory' crime has been some intrinsic factor present in one but absent in the other. It seems more likely that the driving factor has been an underlying concern about the fairness of procedures adopted by prosecutors in the relevant context. Requiring the prosecution to prove fault may be a way in which courts see themselves as contributing to more discriminating prosecution policy, in relation to a given offence.

3.51   Instead of contrasting criminal offences with so-called regulatory offences, we will contrast criminal offences with civil penalties, orders and remedies. These are those penalties, orders and remedies that can be applied to someone without that application necessarily having to be decided through a hearing in a criminal court. On this view, a fine imposed by the Financial Services Authority, and a 'stop now' order issued by a trading standards officer, are civil penalties or orders. Similarly, a parenting order is a civil order because although it must be made by a court, that court need not be a criminal court. It may be that there is an appeal against such penalties or orders to a criminal court. That will not prevent the penalty, order or remedy in question being in the first instance a civil penalty.

---

[40]   *Gammon v Attorney-General for Hong Kong* [1985] AC 1. Lest it be thought that such a deviation must by its nature involve grave danger, it should be kept in mind that even a deviation that vastly improved the safety of the building to be constructed would amount to an offence.

[41]   *R v Blake* [1997] 1 WLR 1167.

[42]   *London Borough of Harrow v Shah* [2000] 1 WLR 83. The defendants were found vicariously liable when unbeknown to them an employee sold a lottery ticket, reasonably believing the purchaser to be over 16 years of age. The court described the defendants as, "honest, decent, and law-abiding shopkeepers" (at 89). The offence is punishable with up to two years' imprisonment.

[43]   *Hart v Anglian Water* [2003] EWCA Crim 2243, (2004) 1 Cr App R (S) 374.

[44]   *Wings Ltd v Ellis* [1985] AC 272, 293.

THE USE OF THE CRIMINAL LAW IN REGULATORY CONTEXTS

3.52   We will now turn to consider the way in which the criminal law is currently used to support, or to lead, regulatory schemes. We do so by considering three very different areas in which the criminal law has this role: truancy, the illegal use of migrant workers, and promoting product safety. The diversity of these contexts helps us to draw up a wider range of what we will at the end of this Part suggest are desirable features of the use of the criminal law in regulatory contexts.

Context 1: truancy and the Education Act 1996

3.53   In 2009, some 67,000 school days were lost through truancy. A common assumption is that truants have taken it upon themselves to miss school. In fact, many truants have their parents' permission to be off school with undocumented illnesses, or are otherwise with their parents at the relevant time when they should be at school, perhaps on holiday. Sometimes truants are looking after siblings at home because parents or other relatives are sick or absent. It has for some time been an offence for a parent or guardian to fail to ensure that a child attends school regularly.

The regulatory element

3.54   The Government's policy in relation to the reduction of truancy has involved the development of a regulation strategy, and related changes to the structure of criminal offences under the Education Act 1996. Under the regulatory strategy, for example, parenting contracts may (if the parents agree) be used to help to secure parents' co-operation in ensuring that their children attend school.[45] In the event that such measures are not effective, non-compliance must be brought to the attention of the court in any subsequent criminal prosecution.[46]

---

[45]   See, for example, s 19 of the Anti-Social Behaviour Act 2003 and the Crime and Disorder Act 1998.

[46]   Department for Education and Skills, *Ensuring Regular Attendance at School* (2003) paras 53 to 57.

3.55 Next up on the ladder of intervention are parenting orders. Whilst aimed principally at involving parents in the prevention of anti-social behaviour by their children, these orders can require the parent, amongst other things, to take steps to ensure that their children attend school regularly. Breach of a parenting order, without reasonable excuse, is an offence punishable by a fine of up to £1000 in the magistrates' court, although it is not a recordable offence for the purposes of the Police and Criminal Evidence Act 1984.[47] This is, in essence, an offence that supports a regulatory strategy, in that parenting orders are devised and requested at court by the relevant authority. It is also an example of a two-step prohibition. A two-step prohibition involves a civil order, as the first step, and then a criminal offence constituted by breach of the civil order, as a second step.[48] This is a phenomenon that we consider in more detail below.[49]

The statutory offences

3.56 Then, there are the statutory offences.

3.57 By virtue of section 444(1) of the Education Act 1996, if a school-age child who is a registered pupil fails to attend regularly at school, the parent is guilty of an offence punishable by a fine up to £1000.[50] This is the traditional offence.

3.58 There is no defence to this offence of due diligence shown, or of impossibility. So, it is no defence that, for example, parental disability, fear of an aggressive teenager's reaction (short of duress, in law), or the need to ensure several children attending different schools all attend regularly, means that it is not in practice possible to ensure that the child in question attends school regularly. Having said that, there is liable to be a fault element in the offence in practice, albeit not one that need expressly be proven. Given that the offence is only committed if a child fails to attend school regularly, and is not committed on the first instance of non-attendance, it is likely that in most instances a parent or guardian will have had some opportunity to ensure that their child does attend school regularly.

---

[47] Youth Justice Board, Disposals: Parenting Orders, http://www.yjb.gov.uk/en-gb/practitioners/CourtsAndOrders/Disposals/ParentingOrder/ (last visited 8 June 2010).

[48] See A P Simester and A von Hirsch, "Regulating Offensive Conduct through Two-Step Prohibitions", in A von Hirsch and A P Simester, *Incivilities: Regulating Offensive Behaviour* (2006).

[49] See paras 3.89 to 3.94 below.

[50] In practice, offenders sentenced under the Education Act 1996 are poor, and receive correspondingly low fines.

3.59   There are some special, context-specific defences to the offence. For example, under section 444(5), it is a defence if the school at which the child is registered is not within walking distance of the child's residence.[51] It is important to bear in mind, when considering possible defences to otherwise strict liability offences, that a range of context-specific defences may sometimes be a better way of doing justice than the provision of a more general due diligence defence. It may provide both fairer and more certain law, from the perspective of both prosecutors and potential offenders, so long as it in practice covers the issues bearing on what it means to show due diligence in the relevant context.

3.60   Prior to recent changes, the reliance on this offence alone did not in our view amount to a good use of the criminal law. On the one hand, the strict nature of liability meant that the offence could in theory be committed in some absurd circumstances, as when a single parent is banned by an Anti-Social Behaviour Order ("ASBO") from going into an area that includes the school, and so by compliance with the ASBO thereby fails to ensure a child's regular attendance. On the other hand, even in cases of persistent and wilful neglect, the maximum fine might prove to be inadequate to satisfy the demands of retribution and deterrence.

3.61   In 2000, however, a new, more serious offence was added, buttressing the offence under section 444(1).[52] The new offence is committed if, in the circumstances described in section 444(1), the parent knew that the child was not attending school regularly but failed without reasonable justification to cause the child to do so. This offence is punishable by a fine of up to £2,500, three months' imprisonment, or both.

3.62   In the first case taken involving the more serious offence, D had been visited 71 times in 12 months by social services seeking to secure her daughter's regular attendance at school. She had also been in breach of a parenting order. In May 2002, D was sentenced to 60 days' imprisonment (reduced, on appeal, to 28 days). When she re-offended two years later, she was sentenced to a further 28 days in prison.

3.63   The use of imprisonment in a case involving a mother with school-age children is a drastic step. However, the justification for it in this case is clearly that only such a sentence could support the Education and Welfare Services more generally in their attempts, at earlier stages, to take a graduated approach involving a compliance strategy.[53]

---

[51]   Walking distance being stated as 2 miles or 3.218688 kilometres for a child under eight and for a child eight and over 3 miles or 4.828032 kilometres, measured by the nearest available route.

[52]   Section 444(1A) of the Education Act 1996, added by s 72(1) of the Criminal Justice and Court Services Act 2000.

[53]   A year on from the first conviction, D's eldest daughter won a school prize for English.

3.64   A further advantage may be gained if compliance authorities know that the courts will, if ultimately called upon to do so, take a firm line on the demands of retribution in particular (as well as deterrence). Such knowledge arguably makes it more likely that regulators or other appropriate authorities will, at first, pursue non-criminal options aimed at securing compliance by consent. They will do this because they have confidence that the courts will accept that the criminal process stands at the apex of a response pyramid, where breach of standards is concerned. We are, of course, not suggesting that only the use of imprisonment is an adequate response to a regulator's decision finally to bring a criminal prosecution against a persistent offender. The fact that Parliament has provided for fines as an alternative, as well as an addition to, imprisonment, shows that this is not the case.

3.65   In the period 2000 to 2006, 72 parents were sent to jail for the more serious offence, whilst some 16,500 received spot fines, and a further 4,700 were convicted in court of one or other offence under section 444. These aggregate figures conceal a clear increase in the period, year on year, in the number of people respectively convicted, imprisoned, or fined for committing one or other of the offences.

3.66   At this point it is very important to say that the introduction of the more serious offence casts serious doubt on the value of continuing with the less serious one. This is not simply because there is already a range of non-criminal regulatory steps that the authorities can take (such as making parenting orders, or agreeing parenting contracts) that can address parental neglect in a more positive way. It is also because there may be scope in this area for the introduction of formal warnings, formal notices that behaviour must improve, and civil penalties, to be administered by child welfare authorities. The penalties might, for example, be comprised of fines based on a certain amount for each day of school missed by the child in question.

The relationship of the regulatory element to the statutory offences

3.67   We have noted that a parent or guardian's record in complying with parenting orders or contracts, as alternative to prosecution, must be brought before the court when an offence has been successfully prosecuted under section 444. That kind of information is essential to ensuring that the courts hand down the right kinds of sentence, following an authority's successful decision to prosecute. In her work on our behalf, Professor Black noted the potentially adverse consequences of sentencing decisions taken in the absence of adequate contextual information of this kind.[54]

---

[54]   See Appendix A.

3.68   It is also important to note that, on the contrary, where a prosecution is brought by an appropriate authority, and there is no evidence of other steps having been taken up to that point to secure compliance by the defendant, under the 1996 Act, the court has the power to order that such steps be taken before the prosecution can proceed.[55] Section 447(2) of the 1996 Act provides that:

> The court … may direct the local education authority instituting the proceedings to apply for an education supervision order with respect to the child unless the authority, having consulted the appropriate local authority, decide that the child's welfare will be satisfactorily safeguarded even though no education supervision order is made.

3.69   Seeking to forge these kinds of connections between regulatory intervention, and the intervention of the criminal courts, must help to create a better-ordered relationship between the two.

Our analysis

3.70   We broadly commend the approach to offence construction in this field, and the way in which it has been related to the regulatory element. On this approach, an Act creates an offence ladder. The ladder is constituted by an offence or offences carrying low to moderate punishments, and an offence or offences requiring proof of high-level fault with more severe punishments available. However, in regulatory contexts, great care must be taken to ensure that there is a real need for low-level offences at the bottom of the offence ladder. Where there are flexible non-criminal regulatory steps that can be taken both to encourage good behaviour and to deter unacceptable behaviour, these steps may in many cases make low-level offences redundant.

3.71   In this context, the offence constituted by breach of a parenting order is on the same level, in terms of available sentence (a fine of £1000 at most), as the minor statutory offence under section 444. That might suggest that the minor offence under section 444 now has little or no role to play in this field. However, it must be kept in mind that parenting orders are not solely or mainly devised for use in this context, but are chiefly a means of seeking to secure parents' involvement in preventing their children engaging in anti-social behaviour. So, it would not be right to express any concluded view on the issue, although we have tentatively suggested that a penalty system operated by child welfare authorities could replace section 444.[56]

---

[55]   Obviously, it may be that it is the great seriousness of the offence that explains why the prosecution has been brought, and a compliance strategy not pursued, in which case such a power would not be used.

[56]   See para 3.66 above.

Context 2: illegal use of migrant workers

3.72   Concern has increased over the last 10 to 15 years about the number of, and the abuse of, illegal migrant workers in Britain.[57] This has led to a number of initiatives aimed at, amongst other things, deterring employers from hiring illegal migrant workers.

The traditional single offence approach

3.73   The main control on illegal migrant working used to be the criminal offence under section 8 of the Asylum and Immigration Act 1996 (as amended by section 147 of the Nationality, Immigration and Asylum Act 2002). In brief, section 8 made it an offence to employ someone who was not entitled to work in the UK. There was a defence to this offence, if the employer had made certain document checks prior to the point of recruitment to establish a person's entitlement to work and had retained copies of the documents checked.[58]

3.74   As we said in relation to the defence to the offence under section 444 of the Education Act 1996, it is perfectly acceptable that a specialised offence should have a specialised defence, rather than a more general due diligence defence (or the like). This is acceptable, so long as, in substance, the specialised defence focuses on the issues at the heart of due diligence in the context in question.

3.75   However, a familiar problem arose in relation to section 8. It was a summary offence, punishable by a maximum of a £5000 fine. Problems with the cost of mounting successful investigations and prosecutions – and the disappointing response of the courts, in terms of sentencing – meant that rates of prosecution were low. Typically, between 1998 and 2004, only a single prosecution a year would be undertaken.[59]

3.76   When prosecutions were taken, the courts commonly imposed fines far below the maximum, and bearing little relation to the costs of bringing the prosecution. For example, a prosecution typically cost between £1000 and £2000 in staff time alone in the year 2004 to 2005, but the fines imposed were more likely to be three, not four, figure sums. As we have said, Professor Black has highlighted how easily a negative cycle can develop, in which cost and evidentiary issues mean that bringing prosecutions seems only questionably to be in the public interest, and the low level of fines imposed when successful prosecutions are brought reinforces that perception amongst prosecutors.[60]

---

[57]   See, for example, Home Office, *Secure Borders, Safe Havens: Integration with Diversity in Modern Britain* (February 2002) Cm 5387; *Controlling Our Borders: Making Migration Work for Britain* (February 2005) Cm 6478.

[58]   There have been efforts to tighten up the document checking requirements, for the purposes of section 8: see the Immigration (Restrictions on Employment) Order SI 2004 No 755.

[59]   Although, in this period, the Immigration Service did mount a much larger number of operations to catch illegal workers: 390 such operations in 2003, and 1098 in 2004.

[60]   See Appendix A.

The modified approach

3.77   In 2004, the section 8 offence was made triable either way, with the possibility of an unlimited fine being imposed following trial on indictment.[61] With the benefit of hindsight, we doubt if this was the right approach. In principle, it is undesirable simply to increase maximum penalties, or make offences that were previously summary only triable on indictment, without considering the way that the whole offence is itself in need of change. As things turned out, the change in 2004 was only a temporary patch. A new approach was adopted under the Immigration, Asylum and Nationality Act 2006.

3.78   First, under section 15 of the Immigration, Asylum and Nationality Act 2006, a civil penalty regime was introduced, to be administered by the UK Border Agency, through the Illegal Working Civil Penalty Unit.[62] It is designed largely to replace the work done by section 8 of the 1996 Act, and hence to be mainly (but not solely) focused on instances in which illegal migrant working has gone on because an employer has carelessly failed to complete adequate document checks.[63]

3.79   In the year 2004 to 2005, the Government estimated the cost of pursuing to a conclusion a civil penalty action against someone as around £250, as opposed to the £1000 to £2000 for a section 8 prosecution. The civil penalty could be up to £10,000 for each worker, but typically the penalty has been (in total) £5000 on each employer.[64] Even so, this is on average far higher than the fines typically imposed by the courts under section 8 of the 1996 Act. The highest civil penalty imposed in 2008 was £52,500, as compared with the theoretical maximum fine of £5000 under section 8.

3.80   Secondly, a new criminal offence was introduced, which was intended to accommodate more serious cases where a purely civil penalty was insufficient to reflect the employer's wrongdoing. As the Government put it in 2005, in its Regulatory Impact Assessment for the then Immigration, Asylum and Nationality Bill:

---

[61]   Asylum and Immigration (Treatment of Claimants etc) Act 2004, s 6.

[62]   It came into force in February 2008.

[63]   See Home Office, *Illegal Working Task Force Regulatory Impact Assessment for Immigration, Asylum and Nationality Bill* (June 2005) para 16. Guidance is issued to employers on how to comply with the law so as to avoid potential liability to civil penalties.

[64]   A person issued with a civil penalty may object to the UK Border Agency, or appeal against the service of the penalty to the County Court (in England and Wales).

The current section 8 legislation does not distinguish between an employer who employs an illegal worker through inadequate recruitment practices – an act of negligence – and an employer who knowingly employs an illegal worker – an act of deliberate criminality. The current legislation makes clear that an employer loses his defence if he knew an employee was not entitled to work at the point of recruitment but, in terms of sanctions for non-compliance, the legislation treats all employers the same way regardless of knowledge. Creating a knowing offence would remedy this.[65]

3.81 Consequently, section 21 of the Immigration, Asylum and Nationality Act 2006 now provides that someone commits an offence if he employs another ("the employee") knowing that the employee is an adult subject to immigration control and that he has not been granted leave to enter or remain in the United Kingdom, or his leave to enter or remain in the United Kingdom is invalid, has ceased to have effect (whether by reason of curtailment, revocation, cancellation, passage of time or otherwise), or is subject to a condition preventing him from accepting the employment. Upon conviction at trial on indictment, an offender may be sentenced to up to two years' imprisonment, to an unlimited fine, or to both.

Our analysis

3.82 We regard this use of the criminal law in this context as an appropriate form of use. The difference from (and improvement on) the approach to its use under the Education Act 1996, is that the criminal law is being used to support a regulatory scheme involving the imposition of civil penalties for low-level wrongdoing. The criminal law is being employed to target the worst offenders, namely those who engage in deliberate (knowing) wrongdoing, and maximum penalties for engaging in such conduct are set accordingly. Consequently, the minor offence under section 8 of the Asylum and Immigration Act 1996 has seemingly been made by and large redundant, unlike the minor offence in section 444 of the Education Act 1996.

Context 3: promoting product safety

3.83 Finally, we will briefly consider the contribution of the Consumer Protection Act 1987 ("the 1987 Act") towards the greater protection of consumers from unsafe products. A key function of the Act was to provide better remedies for consumers in civil law. However, Professor Cartwright argues that the criminal law has tended to be the primary means by which the state has sought to protect consumers from unsafe products.[66]

---

[65] Home Office, *Illegal Working Task Force Regulatory Impact Assessment for Immigration, Asylum and Nationality Bill* (June 2005) paras 18 to 19.

[66] P Cartwright, *Consumer Protection and the Criminal Law* (2001) p 63.

Offences and defences in the Consumer Protection Act 1987

3.84   The 1987 Act made it an offence to supply consumer goods that did not comply with a general safety requirement. In brief, this requirement was for goods to be reasonably safe, having regard to all the circumstances, where 'safe' meant that there was no risk or only a risk reduced to the minimum.[67] The offence can be met with a sentence of imprisonment of up to six months. The main offence was as follows:

> 10.— (1) A person shall be guilty of an offence if he—
>
> (a)   supplies any consumer goods which fail to comply with the general safety requirement;[68]
>
> (b)   offers or agrees to supply any such goods; or
>
> (c)   exposes or possesses any such goods for supply.

3.85   On the face of it, this appears to be a strict liability offence, but in fact the offence is made subject to two kinds of defence. The first kind, which we have already encountered, involve specialised context-dependent defences. Some of these can be found in section 10(3):

> For the purposes of this section consumer goods shall not be regarded as failing to comply with the general safety requirement in respect of—
>
> (a)   anything which is shown to be attributable to compliance with any requirement imposed by or under any enactment or with any Community obligation;
>
> (b)   any failure to do more in relation to any matter than is required by—
>
>> (i)   any safety regulations imposing requirements with respect to that matter;
>>
>> (ii)   any standards of safety approved for the purposes of this subsection by or under any such regulations and imposing requirements with respect to that matter;
>>
>> (iii)   any provision of any enactment or subordinate legislation imposing such requirements with respect to that matter as are designated for the purposes of this subsection by any such regulations.

3.86   In spite of the fact that such context specific defences have been provided, the 1987 Act goes further. It also includes a more general defence in section 10(4)(b)(ii) that:

---

[67]   P Cartwright, *Consumer Protection and the Criminal Law* (2001) p 137.

[68]   This lengthy requirement is defined in s 10(2) of the Consumer Protection Act 1987.

At the time he [D] supplied the goods or offered or agreed to supply them or exposed or possessed them for supply, he neither knew nor had reasonable grounds for believing that the goods failed to comply with the general safety requirement.

3.87 Similarly, section 39 of the 1987 Act provides that:

Subject to the following provisions of this section, in proceedings against any person for an offence to which this section applies it shall be a defence for that person to show that he took all reasonable steps and exercised all due diligence to avoid committing the offence.

3.88 We have set out these provisions in some detail, because they show how the provision of specialised, context-dependent defences is not inconsistent with providing more general defences. These are defences focused on having neither knowledge nor reasonable grounds for believing that the facts are such that one is acting lawfully, or, that one took all reasonable steps and exercised all due diligence to avoid committing the offence.

Regulatory intervention under the Consumer Protection Act 1987

3.89 The 1987 Act also made it possible for the Secretary of State to create safety regulations, and introduced enforcement measures such as prohibition notices, notices to warn and suspension notices.[69] Breaches of such notices are a criminal offence.[70] However, in each case, there is either an entitlement to make representations that the notice should not be issued (prohibition notices), a consultation process before the issuing of the notice (notices to warn), or an opportunity at law to have the notice set aside (suspension notices).[71] This kind of process-based fairness, fairness in the way enforcement is carried out, is as or more important than including a fault element or defence in a substantive offence. This is because process-based fairness involves the development of sound ethical relations between regulators and those whose activities they must regulate.

3.90 These enforcement measures are an example of the two-step prohibitions that were outlined earlier.[72] As we explained, the first step involves a ban, another kind of mandatory requirement, a warning, or some other indication that behaviour must change, that is imposed as a matter of civil law. The two-step nature of these measures comes about if and when breach of, for example, a stop notice is treated as a criminal offence.[73] The second step involves the possibility of a criminal prosecution in respect of any breach of the civil order. This is indirect, as opposed to direct criminalisation.

---

[69] P Cartwright, *Consumer Protection and the Criminal Law* (2001) p 137.

[70] See ss 13(1) and 14(1) of the Consumer Protection Act 1987. Under the Act, authorised officers are also entitled to make sample purchases, to see if regulations have been contravened.

[71] P Cartwright, *Consumer Protection and the Criminal Law* (2001) pp 232 to 235.

[72] See para 3.55 above.

[73] In some instances, of course, a two-step prohibition could in theory involve only a financial civil penalty for breach of the original notice or undertaking.

3.91   A recent example, in a broader context, is the creation of the offence, contrary to the Regulatory Enforcement and Sanctions Act 2008, of failing to comply with a stop notice issued pursuant to that Act.[74] Where it is appropriate to target individual offenders in some particular respect, and perhaps especially individual businesses, two-step enforcement laws may amount to a fair and reasonable use of the criminal law as a back-up for the civil law.

3.92   The fairness of two-step prohibitions depends on the extent to which, amongst other things, (a) it is possible for the potential offender to seek to engage in consultation over the nature and scope of the initial, civil order (b) the order is clear and certain, and gives adequate opportunity for the offender to comply with it, and (c) the punishment for breach is not disproportionate to the wrong done.

3.93   It is likely to be not only fairer but also more efficient and economic to use the criminal law in this way, in regulatory contexts. This is because it is likely that only a minority of those subject to regulation issued with a stop notice will go on to breach this notice in circumstances dictating that it is now appropriate to commence criminal proceedings against the offender in question.

3.94   When used in regulatory contexts, two-step prohibitions have one of the hallmarks of regulation, in that they almost always involve an expert dimension to the decision to employ them at all, or in a certain way. Their effectiveness is linked both to the general knowledge and experience of the regulatory authority of what works in relation to certain types of activity in the field, and to the authority's particular knowledge of the person in breach of standards and the circumstances that gave rise to that breach.

3.95   In that regard, the responsibility for enforcing the criminal law and regulations, as well as for seeking to gain the co-operation of businesses in improving standards, lies typically with Trading Standards Officers operating in their local areas. The Fair Trading Team at one County Council describes its role in relation to the protection of consumers as follows:

> Working with a business is generally seen as the best way of achieving compliance, but in the more serious cases, for example, those involving dishonesty or wilful neglect, investigations will be undertaken and more formal action considered. In these cases the full range of enforcement powers are available. Depending on the circumstances, these will include seeking an assurance from the business as to their future conduct, sending a warning letter, obtaining a court order preventing similar conduct in the future, issuing a caution or ultimately taking a prosecution. Such actions can be taken against the owners of the business, but in many cases individual employees can be liable too. Offending goods, for example counterfeit items, are likely to be seized and subsequently destroyed and in the most serious of cases offenders can be jailed.[75]

---

[74]   Regulatory Enforcement and Sanctions Act 2008, s 49(1).

[75]   Hampshire County Council, "About Trading Standards" http://www3.hants.gov.uk/tradingstandards/tradingstandards-abouttradingstandards.htm (last visited 15 July 2010).

3.96 Regulations in the area of consumer safety, involving the creation of criminal liability, continue to be made, sometimes in response to European legislation. These are considered next.

Two approaches to relating regulation to criminal law

3.97 In 2008, further regulations were made under delegated powers, to protect consumers. Amongst other things, the Consumer Protection from Unfair Trading Regulations 2008[76] create a number of criminal offences.[77] An example is the prohibition of unfair commercial practices under regulation 3:

> 3.— (1) Unfair commercial practices are prohibited.
>
> (2) Paragraphs (3) and (4) set out the circumstances when a commercial practice is unfair.
>
> (3) A commercial practice is unfair if—
>
>> (a) it contravenes the requirements of professional diligence; and
>>
>> (b) it materially distorts or is likely to materially distort the economic behaviour of the average consumer with regard to the product.
>
> (4) A commercial practice is unfair if—
>
>> (a) it is a misleading action under the provisions of regulation 5;
>>
>> (b) it is a misleading omission under the provisions of regulation 6;
>>
>> (c) it is aggressive under the provisions of regulation 7; …

3.98 Another example is found under regulation 8:

> 8.— (1) A trader is guilty of an offence if—
>
>> (a) he knowingly or recklessly engages in a commercial practice which contravenes the requirements of professional diligence under regulation 3(3)(a); and
>>
>> (b) the practice materially distorts or is likely to materially distort the economic behaviour of the average consumer with regard to the product under regulation 3(3)(b).

---

[76] SI 2008 No 1277.

[77] According to the explanatory note, "these Regulations implement Directive 2005/29/EC of the European Parliament and of the Council concerning unfair business-to-consumer commercial practices ('the Directive') (OJ No L-149, 11.6.2005, p 220). These Regulations also implement article 6.2 Directive 1999/44/EC … on certain aspects of the sale of consumer goods and associated guarantees (OJ No L171, 7.7.1999, p 12)".

3.99 The penalty for these offences, and others, is found in regulation 13:

> 13.— A person guilty of an offence under regulation 8, 9, 10, 11 or 12 shall be liable—
>
> (a) on summary conviction, to a fine not exceeding the statutory maximum; or
>
> (b) on conviction on indictment, to a fine or imprisonment for a term not exceeding two years or both.

3.100 The first significant point about the offences created, in this context, is that they all include fault elements. For example, under regulation 8, it is only an offence to contravene the requirements of professional diligence if D does so knowingly or recklessly. In so far as most of the other offences are concerned, it is, for example, a defence under regulation 17 to show that:

> (a) The commission of the offence was due to:
>
> (i) a mistake;
>
> (ii) reliance on information supplied to him by another person;
>
> (iii) the act or default of another person;
>
> (iv) an accident; or
>
> (v) another cause beyond his [D's] control; and
>
> (b) that he [D] took all reasonable precautions and exercised all due diligence to avoid the commission of such an offence by himself or any person under his control.

3.101 The second point of significance about the offences created is that, in so far as fault requirements are concerned, they broadly reflect what can be called a non-hierarchical approach, when put together with the offence created by primary legislation under the 1987 Act (discussed earlier). In other words, the fault elements, defences, or elements of process-based fairness applicable to the two-step prohibitions and offences created by regulation are as (or sometimes more) generous than those applicable under primary legislation.

3.102 This approach stands in contrast to the hierarchical approach adopted to regulatory intervention and offences aimed at parents of persistently truant children under the Education Act 1996, and at employers of illegal migrant workers under the Immigration, Asylum and Nationality Act 2006. In relation to those two Acts, one finds a hierarchical approach: less generous (or no) fault or defence elements applicable to the civil penalties or to the minor offence, and then a more generous fault requirement applicable to the serious offence.

The compliance argument, in relation to European law

3.103 As indicated above, many modern criminal offences in the field of consumer law are an attempt to give effect to European law. Although the numbers given here involve a substantial element of value judgment about the nature of the offence, of the 73 regulations created by the Department for Business, Innovation and Skills (BIS) in 2008, something like 15 were of direct relevance to consumer interests. For example, in 2008, BIS was successful in bringing on to the statute book the Consumer Protection from Unfair Trading Regulations 2008,[78] in response to two European Directives.[79]

3.104 The 2008 regulations create eight criminal offences. These prohibit a range of unfair commercial practices, such as aggressive commercial practices, those that involve misleading omissions, and those that contravene obligations of professional diligence. Almost all of these regulations say that someone found guilty of an offence (triable either way) can be sentenced to up to two years' imprisonment or an unlimited fine, following conviction on indictment. It may be helpful to give an indication of the sort of crime to which such a maximum sentence is attached in the general law of criminal offences. It is, for example, the same maximum sentence as is available for incest with an adult relative, for exposure, and for voyeurism, under the Sexual Offences Act 2003.[80]

3.105 It is very common to hear the argument that the increase in the number and range of criminal offences on the statute book is due to the fact that the creation of such offences is the simplest and most effective way, as well as in practice often being the only way, to implement European Directives requiring punishment and deterrence. We believe that, with the passage of the Regulatory Enforcement and Sanctions Act 2008, that argument has lost a good deal of force. This is because that Act makes it possible to create two-step prohibitions better calculated to secure compliance with the law than the proliferation of offences involving direct criminalisation. We note that breach of, for example, a stop notice under section 49(1) of the 2008 Act, carries a maximum sentence, following conviction on indictment, of two years' imprisonment.

3.106 We suggest that a much simpler response to the European Directives at issue here would have been to grant power to a relevant authority (a local authority or trading standards officer) to issue a monetary penalty, stop notice or other similar requirement, in respect of the conduct as set out in the Directive. The only criminal offences would then be the ones concerned with breach of stop notices, failure to pay civil penalties, and so on.

3.107 More generally, the indirect criminalisation approach – defining conduct specified in a Directive as appropriate for two-step prohibition – promises to obviate the need for much highly specialised and very narrowly focused direct criminalisation. Complaints about direct criminalisation of this sort were already being made more than 200 years ago by, amongst others, Jeremy Bentham:

---

[78] SI 2008 No 1277.

[79] See n 77 above.

[80] See, respectively, ss 64(1), 66(1) and 67(1) of the Sexual Offences Act 2003.

The country squire, who has his turnips stolen, goes to work and gets a bloody law against stealing turnips. It exceeds the utmost stretch of his comprehension to conceive that the next year the same catastrophe may happen to his potatoes. For two general rules ... in modern British legislation are: never to move a finger until your passions are inflamed, nor ever to look further than your nose.[81]

3.108 For example, the Transmissible Spongiform Encephalopathies (England) Regulations 2008[82] created or re-created over 100 criminal offences, in response to European Directives.[83] We find it hard to believe that these offences, or most of them, could not have been dealt with through, for example, a combination of monetary penalties and two-step procedures, such as those created by the Regulatory Enforcement and Sanctions Act 2008.

Our analysis

3.109 The non-hierarchical approach to consumer protection offences is commendable, for its use of fault and defence elements in the creation of those offences. The reliance on elements of process-fairness, in the form of an obligation to consult, or an opportunity to make representations about, a prospective measure, is also commendable.

3.110 Having said that, there is a need to permit flexibility in approach, across all areas of regulation, when considering the relationship between civil penalties, offences created under regulations, and offences created by primary legislation. Consequently, we do not believe that there is any reason to prioritise the non-hierarchical approach over the hierarchical approach employed in other regulatory legislation.

---

[81] J Bentham, Bentham MSS in the library of the University College, London cxl 92, cited in G Postema, *Bentham and the Common Law* Tradition (1986) p 264.

[82] SI 2008 No 1881.

[83] The explanatory note says, "the Regulations, which apply in England, revoke and remake with amendments the Transmissible Spongiform Encephalopathies (No 2) Regulations 2006 (SI 2006/1228), which enforced Regulation (EC) No 999/2001 of the European Parliament and of the Council laying down rules for the prevention, control and eradication of certain transmissible spongiform encephalopathies (OJ No L 147, 31.5.2001, p 1) as amended ("the Community TSE Regulation"), These Regulations now implement Commission Decision 2007/411 prohibiting the placing on the market of products derived from bovine animals born or reared within the United Kingdom before 1 August 1996 for any purpose and exempting such animals from certain control and eradication measures laid down in Regulation (EC) No 999/2001 and repealing Decision 2005/598 (OJ No L 155, 15.6.2007, p 74).

3.111 However, as indicated above,[84] we have reservations about the possible over-use of direct, individualised offences in this and other, related fields. Our concerns would be met if greater reliance was henceforth placed systematically on a two-step approach, such as that made possible by the Regulatory Enforcement and Sanctions Act 2008. The approach of this Act prioritises civil action to secure compliance over immediate criminalisation. It is only a subsequent failure to comply with the civil obligation that amounts to a criminal offence. This avoids the need for the proliferation of offences as a response to relevant European Directives.

3.112 Finally, we have concerns about the use of delegated powers to create criminal offences, especially when these offences can be met with a sentence of imprisonment. These will be addressed below.

OVERLAPPING, DUPLICATION AND PLACEMENT OF OFFENCES

3.113 Minor but important contributing factors to the excess of criminal legislation in England and Wales are the overlapping and duplication of offences. This can be found in a number of places, of which we will give only a few examples.

3.114 One example involves some parts of the Firearms Act 1968. We are not reviewing that legislation, as such, in the current project. However a feature of the 1968 Act, shared by more modern statutes using the criminal law to support a regulatory scheme,[85] is that important offences are created that may be unnecessary. This is because they are covered by more general offences in the criminal law, such as the offence of attempting to commit an indictable offence, contrary to the Criminal Attempts Act 1981, or the offences of fraud, contrary to the Fraud Act 2006.

Attempts to commit crimes

3.115 First, let us consider offences created in the inchoate mode, apparently without regard for the relationship between those offences and the general law governing inchoate offences. In the 1968 Act, there are unnecessary overlaps in this field in some of the aggravated offences (although it is perhaps some mitigation that the 1968 Act preceded the Criminal Law Act 1977, dealing with conspiracy, and the Criminal Attempts Act 1981).

3.116 For example, section 17 of the 1968 Act makes it an indictable offence to make *or attempt to make* use of a firearm with intent to resist arrest. It is, of course, in a way understandable that, in this context, the attempt to make use of a firearm should be wrapped up in the same offence as the actual making use of a firearm. However, it is questionable whether as a matter of legal principle that is the right approach.

[84] See para 3.20 above.

[85] See, for example, the Animal Welfare Act 2006.

3.117   The Criminal Attempts Act 1981 is quite general in its application. Section 1 of the 1981 Act makes criminal a more than merely preparatory act done with the intent to commit an indictable offence. It follows that the 1981 Act can be applied to the offence under section 17 of the Firearms Act 1968 because it is an indictable offence. So, a person can be charged with an attempt (contrary to the 1981 Act) *to attempt* to make use of a firearm to resist arrest etc (contrary to the 1968 Act), as well as with an attempt (contrary to the 1981 Act) actually to make use of a firearm (contrary to the 1968 Act). The former charge appears to cast the net of liability too wide. The latter charge is problematic for a different reason, although that reason also affects the former charge.

3.118   A charge (under the 1981 Act) of attempting to make use of a firearm to resist arrest will be governed by the rules that the courts have painstakingly set out concerning when an act can be more than merely preparatory to the commission of an offence and hence amount to an attempt under the 1981 Act.[86] These rules will not necessarily apply to the use of the word "attempt" in section 17 of the 1968 Act. So, there is inevitably going to be uncertainty over the meaning of attempt in section 17 of the 1968 Act, as there will be in relation to each and every offence under statute that makes special provision for attempts (that is, provision outside the 1981 Act).[87] In relation, specifically, to the possibility that someone might be charged (under the 1981 Act) with an attempt to attempt (under the 1968 Act) to make use of a firearm to resist arrest, it is not an attractive prospect that two different meanings could in theory be given to the meaning of attempt.

3.119   In an ideal world, attempts to commit indictable offences would be left to be dealt with by the 1981 Act, conspiracies to be dealt with by the 1977 Act, and so on.

3.120   As we can now see, the same point can be made in relation to the offences of assisting and encouraging crime, contrary to the Serious Crime Act 2007.

Assisting and encouraging crime

3.121   Consider the offences of having a firearm in one's possession with intent to enable another person to endanger life with it (section 16 of the Firearms Act 1968), or with intent to enable another person to use it to make a third party believe that unlawful violence will be used against someone (section 16A of the 1968 Act). It seems almost certain that both of these offences are now covered by the offence of *assisting* the commission of a section 16 offence, contrary to the Serious Crime Act 2007.[88] The section 16 offences are arguably largely redundant.

---

[86]   See now Conspiracy and Attempts (2009) Law Com No 318.

[87]   See, for example, s 8(a) of the Animal Welfare Act 2006, which reads: "A person commits an offence if he – causes an animal fight to take place, or attempts to do so … ".

[88]   The same point could be made about offences under the Animal Welfare Act 2006. For example, the offence contrary to s 8(b) to (i) reads, "A person commits an offence if he … knowingly receives money for admission to an animal fight; knowingly publicises a proposed animal fight; provides information about an animal fight to another with the intention of enabling or encouraging attendance at the fight … ". All these offences would appear to be covered by the offences of encouraging or assisting the causing of an animal fight to take place.

3.122   Parliament has continued to create offences clearly already covered by the Serious Crimes Act 2007. One example is engaging in an activity knowing or intending that it will enable or facilitate the commission by another person of an offence, contrary to article 5 of the Landsbanki Freezing Order 2008[89] Another example is permitting another person to carry on a specified gas storage operation without a licence, contrary to section 8(2) of the Energy Act 2008.[90]

Fraud and fraud-like offences

3.123   Let us now consider the use of tailor-made fraud and dishonesty offences, employed not only in the Firearms Act 1968 but very widely across many regulatory fields. In the Firearms Act 1968, there is an offence, contrary to section 7(2), of making a false statement in relation to obtaining a (temporary) police permit to have a firearm.[91] Even at the time that this offence was created, it was probably in any event an instance of obtaining property by false pretences (deception), contrary to the general law of theft and deception. It seems highly likely that it is covered by the substantive offence of fraud by false representation under the Fraud Act 2006, or by the offence of attempting to commit an offence contrary to that Act.

3.124   Overlaps of this kind are common in regulatory law. For example, in 2008, around 30 fraud or fraud-related offences were created in regulatory contexts.[92] A generic example is providing false information for the purpose of obtaining a licence.[93] More particular examples include some of the offences contrary to the Health and Social Care Act 2008, concerning false descriptions. Section 35 reads:

> (1) Any person who, with intent to deceive any person—
>
> > (a) applies any name to any concern carried on in England or to any premises in England, or
> >
> > (b) in any way describes such a concern or such premises or holds such a concern or such premises out,
>
> so as to indicate, or reasonably be understood to indicate, that the carrying on of the concern is a regulated activity or that the premises are used for the carrying on of a regulated activity is guilty of an offence unless the conditions in subsection (2) are met.

---

[89]   SI 2008 No 2668. This is an indictable offence with a maximum sentence of two years' imprisonment. See article 9(1)(b) of the Landsbanki Freezing Order 2008.

[90]   In general, when causing and permitting are placed together in a criminal statute, the courts will read in a fault requirement to the causing-or-permitting offence. This means that when that offence relates to causing or permitting another person to commit the main offence, it is effectively covered in almost all circumstances by the offences in Part II of the Serious Crime Act 2007.

[91]   See also s 9(3) of the Firearms Act 1968.

[92]   It is hard to be precise because the offences do not always lend themselves to clear categorisation

[93]   Counter Terrorism Act 2008, Sch 7, part 7, para 31; Energy Act 2008, ss 9(3) and 23(5) of the Landsbanki Freezing Order 2008.

(2) Those conditions are—

(a) that a person is registered under this Chapter as a service provider in respect of the regulated activity in question, and

(b) that the registration has not been suspended.

(3) Any person who, with intent to deceive any person, in any way describes or holds out any person registered under this Chapter as a service provider in respect of a regulated activity as able to provide a service or do any thing the provision or doing of which would contravene a condition for the time being in force by virtue of this Chapter in relation to the regulated activity is guilty of an offence.

(4) A person guilty of an offence under subsection (1) or (3) is liable on summary conviction to a fine not exceeding level 5 on the standard scale.

(5) In this section "concern" includes any organisation.

3.125 The best that one can say for such complex offences is that they are clearly meant to provide a high degree of compliance with the rule of law, by ensuring that anyone affected may know exactly when they are likely to be prosecuted. However, in regulatory contexts such information can be conveyed by means less top heavy than detailed statutory provisions. Simply having a system that involves pointing out to those affected that they may commit fraud, contrary to the Fraud Act 2006, by committing the offences of fraud by false representation, or fraud by failing to disclose information, should be enough to satisfy the demands of the rule of law.

3.126 Regulatory law also commonly contains a number of offences that could be described as fraud-like. One example in the Firearms Act 1968 is the offence, contrary to section 48(3), of failing to give a true name and address when asked to do so by a constable in connection with a demand to see someone's firearm certificate. More generally, the most common offences of this type are those that consist simply of making a false statement or providing misleading information[94] or of failing to disclose information relevant to a licence application.[95] There are also closely analogous offences of destroying or concealing documents required by a regulatory authority.[96]

---

[94] Health and Social Care Act 2008, s 37(2); Local Transport Act 2008, s 44(ii); Energy Act 2008, s 60; Insurance Accounts Directive (Lloyd's Syndicate and Aggregate Accounts) Regulations SI 2008 No 1950.

[95] Energy Act 2008, s 23(6).

[96] Finance Act 2008, Sch 36, part 8, ss 53(1) and 54(1).

3.127 Such offences are for the most part concerned with dishonest conduct.[97] However, they relieve the prosecuting authority of having to show that the offender had any ulterior intent of the sort required by the Fraud Act 2006: the intention to make a gain, cause a loss (to another), or expose (another) to the risk of loss. Such offences may be perfectly justifiable in context.

3.128 Even so, we will argue in the next chapter that there should be clear distinctions drawn between different versions of these offences. Those that create stigma, by expressly or impliedly saying that the offender has behaved in a dishonest manner, should be treated as criminal offences and should have fault elements to match. Those that make no such claim, because they seek to deter inaccurate form-filling, should attract at most civil penalties, and should be drafted in such a way that they avoid implying that the offender behaved dishonestly even though there is no requirement to prove dishonesty.[98]

Inappropriate placement of offences

3.129 We now turn to instances where criminal offences may be wrongly placed, by being located in regulatory legislation. Wrong placement is not merely a matter of bureaucratic tidiness. It is an important issue touching on the correct labelling of offenders.

3.130 For example, entering a property as trespasser with intent to rape was at one time an offence of burglary under section 9 of the Theft Act 1968. The tenuous connection with offences related to theft was the fact that an invasion of property was concerned. The Sexual Offences Act 2003 rightly took ownership of this offence.[99] The offence has much more in common with preliminary conduct that, although falling short of an attempt to commit a sexual offence, should nonetheless be prohibited.

3.131 An analogous example is provided by the aggravated offences under the Firearms Act 1968. It was previously mentioned that there is an aggravated offence, under section 16 of the Firearms Act 1968, of having in one's possession a firearm or ammunition with intent to endanger life, or to enable another person to endanger life.[100] The offence is triable only on indictment and is punishable by a sentence up to, and including, life imprisonment. It has had added to it (section 16A) a less serious version, in which D has a firearm or ammunition in his possession intending to use it to make – or to enable another to make – another person believe that violence will be used against him or her. Upon conviction at trial on indictment, the offence carries a maximum 10 year prison term.

---

[97] Although it is by no means a requirement in all cases that the offender should have known that, for example, a false statement made was false, at the time he or she made it.

[98] See *Wings Ltd v Ellis* [1985] AC 272.

[99] Sexual Offences Act 2003, s 63.

[100] See para 3.121 above.

3.132   There are other aggravated offences in the Firearms Act 1968. An offence under section 18(1) is committed when D has with him a firearm or imitation firearm with intent to commit an indictable offence. This carries a maximum sentence of life imprisonment. An offence is committed contrary to section 19(1) of the Firearms Act 1968 when D, without lawful authority or reasonable cause has with him in a public place a loaded shotgun, an air weapon, or another kind of firearm or imitation firearm. The offence has a maximum sentence of seven years' imprisonment at trial on indictment (12 months in the case of an imitation firearm). Section 20(1) of the Firearms Act 1968 makes it an offence, punishable with up to seven years' imprisonment at trial on indictment, for D to trespass without reasonable excuse in a building or part of a building, with a firearm or imitation firearm with him.

3.133   What is the difficulty with these offences?

3.134   These aggravated offences are committed in the circumstances described *whether or not* the firearm or ammunition is lawfully held by D, so the offences have no bearing on the regulatory scheme at the heart of the Firearms Act 1968. It is thus arguable that the offences would be equally, if not more, at home in offences against the person legislation (or, in the case of the offence under section 20(1), more at home as an aspect of the offence of burglary[101]).

3.135   The same point could be made about the offence under section 17(1) of making use (or attempting to make use) of a firearm with intent to resist or prevent a lawful arrest.[102] This aggravated offence seems to belong more naturally alongside (that is to say, supporting) the offences in the Offences Against the Person Act 1861 of (a) wounding with intent to resist or prevent lawful apprehension, contrary to section 18, and (b) unlawfully and maliciously wounding or inflicting grievous bodily harm, either with or without a weapon or instrument, contrary to section 20.

LESSONS FROM THE EXAMPLES

3.136   We take the following lessons from the way in which the criminal law is employed in the contexts we have described. We invite comments from consultees on these provisional proposals:

General principles: the limits of criminalisation

3.137   **Proposal 1: The criminal law should only be employed to deal with wrongdoers who deserve the stigma associated with criminal conviction because they have engaged in seriously reprehensible conduct. It should not be used as the primary means to promote regulatory objectives.**

3.138   **Proposal 2: Harm done or risked should be regarded as serious enough to warrant criminalisation only if,**

---

[101]   Contrary to s 9 of the Theft Act 1968.

[102]   See also s 18 of the Firearms Act 1968, which covers the case where D has a firearm or imitation firearm, with intent to resist arrest.

(a) in some circumstances (not just extreme circumstances), an individual could justifiably be sent to prison for a first offence, or

(b) an unlimited fine is necessary to address the seriousness of the wrongdoing in issue, and its consequences.[103]

3.139 **Proposal 3: Low-level criminal offences should be repealed in any instance where the introduction of a civil penalty (or equivalent measure) is likely to do as much to secure appropriate levels of punishment and deterrence.**

General principles: avoiding pointless overlaps between offences

3.140 **Proposal 4: The criminal law should not be used to deal with inchoate offending when it is covered by the existing law governing conspiracy, attempt, and assisting or encouraging crime.**

3.141 **Proposal 5: The criminal law should not be used to deal with fraud when the conduct in question is covered by the Fraud Act 2006.**

General principles: structure and process

3.142 **Proposal 6: Criminal offences should, along with the civil measures that accompany them, form a hierarchy of seriousness.**

3.143 **Proposal 7: More use should be made of process fairness to increase confidence in the criminal justice system. Duties on regulators formally to warn potential offenders that they are subject to liability should be supplemented by granting the courts power to stay proceedings until non-criminal regulatory steps have been taken first, in appropriate cases.**

THE LIMITS OF CRIMINALISATION: WHEN, AND BY WHOM, SHOULD CRIMINAL OFFENCES BE CREATED?

3.144 In underpinning the case for provisional proposals 1 and 2,[104] it is important briefly to consider the threshold tests currently used, or recommended, for the creation of criminal offences. In our view, to promote principled and restricted use of the criminal law, it is unlikely to prove sufficient simply to say that criminal offences should only be targeted at seriously reprehensible conduct or at conduct where only imprisonment or an unlimited fine will suffice to meet the demands of retribution and deterrence. This will not prove sufficient if there are too many bodies with the power to create criminal offences whenever they like.[105]

3.145 Accordingly, in support of provisional proposals 1 and 2, we also take the provisional view that criminal offences should be created and (other than in relation to minor details[106]) amended only through primary legislation.

---

[103] Putting aside factors such as whether the individual has previous convictions for other offences, and so on.

[104] At paras 3.137 and 3.138 above.

[105] In our analysis of consumer protection law, we saw an example earlier of imprisonable offences being created through delegated legislation: see para 3.83 and following above.

[106] What this qualification may turn out to mean in practice is not for us to address here.

Appearance and reality

3.146 In our view, there is little room for doubt that the granting of powers to create criminal offences through secondary legislation has been an important factor in the growth of the criminal law. Official statements about when criminal offences can be created tend to take a restrictive view. Unfortunately, that view is liable to lull people into a false sense of security. This is because in statutes creating or furthering a regulatory scheme, there is commonly a much more generous breadth to the basis on which criminal offences can be created through secondary legislation than is acknowledged in official statements.

3.147 So far as official statements are concerned, for example, Lord Williams said on behalf of the Government, in reply to a Parliamentary question in 1999, that criminal offences "should be created only when *absolutely necessary*".[107] In a slightly less restrictive, but nonetheless firm, way, the joint guidance issued on the creation of criminal laws by the Ministry of Justice and what is now the Department for Business, Innovation and Skills by departments says:

> If you are considering creating a regulatory offence, you need to consider carefully whether the behaviour warrants the intervention of the criminal law, and what alternatives there may be to criminal offences. If you are consolidating existing offences, you still need to consider whether the offences continue to be necessary and proportionate. Just because something has, historically, been a criminal offence is not justification in its own right.[108]

3.148 These official statements, emphasising that the creation of a criminal offence must be, amongst other things, 'necessary' should be contrasted with the much broader basis some statutes have given to the power to create such offences. More typically, in such statutes, it is stipulated that such a power can be used whenever it is expedient, or something of a kind much more generous to the law-creator.

3.149 For example, under section 12 of the Animal Welfare Act 2006, the appropriate national authority may make such regulations as it "*thinks fit* for the purpose of promoting the welfare of animals ..." (emphasis added). Such regulations may include criminal offences, and what is more, breach of these offences may lead to a sentence of imprisonment. Under section 32(3) of this Act:

> A person guilty of an offence under regulations under section 12 ... shall be liable on summary conviction to such penalty by way of imprisonment or fine as may be provided by regulations under that section.

---

[107] Written reply to a question from Lord Dholakia, Written Answer, *Hansard* (HL), 18 June 1999, vol 602, col WA57 to 58 (our emphasis).

[108] Ministry of Justice and the Department for Business, Enterprise and Regulatory Reform, *Guidance on Creating New Regulatory Penalties* (26 January 2009), para 18 (our emphasis).

3.150 To give hypothetical examples, it follows that the national authority could, if it saw fit, make it an imprisonable offence for someone to stroke a pet's fur the wrong way, to play loud music in the presence of a pet, or for someone to tether a dog outside a supermarket, if to do so risks exposing the dog to getting wet in the rain.

3.151 Powers expressed in such broad terms as section 12, when they are used to create criminal offences, undermine official endorsement of and guidance on the (more restrictive) use of the criminal law. The existence and use of such powers also risks bringing the criminal law more generally into disrepute.[109]

3.152 It would, of course, be possible to seek to meet this point by tightening up the basis on which regulators can create criminal offences. This might be done by replacing 'thinks fit' tests with tests of necessity, if the creation of an offence is to be justified. In our view, this would not be an adequate response. In practice, it will prove too hard to distinguish cases where a regulator thought it fit to create an offence, from cases where he or she thought it necessary to create that offence.

3.153 Moreover, this objection cannot easily be met by saying that the test should be whether the offence was objectively necessary rather than merely necessary in the eyes of the regulator. This is for the simple reason that if an expert body – a regulator – was really needed in the first place to decide how, through regulation, to secure best practice in a given area, it ought to be conceded that such a body is in the best position to judge what is indeed necessary to achieve that aim.

3.154 If this point is right, then the proper direction for reform is not to seek to fetter regulators' discretion to decide what will best promote sound practice in the area subject to regulation, but to exclude criminal law-creation from the regulators' armoury.[110]

Conclusion

3.155 Criminalisation is an area in which it is particularly important that there is no gap between what Government and officials say about the basis on which offences are created, and the facts. Recent years have seen growth of a number of alternatives to direct criminalisation.[111] This development means that it should no longer be necessary to grant powers to regulators or other delegated authorities to create criminal offences in order effectively to pursue their aims.

---

[109] See A Ashworth, "Is the Criminal Law a Lost Cause?" (2000) 116 *Law Quarterly Review* 225. It follows that we call into question the wisdom underlying The Regulatory Enforcement and Sanctions Act 2008, s.62, that broadened the powers to create criminal offences through secondary legislation.

[110] It is important to note that we cast no doubt here on the importance of permitting regulatory bodies to instigate and pursue criminal prosecutions, in appropriate cases. It is only the creation by such bodies of criminal offences that is in issue here.

[111] Such as the alternatives created by the Regulatory Enforcement and Sanctions Act 2008.

3.156 Beyond that, where wrongful conduct is so serious that such alternatives to offences are an insufficient response, the creation of an offence – which will be imprisonable or subject to an unlimited fine, on our proposals[112] – must be *necessary* to meet the demands of retribution and deterrence, as official guidance currently insists. In order to ensure that the necessity test is satisfied, nothing should suffice by way of scrutiny short of that provided by the primary legislative process itself.

3.157 It would not be an exaggeration to say that the question of when a criminal offence should be created is one with some constitutional significance.[113] Parliament's responsibility for the administration of criminal justice is a key part of its relationship with those within the jurisdiction (whether or not British citizens). It is also increasingly important to its responsibility for giving effect to the UK's European and international obligations. Sound principles of criminalisation can make a significant contribution to a better constitutional relationship between Parliament and the people.

3.158 Consequently, we provisionally propose that:

> **Proposal 8: Criminal offences should be created and (other than in relation to minor details) amended only through primary legislation.**

APPEALING AGAINST REGULATORY MEASURES

3.159 If our proposals were adopted, more use would be made than at present of civil penalties, two-step prohibitions, and other non-criminal means of securing regulatory compliance and deterring people from failures to comply. Upon conviction for a criminal offence, the person convicted may have their case re-heard or appealed (depending on the circumstances) in a superior court. What should the approach be, when someone is subjected to a civil penalty, or the like?

3.160 In his review of the criminal courts in 2003,[114] Lord Justice Auld was of the opinion that some matters such as "certain types of financial and regulatory offences",[115] could be removed from the criminal justice system and placed under the jurisdiction of regulatory authorities such as Financial Services Authority. He referred to a view expressed by the then Director of the Serious Fraud Office, Rosalind Wright, that, some offences could be de-criminalised and made regulatory infringements if they were the sort of offences, 'that can be dealt with by, effectively, taking someone off the road by removing their licence'.[116]

---

[112] Proposal 2: see para 3.138 above.

[113] See, for example, F W Maitland, *The Constitutional History of England* (1919) p 478, "I think, however, that a lecturer on constitutional law is bound to try to bring out the relation between what we call "the government" and 'the administration of justice".

[114] Rt Hon LJ Auld, *A Review of the Criminal Courts of England and Wales* (September 2001).

[115] Above, part 9, para 48.

[116] Above, part 9, para 50.

3.161   We cast no doubt on the wisdom of Lord Justice Auld's recommendations, and they provided a sound basis for reform. However, a significant aspect of the kind of de-criminalisation that he recommended is that it requires there to be an administrative body with powers not only to investigate (and sometimes to create) the relevant regulatory offences, and to find them proven or not proven, but also to instigate a system of appeals against its own findings. In effect, each regulatory authority must set up a parallel system of administrative justice, to some extent to mirror, but to a substantial extent to depart from, the ordinary criminal process.

3.162   There are many advantages to such parallel systems. Perhaps the most important is the expertise that the involvement of specialists brings to the investigation and (where appropriate) hearing or trial, (where relevant) to the punishment of wrongdoers, and to decision-making about appropriate preventative measures such as the withdrawal of practising licences.[117]

3.163   One disadvantage comes, ironically, from one of the strengths of specialised systems. That is the risk that those investigating, hearing and determining will not be sufficiently independent and impartial to satisfy the fair trial requirements of article 6 of the European Convention on Human Rights, and sometimes also the requirements of other articles of the Convention such as article 8 (protecting private and family life). In any regulatory scheme there may be a problem that, in effect, the regulator is investigator, prosecutor, judge, jury, and (quite possibly) court of appeal in his or her own cause.

3.164   This was an issue at stake in relation to the role of the body – the Independent Safeguarding Authority (ISA) – charged with deciding whether to ban unsuitable individuals from working with children or vulnerable adults. The House of Lords found a need for full and independent hearing on the merits in such cases.[118] During the legislative process leading up to the passing of the Safeguarding Vulnerable Groups Act 2006, the issues had to be fully considered by the Joint Committee on Human Rights. The Joint Committee concluded that the decision-making processes of the ISA would not be sufficiently independent from Government, were it not for the inclusion of the possibilities that (a) there could be a review of the facts by the Care Standards Tribunal, and (b) there was a final appeal to the Court of Appeal on a point of law.[119]

3.165   We do not mention this to cast any doubt whatsoever on the integrity and fairness of the ISA's procedures. The example is relevant for a different reason.

---

[117] See the analysis of court deficiencies, in that regard, by Professor Black, Appendix A.

[118] *R (Wright) v Secretary of State for Health* [2009] UKHL 3, [2009] AC 739.

[119] Joint Committee on Human Rights, *Twenty-Fifth Report* (July 2006) http://www.publications.parliament.uk/pa/jt200506/jtselect/jtrights/241/24105.htm#a7 (last visited 15 June 2010); see now also section 4 of the Safeguarding Vulnerable Groups Act 2006.

3.166   There are clearly difficulties and complexities in setting up alternative procedures in regulatory contexts that meet the requirements of article 6, amongst other articles. That being so, it is highly desirable that use is made of the courts in all instances in which regulators may impose civil penalties, or two-step prohibitions, or the like. The best use to which the courts may be put can vary from one regulatory context to the next. In our view, the role of courts, in relation to the imposition of penalties by regulators, is likely to be most effective and helpful if, in broad terms, it takes the form of re-hearing or appeal (if only on a point of law).[120]

3.167   The Firearms Act 1968 provides for an appeal against the revocation by the police of a firearms certificate to the Crown Court.[121] This is the equivalent of an appeal from a magistrates' court to the Crown Court, where the appeal takes the form of a re-hearing of the whole case. Appeals to the Upper Tribunal against civil penalty decisions taken by the Financial Services Authority also take the form of complete re-hearings.[122]

3.168   Such re-hearings will not necessarily be appropriate in all regulatory contexts. However, we believe that it is now well understood that legislation must provide recourse to the courts in cases where civil penalties or other kinds of set-back to someone's interests have been imposed by a state-sponsored agency.[123] The very minimum requirement is that there should be an appeal on a point of law against the imposition of such measures. Fairness will also be improved if, more generally, there is a means of objecting to the imposition of the penalty to a person or body within the regulatory agency itself. An example is provided by the Regulatory Decisions Committee of the Financial Services Authority, to whom objection may be made about a warning notice that has been issued indicating that further action may be taken by the Financial Services Authority.

3.169   Finally, whilst it may be legitimate to indicate that early admission of guilty and payment of a fee may mean that the fee is discounted,[124] such discounts should in no circumstances be offered in exchange for an agreement not to object, or not to appeal against a penalty.

3.170   Consequently, we provisionally propose that:

---

[120]   See, for example, s 4 of the Safeguarding Vulnerable Groups Act 2006.

[121]   Firearms Act 1986, s 44.

[122]   Financial Services Authority, *FSA Enforcement Information Guide* (April 2010) www.fsa.gov.uk/pages/doing/regulated/law/pdf/enf_procedure.pdf (last visited 13 July 2010).

[123]   For example, under section 17 of the Immigration, Asylum and Nationality Act 2006, an employer on whom a civil penalty has been imposed may object to the imposition to the UK Border Agency's civil penalty compliance team, but may also appeal to the County Court. See: UK Border Agency, Civil Penalties for Employers, www.ukba.homeoffice.gov.uk/employers/preventingillegalworking/penaltiesemployers/ (last visited 13 July 2010).

[124]   For example, such a discount was obtained by JP Morgan Securities Ltd from the FSA, for an early acceptance of a fine for failing properly to separate clients' money from other funds: FSA, *Final Notice* (25 May 2010) Reference No 155240 www.fsa.gov.uk/pubs/final/jpmsl.pdf (last visited 13 July 2010).

Proposal 9: A regulatory scheme that makes provision for the imposition of any civil penalty, or equivalent measure, must also provide for unfettered recourse to the courts to challenge the imposition of that measure, by way of re-hearing or appeal on a point of law.

PART 4
CONSISTENCY AND PRINCIPLE IN USING FAULT ELEMENTS

FAULT AND THE ROLE OF THE CRIMINAL LAW IN REGULATION

4.1 There is great variety in regulatory contexts, and yet further diversity to the risks and harms within each context. In the course of this CP, for example, we have been or will be dealing with (amongst many other pieces of law) criminal offences supporting regulatory aims under the Immigration, Asylum and Nationality Act 2006, the Pensions Act 2004, and the Eggs and Chicks Regulations 2008.[1] Nonetheless, it is possible to establish clarity, consistency and fairness in the way that the criminal law is employed to support regulatory strategies.

4.2 In Part 2, we were concerned with the degree to which, in different areas, there may be reliance on the criminal law to support a regulatory strategy. When the criminal law is employed in support of a regulatory strategy, there have long been questions over the form such laws should take. In particular, it is common to find criticism of the use of strict (essentially, no-fault) liability offences, especially when prison sentences are available upon conviction.

4.3 If the criminal law is in future created only in the form and used in the circumstances that we propose, the issue of strict liability is likely to fade into the background to a considerable extent. This is because the criminal law would then be used to target only the worst instances of wrongdoing and would almost as a matter of course have fault elements (or appropriate defences) in its definition of offences.

4.4 In this Part, therefore, we will concentrate on a different range of important issues that still need attention. By establishing certain principles for the use of fault elements in defining criminal offences, it becomes possible to secure consistency in the use of such principles across very different regulatory regimes. As Professor Ashworth has argued:

> In principle, the boundary between criminal offences and non-criminal "violations" should be set according to consistent criteria, and should not vary with the social context in which the wrongdoing occurs.[2]

4.5 However, our concern is not only with clarity and consistency. In broad terms, the principles that we believe should be developed ought to lead in future to significantly more restricted use of the criminal law in regulatory contexts. In ways that we will now explain, this comes about because of the way in which conduct that is to be the subject of a criminal prohibition must be linked to moral wrongdoing.

---

[1]   SI 2008 No 1718.

[2]   A Ashworth, *Principles of Criminal Law* (5th ed 2006) p 48.

MORAL WRONGDOING AND HARM

Criminal wrongdoing and moral wrongdoing

4.6 The criminal law should be employed only when engagement in the prohibited conduct in question warrants official censure, because it involves a harm-related moral failing, not just a breach of a rule or simple departure from a standard.

4.7 In a regulatory context, it is not enough to justify making engagement in conduct criminal, that the conduct must be deterred or punished in some way.[3] In such contexts, deterrence and punishment are commonly best achieved through vigorous use of some mixture of preventative measures and civil penalties. When the criminal law is (inappropriately) used merely as a substitute for such alternative measures, conviction may generate little stigma, little by way of deterrence may be achieved, and little by way of punishment may be justified. Consequently, the criminal law is liable to fall into disrepute, in the eyes of both prosecutorial agencies, and those subject to regulation, alike.[4]

4.8 The use of the criminal law must be justified by an aim including, but going beyond, achieving a measure of deterrence and punishment as such. The aim must be to create, in part through the process of criminalisation itself, a strong sense of the unacceptability of the conduct in question, within the industry in question and beyond. For that to happen, engagement in the conduct in question must in itself already be in some sense morally wrong, or it must be the case that, given the nature of the conduct, criminalisation will have the desirable effect of creating a justified sense that the conduct is morally wrong.

4.9 In the next section we will deal with the necessity for criminalisation to be harm-related. In this section, we discuss the requirement that a moral failing must also be involved.

4.10 A number of experts on the criminal law have argued how important it is to keep in mind that, by imposing liability, the state will be *officially condemning or censuring* the behaviour in question.[5] Professor Simester has argued in strong terms that:

---

[3] See Part 3. As Professor Gardner aptly puts it, measures falling short of the criminal sanction aim to, "institutionalise clear standards of success and failure where the internal standards are in doubt or come to be widely disregarded": J Gardner, "On the General Part of the Criminal Law", in A Duff (ed), *Philosophy and the Criminal Law: Principle and Critique* (1998) p 231.

[4] See the discussion in the work of Professor Black, Appendix A.

[5] See, further H M Hart, "The Aims of the Criminal Law" (1958) *Law and Contemporary Problems* 401, 404, expressing that view that what distinguishes a criminal sanction is, "the judgment of community condemnation which accompanies and justifies its imposition".

> Convictions are official. They condemn D on behalf of society as a whole. To say that D has a criminal record is to say that he has been labelled as a reprehensible wrongdoer; that the state has made a formal adverse statement about *him*. Moreover, the statement marks D out in such a way that it becomes appropriate, within the community, for the regard in which he is held to be affected ... . The conviction (and indeed the punishment, in its censorious facet) tends not only to censure D for the particular act that is proscribed, but also to undermine D's participation in the society itself.[6]

4.11　There may be some degree of over-statement in the second part of this claim, although it can be argued that it is not far, or should not be far, from the truth where the criminal conviction of an individual is concerned. The claim does need some modification when what is being considered is the role of the criminal law in regulatory contexts where those subject to regulation are likely primarily to be (small) businesses, not individuals.

4.12　Although a criminal conviction may affect the regard in which a company is held in the jurisdiction in which the offence is committed, it may not have such an impact on a multi-national company; or it may not have such an impact on a company that operates largely through subsidiaries or agents. Diversified or global companies do not have the kind of simple one-person identity that an individual offender does. So, adverse statements about the company, or marking out the company, may not have the same effect as making adverse statements about or marking out an individual.

4.13　Moreover, in the light of a conviction, it is always open to a company to re-form (as by merger with another company), re-brand, or re-focus its operations in a way that will substantially diminish the impact of the conviction, in a way that an individual offender does not have much scope to do. So, it is far less likely, in the case of a company, that conviction will undermine D's participation in the society itself.

4.14　Accordingly, our focus will be on the first part of the claim, that criminal conviction involves officially labelling the offender as a reprehensible wrongdoer. As we have said, that should involve confining the scope of the criminal law to conduct that is morally wrong or that will rightly come to be seen as morally wrong if it is made a criminal offence.

4.15　The latter part of this claim may seem circular, but our claim is not that any conduct, if made criminal, will or should automatically become seen from then onwards as morally wrong. Suppose that parking in a prohibited place were made an offence triable only on indictment, with a minimum sentence of 20 years in prison on conviction. That would not tend to make the conduct itself seem morally wrong. On the contrary, it would be the law that was brought into moral disrepute because it was being used to deter and punish conduct in a disproportionate way.

---

[6]　A P Simester, "Is Strict Liability Always Wrong?" in A P Simester, *Appraising Strict Liability* (2005) p 35.

4.16 The latter part of our claim is meant to indicate that there may sometimes be a pressing social need to change people's attitude to some kinds of conduct, making those kinds of conduct seem morally unacceptable when until then they have been tolerated too widely. Criminalisation can play a legitimate role in that process. A well-known example is driving whilst under the influence of alcohol, something tolerated many years ago, but which criminalisation, in the interests of road safety, has turned into a morally unacceptable activity and not just an instance of simple rule-breaking.

4.17 Linking the use of the criminal law with moral wrongdoing does not provide a magic formula for drawing the line between the conduct that may be dealt with through the criminal law, and conduct that should be stopped, deterred or punished in some other way. One obvious reason for that is that people's moral view points differ widely. However, two points need to be made about this common objection to reform based on moral principle.

4.18 First, our aim is to provide guidance on the creation of criminal offences, not to prescribe precisely when this activity is and is not acceptable. We recognise that there must be a considerable margin for differences in view on the scope of morally wrongful harming or risk-taking. Secondly, people's moral differences may be narrowed quite considerably, when they are called to pronounce on the unacceptability of conduct that causes harm, poses a direct risk of harm to others, or will unacceptably increase that risk if left unregulated. There is likely to be more consensus over the manifestations of such morally unacceptable conduct than there might be over conduct that reflects only lifestyle choice and does not cause or threaten harm.

Criminal wrongdoing and harm

General considerations

4.19 In a much discussed and highly influential passage in his work, *On Liberty*, John Stuart Mill said, "the only purpose for which power can be rightfully exercised over any member of a civilised community, against his will, is to prevent harm to others".[7] Mill was not speaking of the criminal law, in particular, although discussion of this passage has been largely examined in that context. When considering regulatory contexts, it is important to keep in mind that the harm principle (as it is commonly called) should apply with full force to the creation of civil penalties as well as to criminal offences.

4.20 Quite how influential Mill's principle is already meant to be in the delivery of public policy is illustrated by the official guidance currently issued jointly by the Ministry of Justice and Department of Business, Education and Regulatory Reform (now the Department of Business, Innovation and Skills) to departments, on the creation of offences and penalties.[8] It begins:

---

[7] J S Mill, *On Liberty* (1859) pp 21 to 22.

[8] Ministry of Justice and the Department for Business, Enterprise and Regulatory Reform, *Guidance on Creating New Regulatory Penalties* (26 January 2009).

> In creating any new civil or criminal sanctions, you should consider the following points: nature and potential harm of the conduct to be targeted ... .[9]

4.21 This guidance makes it implicitly clear that just because conduct is to be targeted with civil sanctions, rather than criminal penalties, does not mean that the harm principle ceases to have an application. Under the guidance, the choice between civil sanction or criminal penalty is determined in part by questions of degree. In relation to implementing an EU obligation, for example, the guidance requires departments to ask the question:

> Does the obligation require "dissuasive and proportionate" sanctions? (In appropriate circumstances this could mean the creation of criminal sanctions).[10]

4.22 In broad terms, this is the right approach. That is to say, the guidance does not seek to rely heavily on an intrinsic distinction in kind between conduct appropriately targeted through the criminal law and conduct better targeted through civil sanctions or private remedies. Instead, the guidance treats that distinction as one of degree. The right question is whether, for example, the nature and degree of unacceptable risk posed by conduct together point towards a need for the deterrent and retributive effect of a criminal sanction, as opposed to a civil penalty, even though that will mean having to prove beyond reasonable doubt that the risk was posed.

4.23 There are two influential factors that should be highlighted when this question is posed.

4.24 First, even if conduct causes harm, or a risk of harm, that will not normally in itself provide a sufficient reason for any kind of prohibition, if there is social or economic utility in permitting people to cause the harm or take the risk that it will occur. Suppose that there is only one clothes manufacturer in a town, and person X sets up a rival business in the town that may harm the existing manufacturer economically. The dis-value of the fact that, in setting up his or her business, person X will cause harm to his or her rival may be outweighed, in public policy terms, by the good that introducing competition will do for the clothes market.

4.25 Secondly, as we have already indicated, it is our provisional view that it is unlikely to be enough to justify using criminalisation to deter and punish conduct that the conduct is harmful or risky, unless there is an element of moral wrongdoing involved in the way that the harm is done or the risk posed. We will turn directly to an examination of what this entails for criminal law creation, following a discussion of the relevance of harm to criminalisation.

Is it crucial how much harm, or risk of harm, was involved?

4.26 In regulatory contexts, it is important not to be too restrictive in one's view of what harm-related conduct may qualify, in principle, for criminalisation.

---

[9] Ministry of Justice and the Department for Business, Enterprise and Regulatory Reform, *Guidance on Creating New Regulatory Penalties* (26 January 2009) p 2 (point 7).

[10] Above, p 3 (point 7).

4.27　There are clearly some kinds or degrees of harmful wrongdoing, or wrongful risk-posing so serious that anything less than criminalisation would be an inadequate response on the part of the state. Murder or rape would be obvious examples where harmful wrongdoing is concerned; and trying to fly a full passenger plane by posing as a qualified pilot would be an obvious example where wrongful risk-posing is concerned. However, seeking to restrict the scope of the criminal law by concentrating primarily on the seriousness of the harm done or of the risk directly posed is not a promising line of approach, especially in regulatory contexts.

4.28　Even outside regulatory contexts, the criminal law sometimes quite properly targets trivial and transient harm, because of the more adverse (harmful) consequences that might otherwise result. An example is battery constituted by the merest non-consensual touching other than in the course of ordinary social contact. Of such transient and trifling harm, Sir William Blackstone said, in a passage accepted as correct by almost all commentators on the criminal law:

> The law cannot draw the line between different degrees of violence, and therefore prohibits the first and lowest stage of it; every man's person being sacred, and no other having a right to meddle with it, in any the slightest manner.[11]

4.29　By way of contrast, some potentially quite serious harms appear to be perfectly adequately dealt with by private law through the facilitation of actions for damages. The negligent causing of harm in breach of a duty of care, defamation and breach of contract are examples. In such examples, the fact that there is someone who suffers loss and has an adequate incentive to sue for damages, rather than the intrinsic nature of the harm, inclines the law to treat these forms of harm as civil rather than criminal wrongs.

4.30　Moreover, regulators may quite properly be asked to deter and punish conduct that is not as such easily categorised as harmful on a simplistic view of that notion. An example that we discussed in Part 3 was the illegal employment of a person with no entitlement to work in the UK.

4.31　For the purposes of criminal law-making in regulatory contexts, generally speaking, more important than harm done is the risk of harm posed. It is normally a central function of regulation to concentrate on risk reduction, whether through education and information campaigns (not considered in this paper), or through deterrence and punishment.

4.32　What is the relationship between the harm principle and risk of harm?

---

[11] Sir W Blackstone, *Commentaries*, vol ii, book iii, at 120.

Risk-based offences

4.33 A well-known example of the use of the criminal law to punish unacceptable risk-taking is the criminal offence of failing to ensure, so far as is reasonably practical, that a system of work is safe.[12] Section 1 of The Health and Safety at Work etc Act 1974 is focused on (broadly speaking) careless failures that lead to unsafe – risky – systems of work being allowed to continue. Perhaps surprisingly, the 1974 Act does not seek to make it a criminal offence actually to cause harm through such failures. The causing of actual harm is left to the general criminal law which, in this area, requires proof of subjective fault if the perpetrator is to be convicted.[13] That is an example of how important a place risk-posing has on the regulatory agenda.

4.34 In this example (health and safety at work), although no harm done need be proved if an offender is to be convicted, there is a link between the nature of the risk – unsafe working practices – and the *direct* causing of physical harm or damage. This link is what legitimates the inclusion of such practices within the scope of the harm principle and it explains their status as criminal offences rather than merely civil wrongs. However, many offences contain no such link, and yet their legal prohibition is not regarded as especially controversial.

4.35 Good examples are laws requiring persons to hold licences or certificates in order to possess, supply or trade in dangerous or potentially dangerous products, such as medicines and firearms,[14] or to give certain kinds of financial advice.[15] When someone does not have a licence for such activities, if harm or the risk of harm comes about at all, in most instances it will come about only through a further, free and informed act. An example would be where the person to whom the product is supplied decides to take the medicine, or use the firearm, or to act on the financial advice in question. In such cases, there is only an indirect link between the prohibited conduct (unlicensed possession, supply, trade, or advice), and harm done or risked.

4.36 The indirect character of the link between harm and the unlicensed possession or supply of potentially dangerous products or unlicensed financial advice might be an argument in favour of treating such conduct as suitable only for regulatory intervention through civil penalty, rather than through criminal law. However, whichever mode or prohibition is adopted, the harm principle must be satisfied if the prohibition is to be legitimate. The harm principle can in fact perfectly well accommodate and explain the existence of licensing offences, even though it cannot tell us what sort of offences (criminal or civil) those offences should be.

---

[12] Heath and Safety at Work etc Act 1974, s 2.

[13] Other than in manslaughter cases, where gross negligence is the fault element. See the discussion in, for example, Smith and Hogan, *Criminal Law* (12th ed 2008), part II. As we will see in Part 5, it is hard to prove subjective fault attributable to a corporate person.

[14] See, for example, s 45 of the Medicines Act 1968, and s 1 of the Firearms Act 1968.

[15] See the Financial Services and Markets Act 2000.

4.37 It is not only when an activity has actually caused or risked harm that it can legitimately be prohibited by appealing to the harm principle. The harm principle is also apt to justify prohibition of the activity if, whether or not individual instances of it cause or risk harm, failing to prohibit that activity in general will lead to an unacceptable level of unwarranted harm done or risked. As Professors Gardner and Shute put it:

> It is no objection under the harm principle that a harmless action was criminalised, nor even that an action with no tendency to cause harm was criminalised. It is enough to meet the demands of the harm principle that, if the action were not criminalised, *that* would be harmful … non-instrumental wrongs, even when they are perfectly harmless in themselves, can pass this test if their criminalisation diminishes the occurrence of them, and the wider occurrence of them would detract from people's prospects – for example, by diminishing some public good … .[16]

4.38 To go back to the examples of licences to engage in certain kinds of activity, it may be that in these circumstances, no harm is either done or risked by the unlicensed person in question who may be acting in a highly responsible way. However, it might be the case more broadly that to leave the conduct in question unregulated through prohibitions on unlicensed activity, would create an unacceptably higher risk of harm being done or loss caused by those in possession of the firearms, medicines or financial advice.

How useful really is the harm principle?

4.39 There are limits to the function of the harm principle as a principle of restraint in the regulatory field. It cannot function as a guide to the precise limits, still less to the exact design of the criminal law. Nonetheless, the harm principle still plays an important role. It forbids the use of criminal or civil penalties to prohibit conduct solely on the ground that the conduct is immoral or solely because if people were deterred by the prohibition it would make them better people, morally speaking. However, this role for the harm principle is not especially important in most regulatory fields.

4.40 Having said that, we have indicated that when it is proposed to use criminal offences, as opposed to civil penalties, to deter and punish harm-related conduct, the conduct in question must be tainted by an element of moral wrongdoing. That proposal must now be explored in more detail.

The element of moral wrongdoing in criminal wrongdoing

Fault requirements that reflect moral wrongdoing

4.41 Moral wrongdoing in criminal offending is commonly manifested by the way in which, and the extent to which, the offender was at fault in offending. There are many forms of fault element used in the criminal law. Here are some (but by no means all) forms of positive fault requirements that the prosecution must prove:

---

[16] J Gardner and S Shute, "The Wrongness of Rape", in J Horder (ed), *Oxford Essays in Jurisprudence* (4th Series 2000) p 216 (emphasis in original).

- dishonesty;

- intention;

- knowledge;

- recklessness;

- (gross) negligence, or an equivalent state of mind such as the absence of due care, or of reasonable grounds for a belief.

4.42 In principle, D will be, morally speaking, at fault in causing unjustified harm or posing unjustified risk if D is at fault in so doing in one of these ways.

4.43 There is a well-established understanding that, broadly speaking, these kinds of fault form a hierarchy (putting dishonesty on one side, as a special case). In other words, it is, other things being equal, worse to cause harm or to pose unwarranted risk of harm intentionally than knowingly, worse to do it knowingly than recklessly, and worse to do it recklessly than negligently.[17] We find no reason to cast doubt on this hierarchy here. It is, though, important to keep in mind that in regulatory contexts there may only rarely be a need to make fine distinctions between, for example, intention and knowledge, or even between intention and recklessness. In regulatory contexts, the hierarchy is best understood in terms of groupings of fault elements:

Higher level: dishonesty; intention; knowledge, recklessness.

Lower level: negligence, or an equivalent state of mind.

4.44 It should be noted that express use of one of these fault elements may not be necessary, in order for a requirement to prove it to arise. There will inevitably be subtleties in the way that fault elements manifest themselves, and there is nothing wrong with that. For example, offences of obstructing an authorised officer whilst he or she is lawfully conducting an inspection of some kind are quite common in regulatory contexts.[18] In allied legislation, one may also find offences of pretending to be or of personating an authorised officer.[19] Such offences either necessarily involve or, in the case of obstruction, almost certainly imply an element of intention on the part of the perpetrator.

---

[17] In his paper for the Law Commission, published as Appendix B below, Professor Cartwright argues that in consumer protection contexts, 'recklessness' still encompasses some manifestations of gross negligence and thus that there is a degree of overlap between the two. In the light of the decision of the House of Lords in *R v G* [2003] UKHL 50, we believe that recklessness is now a distinct concept, confined to cases in which, very broadly speaking, a risk that it is unjustified to take has been appreciated but ignored.

[18] See, for example, regulation 13(1) of the REACH Enforcement Regulations SI 2008 No 2852.

[19] Above.

4.45 Dishonesty does not always fit neatly into the hierarchy, in part because it is applicable only to certain kinds of offence (such as theft, fraud, and more broadly the provision or withholding of information). It makes little sense to think, for example, of physical harm being inflicted dishonestly. Nonetheless, depending on the circumstances, dishonesty may have the same status, as a form of moral wrongdoing in criminal law, as intention, knowledge, or recklessness.

4.46 Then there are negative fault requirements, where it is for the defendant to show, either as a matter of law or through discharging an evidentiary burden, that he or she was not at fault. Examples would be provisions saying that an offence is not established:

- if D established a 'reasonable excuse' for engaging in the conduct;

- if D showed 'all due diligence' (or the like) in seeking to avoid offending;

- if D showed that he or she had a 'reasonable belief' that facts existed that would have made his or her conduct lawful; or

- if D showed that the commission of the offence was attributable to the conduct of another person.

4.47 We find prominent in these negative fault requirements what are in effect negligence-based, denial-of-fault elements (all due diligence; reasonable belief). These take their place on the lower level of fault elements described above.

4.48 In different ways, should D establish any of these defences, he or she will effectively be showing that his or her transgression should not be open to moral criticism, at least not such as would warrant the imposition of criminal liability for the harm done, or risk posed.

4.49 There is nothing radical about the suggestion that positive or negative fault requirements should in some form generally be essential elements in a criminal offence. Official guidance to departments already says that (generally speaking) it should play such a role:

> A criminal offence is normally made up of two parts – the action and the state of mind of the person doing it. The main categories for the mental state are intention, recklessness or neglect. Some actions may be offences whatever your state of mind. You may need specific defences (such as "due diligence") to make sure that, for example, if the action was inadvertent or unavoidable, it would not constitute an offence.[20]

[20] Ministry of Justice and the Department for Business, Enterprise and Regulatory Reform, *Guidance on Creating New Regulatory Penalties* (26 January 2009), p 6 (point 19).

4.50   What is understandably absent from existing official guidance, which is aimed at individual departments contemplating the creation of criminal offences, is an insistence that usage of particular fault terms should ideally be consistent across regulatory contexts, not only within them. A number of statutes or regulations now provide that, in a regulatory context, it is an offence to obstruct an authorised officer in the performance of his or her duties. It is surely essential that the same test of fault in relation to such an obstruction is used in as many of the contexts as possible in which such an offence is created.

4.51   The notion of obstruction is likely to be interpreted by the courts as necessitating proof of an intention to obstruct, providing the kind of certainty and consistency we seek. It is, though, perhaps regrettable that the point is not routinely made clear in legislation itself. For example, regulation 15(1) of the Eggs and Chicks Regulations 2008 provides that someone is guilty of an offence if they "*intentionally* obstruct an authorised officer acting in the execution of these Regulations". That should not be taken to imply that in analogous provisions under other Acts or Regulations, the absence of the word 'intentionally' means that the offence is committed even in cases where the obstruction is accidental.

4.52   We will make a proposal about the consistency issue below.

4.53   What is needed, before the issue of consistency comes into play, is a guide to the principles for the use of the fault elements described. In this Part, we will try to provide at least some such principles.

4.54   One area where we will not seek to do this systematically concerns the question of when it is right to employ positive rather than negative species of fault requirement. There has been much academic discussion of the question whether criminal offences should always employ positive fault requirements, putting the prosecution to its proof beyond reasonable doubt, or whether (and when) the legislature may rely on negative fault requirements, leaving D to establish his or her moral innocence.

4.55   We will not take a general stand on this issue.[21] This is simply because it would involve being far too prescriptive about the precise character of legislation across so many different fields. In some fields, for example, negative fault elements may be appropriate because those subject to regulation can more easily show that they were not at fault, if indeed they were not, than regulators can establish positive fault requirements. The interests of third parties, such as consumers, may thus be better protected in some areas by a negative fault regime than by a positive fault regime. It is a matter of judgment for the department given the task of introducing a regulatory regime supported by criminal offences.

4.56   However, important progress can be made in other areas. As it is a matter of such great importance in regulatory contexts, we will focus mainly on offences to a greater or lesser extent remote from the causing of harm itself.

---

[21]   At paras 4.62 to 4.82 below, we will discuss a need for higher level fault elements in one area, but that is a slightly different issue.

Proportionate fault elements and criminalisation

4.57 In that respect, our first proposal is that the extent of moral wrongdoing required to justify criminalisation should be related to the degree of harm done or risked. In that regard, it is helpful to focus by way of example on negligence (or its equivalent) as a fault element.

4.58 When great harm is involved, as in rape or manslaughter, (gross) negligence may be used as a species of fault, as a key element of the moral wrong involved in doing the harm in question.[22] Beyond these instances, whether employing negligence as a fault element should be regarded as doing enough to mark the conduct in question out as criminal wrongdoing depends on the nature of the harm or risk of harm at issue. Further, in the case where harm is risked, it may depend on whether the risk is directly or only indirectly posed.

4.59 When the risks are high, or the potential harm is great, a requirement for proof of negligence may rightly be regarded as having the effect of marking out the conduct in question as genuinely criminal. For example, the criminal law prohibits not only dangerous driving,[23] but also driving without due care and attention (a kind of negligence).[24] The former is in principle the graver offence, because the risk of serious harm is liable to be greater when driving is dangerous than when it is merely careless.[25] However, the latter is still an instance in which a risk of (possibly serious) harm was directly posed through unjustifiable lack of care and inattention, albeit possibly involving a lower or more remote risk of harm. The risks of inattention whilst driving are well-known. So, the possible consequences of taking an unjustified risk mean that when this risk is due to a lack of due care and attention, the moral shortcoming involved can justify making the risk-taking criminal.

4.60 By way of contrast, a careless error in, say, completing a grant application form is unlikely to be worthy of criminalisation, even though it involves some element of moral shortcoming. It is simply too remote from posing a direct risk of harm, and even more remote from causing harm itself. Simple failures to comply with bureaucratic requirements, or attempts to comply that may have the effect of misleading another, should not in general lead to criminalisation, even if attributable to negligence. Unless they pose a more or less direct risk of harm, such failures should lead only to a civil penalty or equivalent non-criminal form of action. Such failures should only be open to criminal proceedings if they manifested a higher level fault requirement, such as dishonesty, intention, or recklessness. This claim is explored further below.

4.61 If this is accepted, then we can put forward as our first provisional proposal about fault:

[22] Sexual Offences Act 2003, s 1(1); *Adomako* [1995] 1 AC 171.

[23] Road Traffic Act 1988, s 2.

[24] Road Traffic Act 1988, s 3.

[25] In theory, a car could be driven dangerously even though the driver was not careless in so driving, so there is not any necessary comparability between the offences; but instances where dangerousness and carelessness part company are likely to be rare. An example might be where D is driving lawfully at 50 miles per hour in a lorry, justifiably unaware that someone is clinging to the underneath of his or her vehicle. D's driving poses a danger, but he or she is not driving carelessly.

Proposal 10: Fault elements in criminal offences that are concerned with unjustified risk-taking should be proportionate. This means that the more remote the conduct criminalised from harm done, and the less grave that harm, the more compelling the case for higher-level fault requirements such as dishonesty, intention, knowledge or recklessness.

PROPORTIONALITY ILLUSTRATED: (NOT) PROVIDING INFORMATION

The significance of the issue

4.62 Proposal 10 is one that necessarily operates at quite an abstract level. We believe that consultees will expect us to provide more concrete examples of how our proposal will work to restrict the criminal law. Accordingly, we will now discuss a specific example of widespread importance throughout the field of regulation, where a consistent and principled approach to the use of the criminal law would deliver both fairness to those affected and more restricted use of the criminal law.

4.63 This is the area of law concerned with requirements to provide relevant information to regulatory bodies or other agencies, omissions to provide relevant information to such bodies or agencies, and (more rarely) the wrongful dissemination of such information. It is difficult to exaggerate the importance of this area of regulatory law.

4.64 Almost any business makes frequent or regular contact with Government departments and their agencies through paperwork designed to enable the department or agency to perform a (regulatory) function of some kind. Indeed, even small to medium-sized firms may allocate a specific responsibility to an employee or director to secure the firm's regulatory compliance, in this respect; a large firm may even have a whole compliance department within it. Government departments and their agencies must often also frequently account to one another respecting regulatory compliance, as on issues of health and safety. Individuals, of course, must also have such information contact with Government departments and their agencies whenever they file tax returns, renew driving or other kinds of licences and permissions, and so on.

4.65 Suppose someone is required to fill in forms for different regulatory bodies, providing information in relation to (i) qualification for a licence to engage in a particular kind of business, (ii) the nationality and criminal record (if any) of employees, and (iii) the nature of the marketing to be employed for the firm's products. Let us assume that there is sufficient reason to make it a criminal offence in each case to fail to supply adequate information, or to supply the wrong sort of information, if the transgression in question reflected one of the moral failings just mentioned.

4.66   That being so, it would be undesirable that different kinds of positive or negative fault requirement apply, depending on which body it is that requires the information in question (although there can of course be special reasons why differences obtain). At present, it may well be that one set of provisions makes it an offence to make a false or misleading statement knowingly or recklessly, another set makes it an offence to do this, without reasonable excuse, and the final set of provisions makes it an offence to make a false or misleading statement, unless all due diligence was shown in seeking to ensure the information was accurate. This is confusing and unhelpful, especially to small businesses less likely to have employees whose special task it is to secure regulatory compliance across the board.

A principled approach

4.67   In fact, the proportionality principle that we set out above is to be found in a good deal of regulatory law on this issue. In the regulatory schemes set up by such laws, the provision of the wrong information (false or misleading information) is not a criminal offence unless there is knowledge or recklessness as to its falsity. Mere negligence is not enough, being (as we have seen) further down the scale or hierarchy of fault.

4.68   This approach respects the proportionality principle. It implicitly recognises that the mere provision of inaccurate information, or the simple omission to provide relevant information, may often be very remote from any harm done, or may lead to harm only indirectly. Accordingly, to avoid over-criminalisation, higher level fault elements should be employed to limit the scope of the offences in question.

The Pensions Act 2004

4.69   One example can be found in the Pensions Act 2004. Section 195 creates an offence of providing false or misleading information, wherein the offence is not committed unless knowledge or recklessness is proved:

> (1) Any person who *knowingly or recklessly*[26] provides information which is false or misleading in a material particular is guilty of an offence if the information—
>
> > (a) is provided in purported compliance with a requirement under—
> >
> > > (i) section 190 (information to be provided to the Board etc),
> > >
> > > (ii) section 191 (notices requiring provision of information), or
> > >
> > > (iii) section 192 (entry of premises), or

---

[26] Emphasis added.

(b) is provided otherwise than as mentioned in paragraph (a) but in circumstances in which the person providing the information intends, or could reasonably be expected to know, that it would be used by the Board for the purposes of exercising its functions under this Act.

(2) Any person guilty of an offence under subsection (1) is liable—

(a) on summary conviction, to a fine not exceeding the statutory maximum;

(b) on conviction on indictment, to a fine or imprisonment for a term not exceeding two years, or both.

The Local Transport Act 2008

4.70   Similarly, as a result of section 44 of the Local Transport Act 2008:

(11) A person is guilty of an offence under this subsection if—

(a) the person provides information in accordance with a requirement imposed by virtue of subsection (7)(c),

(b) the information is false or misleading in a material particular, and

(c) the person *knows* that it is *or is reckless* as to whether it is.[27]

(12) A person who is guilty of an offence under subsection (11) is liable on summary conviction to a fine not exceeding level 4 on the standard scale.[28]

4.71   Such provisions, which insist on proof of knowledge or recklessness, are common. They rightly avoid reliance on wrongdoing constituted merely by negligence, in making conduct in relation to mis-statements criminal.

The Medicines Act 1968

4.72   Even when the matter is as weighty as the provision of information in relation to an application for a licence to manufacture, sell or supply medicine, a proof-of-knowledge requirement is included in the relevant offence, contrary to section 45(6) of the Medicines Act 1968. The section reads:

Any person who, in giving any information which he is required to give … makes a statement which he knows to be false in a material particular shall be guilty of an offence.[29]

---

[27]   Emphasis added.

[28]   The large difference in possible maximum penalties under these two Acts is a matter addressed elsewhere in the CP. In the next Part, we suggest that if conduct is worthy of punishment only by a fine, then it would be better dealt with by a regulatory penalty.

[29]   Following conviction on indictment for this offence, an unlimited fine or up to two years' imprisonment may be imposed by way of penalty: s 45(8)(b) of the Medicines Act 1968.

4.73   The provision is perhaps rather generous to applicants, in that giving information that one realises may be false (recklessness) would seem to be equally worthy of inclusion within the scope of the offence. The main point is that the remoteness of possible harm from the simple failure to provide relevant information is treated here as a reason to employ only restricted (subjective) forms of fault element, excluding negligence.

The Eggs and Chicks Regulations 2008[30]

4.74   Contrast these examples with regulation 15(1)(c) of the Eggs and Chicks Regulations 2008/1718. These are meant to address marketing standards for eggs, for hatching and farmyard poultry chicks and regulation 15(1)(c) deals with obstruction. It reads:

> 15.—(1) A person is guilty of an offence if—
>
> (a) they intentionally obstruct an authorised officer acting in the execution of these Regulations;
>
> (b) without reasonable excuse, they fail to give an authorised officer acting in the execution of these Regulations any assistance or information which that person may reasonably require of them for the performance of the authorised officer's functions under these Regulations;
>
> (c) they give to an authorised officer acting in the execution of these Regulations any information which they know, or ought reasonably to know, to be false or misleading; or
>
> (d) without reasonable excuse, they fail to produce a record when required to do so by an authorised officer acting in the execution of these Regulations.

4.75   Moreover, regulation 19 provides that:

> A person guilty of an offence specified in regulation 4, 7, 13(8), 14(5) or 15(1) is liable on summary conviction to a fine not exceeding level 5 on the standard scale.

4.76   In this example, regulation 15(1)(c) falls short of our requirement that moral wrongdoing sufficient to justify criminalisation must be properly related to the harm done or risked. Regulation 15(1)(c) makes it an offence to give information to an authorised officer which D ought reasonably to know is false or misleading. So, regulation 15(1)(c) imposes criminal liability for a kind of negligent conduct (not knowing what one should know) in relation to a risk of harm that may well be quite remote. Accordingly, this is an example of over-extensive criminalisation.

---

[30] SI 2008 No 1718.

4.77　This is so even though the maximum penalty is quite low, and even though (it would seem) the fault requirement is a positive one that involves the prosecution in discharging the burden of proof in relation to what ought reasonably to have been known. There is a strong case for imposing criminal liability in this kind of case, only if there is dishonesty, intention or recklessness, in relation to false or misleading information provided.[31]

The Education and Skills Act 2008

4.78　These examples should now be contrasted with the analogous provision in section 90 of the Education and Skills Act 2008. In one way, the provision is quite similar to regulation 15(1)(c), in that it renders someone criminally liable for a bureaucratic transgression, on the basis of negligence. Section 90 concerns the wrongful release of information about an adult on an education or training programme. According to section 90, the provision of information to the wrong person about an adult's participation in education and training (and the relationship of that participation to that person's entitlement to benefit) is an offence with only a negative fault requirement, meaning D must prove his or her own moral innocence. Section 90 reads:

> (1) This section applies to information—
>
> > (a) used in reliance on section 87(1)(a), or
> >
> > (b) disclosed in reliance on section 87(1)(b) or 88.
>
> (2) A person commits an offence if—
>
> > (a) the person discloses the information to another otherwise than in connection with the exercise of an assessment function of the Secretary of State or a devolved authority, and
> >
> > (b) the information relates to a person whose identity is specified in or can be deduced from the disclosure.
>
> (3) It is a defence to prove that a person charged with the offence reasonably believed—
>
> > (a) that the disclosure was lawful, or
> >
> > (b) that the information had already and lawfully been made available to the public.
>
> (4) A person guilty of an offence under this section is liable—
>
> > (a) on conviction on indictment, to imprisonment for a term not exceeding 2 years or to a fine or to both;

---

[31] We will not deal here with the policy issues raised by, for example, the offence in regulation 15(1)(c) of the Eggs and Chicks Regulations 2008 of failing, without reasonable excuse, to assist an authorised officer, when reasonably required to do so. A question certainly arises over whether the existence of such an offence is proportionate to the goal to be achieved by the regulations. It is, perhaps, a rather different matter where the offence (set out in 15(1)(a)) is positive obstruction of an authorised officer.

(b) on summary conviction, to imprisonment for a term not exceeding 12 months or to a fine not exceeding the statutory maximum or to both.

4.79 In this instance, by way of contrast with regulation 15(1)(c) of the Eggs and Chicks Regulations 2008,[32] it is arguable that a lesser fault requirement than, say, dishonest, intentional or reckless disclosure, is warranted. This is because the disclosure in question involves a direct violation of someone's privacy, and thus involves a much more direct (threat of) harm done than the wrongdoing at issue in regulation 15(1)(c). Carelessness in making an error, manifested by (say) the absence of a reasonable belief that the disclosure in issue was lawful, is accordingly more justifiably regarded as making criminalisation legitimate, than it would be had some less inherently damaging disclosure been involved.

4.80 However, this is a marginal and controversial case.

Conclusion

4.81 Clarity and consistency, as well as fairness, should be essential elements of any offence applicable, in particular, to businesses faced with bureaucratic demands from a number of different agencies for information, on pain of criminal penalty for failure to comply. Those subject to such laws should be able to rely on a simple rule of thumb. Consequently, we propose:

> **Proposal 11: In relation to wrongdoing bearing on the simple provision of (or failure to provide) information, people should not be subject to criminal proceedings – even if they may still face civil penalties – unless their wrongdoing was knowing or reckless.[33]**

SECURING CONSISTENCY IN ALL REGULATORY CONTEXTS

4.82 We mentioned earlier that what is absent from existing official guidance aimed at individual departments contemplating the creation of criminal offences is an insistence that usage of particular fault terms should ideally be consistent across regulatory contexts, not only within them.

4.83 Now that we have some principles governing fault that can be applied across the board in regulatory contexts our third provisional proposal is thus that:

---

[32] SI 2008 No 1718.

[33] It is important to emphasise that our concern here is with the simple provision of the wrong or incomplete information, and so on, to a regulatory agency. Where false or misleading statements are knowingly or recklessly made in a dishonest way, with a view to gain or to imposing (the risk of) loss on another, they will fall foul of the Fraud Act 2006; and rightly so.

Proposal 12: The Ministry of Justice, in collaboration with other departments and agencies, should seek to ensure not only that proportionate fault elements are an essential part of criminal offences created to support regulatory aims, but also that there is consistency and clarity in the use of such elements when the offence in question is to be used by departments and agencies for a similar purpose.

PART 5
STATUTORY INTERPRETATION AND THE STATUS OF THE IDENTIFICATION DOCTRINE

INTRODUCTION

5.1 Corporations are recognised as separate legal persons;[1] they have a legal identity that is distinct from the natural persons who together make up the corporation. As Smith and Hogan remark, this "presents the opportunity, in theory, of imposing liability on the corporation separately from any criminal liability which might be imposed on the individual members for any wrongdoing".[2] This possibility is supported by the established rule of statutory interpretation that, in the absence of a contrary intention, the word "person" in a statute should be interpreted as extending to corporations.[3]

5.2 Previously corporations were thought not to be indictable for procedural reasons,[4] but these barriers have now been removed by legislation.[5] Clearly, corporations, as abstract entities, can only act through their servants or agents. In order for liability to be imposed on the corporation itself it is therefore necessary to attribute to it the acts and state of mind of a natural person(s). The issues that then arise are how the acts and state of mind of individuals can be attributed to the corporation, and which individual's acts and states of minds *should* be attributed to the corporation.

5.3 Two main techniques have now been developed for attributing to a corporation the acts and states of mind of the individuals who comprise it; vicarious liability and the 'identification' doctrine.

---

[1] *Salomon v Salomon* [1897] AC 22.

[2] *Smith & Hogan, Criminal Law* (12th ed 2008) p 245.

[3] Interpretation Act 1978, s 5 and Sch 1. Some further helpful theoretical analysis can be found in the paper written by Professor Wells, published as Appendix C.

[4] *Anon* (1701) 12 Mod 560, 88 ER 1518, note, by Holt CJ.

[5] Section 33(3) of the Criminal Justice Act 1925 provides that a corporation may enter a plea by a representative, or if the corporation fails to do so the court shall order a plea of not guilty to be entered and the trial shall proceed as though the corporation entered a not guilty plea. Section 1 of the Criminal Law Act 1967 also abolished the distinction between felonies and misdemeanours, thereby removing the obstacle that a corporation could not be indicted for a felony.

5.4 Vicarious liability holds the employer liable for the acts of their employee.[6] The courts had no difficulty in holding a corporation liable in this way, just as an individual employer would be for the acts of an employee. As a general rule, vicarious liability does not form part of the criminal law. The employer is not normally criminally responsible for the acts of his or her employee/agent. An important exception is that vicarious liability can be incurred in the criminal law by way of statutory offences that impose an absolute duty on the employer, even where they have not authorised or consented to the act. Whether a statutory provision imposes such vicarious liability is a matter of construction.[7]

5.5 In *Mousell Brothers Ltd v London & North Western Railway Co*[8] the appellant was required, under section 98 of the Railways Clauses Consolidation Act 1845, to provide the collector of tolls for the railway with an exact account of the goods to be carried. False accounting with intent to avoid the payment of the tolls was an offence under section 99 of the Act. On two occasions the appellant had delivered lorry loads of goods for carriage and the driver had handed over a consignment note falsely describing the loads. The magistrate found as a fact that the false description had been provided on the instructions of the manager, who had authority to complete the accounts. It was not suggested however that the directors of the company were party to the false descriptions. The company was held liable for the offence committed by their manager. Giving judgment Viscount Reading said:

> I think, looking at the language and the purpose of this Act, that the Legislature intended to fix responsibility for this quasi-criminal act upon the principal if the forbidden acts were done by his servant within the scope of his employment. If that is the true view, there is nothing to distinguish a limited company from any other principal, and the Defendants are properly made liable for the acts of [the manager].[9]

5.6 From our point of view, the opening words of this passage are highly significant. They show that at this early stage, the courts were taking an approach to the nature and scope of corporate liability that was tied to the language and purpose of the individual statute in question. They were not principally concerned with the development of abstract rules of liability that were then to be imposed across the board, without regard to the context.

5.7 This context-based, interpretive approach to crimes created by statute is an approach that we believe should have a stronger influence than it currently does in the modern law, as we will now go on to argue.

---

[6] See the discussion in Professor Wells' paper, Appendix C, paras C.47 to C.52.

[7] *Mousell Bros Ltd v London and North-Western Railway Co* [1917] 2 KB 836, 845 by Atkin J.

[8] [1917] 2 KB 836.

[9] *Mousell Brothers Ltd v London & North Western Railway Co* [1917] 2 KB 836, 845.

The identification doctrine

5.8 The second method of attributing to a corporation the acts and state of mind of certain individuals is known as the 'identification doctrine' or the directing mind theory. In essence this method attributes to or identifies with the corporation the acts and state of mind of those individuals who are part of the 'directing mind and will' of the corporation.[10]

5.9 This doctrine treats the acts and states of mind of those individuals who are the directing mind and will of the corporation as the acts or state of mind of the corporation itself. Described as "the concept of corporate alter ego",[11] the doctrine is a "two step analysis [that] first identifies the perpetrator of the crime, and then asks whether he or she is a person who can be said to embody the company's mind and will".[12] We examine the question of who falls into that category below.

5.10 The application of the identification doctrine to criminal law enabled liability to be imposed on a corporation for virtually any offence, including those that require a culpable state of mind. The only offences where the doctrine is inapplicable are those that are not punishable by a fine (such as murder) and offences such as rape and bigamy where the corporation would lack a basic qualification for liability.[13] It is arguable that it has never been clear to what extent the identification doctrine is a doctrine of general application, like the rule that criminal liability can only be incurred once someone is aged 10 or older.

5.11 This lack of clarity has manifested itself in recent cases that have brought the scope and application of the doctrine into question. The individuals said to form part of the directing mind and will have not been consistently so regarded in the case law, the distinction between the application of vicarious liability and the identification doctrine has not always been clear, and recent judgments have sometimes directly challenged the application and status of the doctrine. Parliament has not yet sought to resolve these problems by, for example, providing a statutory definition of the nature and scope of the identification doctrine, or by consistently making clear, when a criminal offence is created, the basis on which a company may be found liable for that offence. By way of contrast, as we will see in Part 7, it is very common for primary legislation to make clear the basis on which directors (or equivalent persons) can be found individually liable for offences committed by their companies. This is so, even though the statute in question says nothing about the basis on which the company itself might be found criminally liable.

5.12 In this part, we examine the emergence of the identification doctrine in the common law as a method of attributing corporate criminal liability. We then analyse how the doctrine has been applied, review the recent cases challenging the status of the doctrine, and assess the continued appropriateness of the doctrine as the primary means of establishing corporate criminal liability.

---

[10] See *Archbold* (2010) para 17-30.

[11] G R Sullivan, "The Attribution of Culpability to Limited Companies" (1996) 55(3) *Cambridge Law Journal* 515, 515.

[12] J Gobert, "Corporate criminality: four models of fault" (1994) 14(3) *Legal Studies* 393, 395.

[13] *Blackstone's Criminal Practice* (2010) A5.17.

THE EMERGENCE OF THE IDENTIFICATION DOCTRINE IN COMMON LAW

5.13 By the beginning of the nineteenth century courts had accepted that corporations could be guilty of regulatory offences through the doctrine of vicarious liability. However, establishing corporate liability for offences requiring a particular state of mind was more difficult and, as noted above, was not addressed by the courts until much later on.[14]

Liability for *mens rea* offences: before the identification doctrine

Origins of the identification doctrine

5.14 The origins of the identification doctrine lie in the civil case *Lennard's Carrying Co Ltd v Asiatic Petroleum Co Ltd.*[15] In this case the statute referred to "actual fault or privity" and the court held that the privity of the company's manager was the privity of the company itself. The principle underlying what has come to be known as the identification doctrine was expressed by Viscount Haldane in the following oft-cited passage:

> A corporation is an abstraction. It has no mind of its own any more than it has a body of its own; its active and directing will must consequently be sought in the person of somebody who for some purposes may be called an agent, but who is really the directing mind and will of the corporation, the very ego and centre of the personality of the corporation.[16]

5.15 The principle espoused in *Lennard's* was then followed in various shipping cases, the courts making explicit use of directing mind theory.

The 1944 cases: personal criminal liability for companies

5.16 The following three cases have been taken to show the first appearance in the *criminal* law of the doctrine of identification.[17] Amanda Pinto QC and Martin Evans have suggested that, following these cases, from 1944 a company could be liable on the basis that certain acts of certain employees were to be regarded as the acts of the company itself and that "this is direct, personal liability, not vicarious liability".[18] The approach in these cases can therefore be distinguished from the earlier ones where vicarious liability was adopted. It is widely recognised as the point at which what is now known as the identification doctrine was adopted by the criminal law.

---

[14] See para 5.4 above.

[15] [1915] AC 705.

[16] *Lennard's Carrying Co Ltd v Asiatic Petroleum Co Ltd* [1915] AC 705, 713.

[17] A Pinto QC and M Evans, *Corporate Criminal Liability* (2003) pp 39 to 46.

[18] Above, p 39.

Director of Public Prosecutions v Kent & Sussex Contractors Ltd[19]

5.17   In this case the company was prosecuted for issuing a record which it knew to be false in a material particular. The records had been submitted by the transport manager, on behalf of the company, in order to obtain petrol coupons. The magistrate acquitted the defendant company on the grounds that the offence required "an act of will or state of mind". Whilst it was found that the record was false in the material particular alleged to the knowledge of the transport manager, this knowledge could not be imputed to the company.

5.18   On appeal the Divisional Court reversed the decision, holding that the company could be convicted of the offences charged. The court held that, as a company could only act through those empowered to speak or act on its behalf, the state of mind of those individuals could be imputed to the company.

5.19   In delivering his judgment Viscount Caldecote rejected an application of vicarious liability, stating that:

> Although the directors or general manager of a company are its agents, they are something more. A company is incapable of acting or speaking or even of thinking except in so far as its officers have acted, spoken or thought ... . It is unnecessary, in my view, to inquire whether it is proved that the company's officers acted on its behalf. The officers are the company for this purpose ... .[20]

5.20   The judgment of Mr Justice Hallett also marked this case as a turning point in corporate criminal liability. Having referred to the Interpretation Act 1889, he stated that he believed:

> There has been a development in the attitude of the Court arising from the large part played in modern times by limited liability companies ... the theoretical difficulty of imputing criminal intention is no longer felt to the same extent.[21]

R v ICR Haulage Ltd[22]

5.21   Before the hearing in this case objection was brought on behalf of the company that an indictment alleging a common law conspiracy, requiring proof of fault, could not lie against a limited company. The commissioner of the assize refused to quash the indictment.

---

[19]   [1944] KB 146.

[20]   *DPP v Kent & Sussex Contractors Ltd* [1944] KB 146,155.

[21]   Above, 157.

[22]   [1944] KB 551.

5.22 This case had arisen out of a contract for the supply and delivery of hardcore and ballast between ICR Haulage and Rice & Sons Ltd, a public works contractor. The defendants were the company (ICR Haulage), the managing director, two ICR drivers and two Rice & Sons employees. The prosecution alleged that they had conspired together to defraud Rice & Sons Ltd by charging it for more than was delivered. The common law offence of conspiring to defraud required proof of a criminal state of mind. The defendants were all convicted. On appeal it was again argued that the company itself could not be indicted for conspiracy as that offence involved proof of fault as an essential ingredient.

5.23 The appeal was rejected, approving of *DPP v Kent & Sussex Contractors*. Mr Justice Stable stated that:

> Where in any particular case there is evidence to go to a jury that the criminal act of an agent, including his state of mind, intention, knowledge or belief is the act of the company, … must depend on the nature of the charge, the relative position of the officer or agent, and the other relevant facts and circumstances of the case.[23]

5.24 It has been noted that this was particularly easy to determine on the facts of the case because the managing director of ICR Haulage (Mr Robarts) was also a defendant. He took all the decisions of the company effectively acting as a one-man band. His acts were therefore clearly the acts of the company.[24]

Moore v I Bresler Ltd[25]

5.25 I Bresler Ltd, Sydney Bresler (the company secretary and general manager) and the sales manager of the company's Nottingham branch, were convicted under section 35(2) of the Finance (No 2) Act 1940 of the offence of making use of a document which was false in a material particular with intent to deceive. The (non-corporate) individual defendants had submitted tax returns which showed a lower sales figure than should have been the case. The Recorder found that the (non-corporate) individuals' misconduct was outside the scope of their authority and that the company was the victim of the fraud rather than an offender.

5.26 However, the Divisional Court rejected this argument. It did not regard as significant the fact that the company was the victim of the fraud. The court considered the issue to be whether the individuals were acting within their authority, not whether they were acting contrary to the company's best interests. In that regard, giving judgment Viscount Caldecote stated that:

---

[23] *ICR Haulage Co Ltd* [1944] KB 551, 559.

[24] A Pinto QC and M Evans, *Corporate Criminal Liability* (2003) p 42.

[25] [1944] 2 All ER 515.

These two men were important officials of the company, and when they made statements and rendered returns which were proved in this case, they were clearly making those statements and giving those returns as officers of the company, the proper officers to make those returns. Their acts, therefore … were the acts of the company.[26]

5.27 Addressing the issue of whose acts could be imputed to the company for this purpose, Mr Justice Humphreys stated that:

It is difficult to imagine two persons whose acts would more effectively bind the company or who could be said on the terms of their employment to be more obviously agents for the purpose of the company than the secretary and general manager of that branch and the sales manager of that branch.

5.28 We question how decisive these cases really are, in establishing a generalised identification doctrine, although they certainly impose liability other than through the use of the doctrine of vicarious responsibility. None of them provide guidance on the extent of the identification doctrine. None of them specifically address the category of persons whose acts and states of mind can be imputed to the company in this way.[27] Moreover, a point that may explain the courts' silence on such matters, the judges are at pains to emphasis the context-sensitive nature of a decision to attribute liability to the company for the acts of the particular agents in the case at hand.

5.29 For example, in the *ICR Haulage* case, Mr Justice Stable said:

We are not deciding that in every case where an agent of a limited company acting in its business commits a crime the company is automatically to be held criminally responsible.[28]

Development of the doctrine

5.30 Some evidence for the emergence a new doctrine with a defined scope, whereby the acts and states of mind of certain employees are considered to be the acts and states of mind of the corporation itself, was provided by Lord Denning in the civil case of *H L Bolton (Engineering) Co Ltd v T J Graham & Sons Ltd.*[29] He said:

---

[26] *Moore v I Bresler Ltd* [1944] 2 All ER 515, 516 to 517.

[27] C Wells, *Corporations and Criminal Responsibility* (2nd ed 2001) p 95.

[28] *ICR Haulage Co Ltd* [1944] 1 KB 551, 559.

[29] [1957] 1 QB 159.

A company in many ways may be likened to a human body. It has a brain and a nerve centre which controls what it does. It also has hands which hold the tools and act in accordance with directions from the centre. Some of the people in the company are mere servants and agents who are nothing more than the hands to do the work and cannot be said to represent the mind or will. Others are directors and managers who *represent the directing mind and will of the company*, and control what it does. The state of mind of these managers is the state of mind of the company and is treated by the law as such.[30]

5.31 Lord Denning went on to state, without this being necessary for the decision, that:

So also in the criminal law, in cases where the law requires a guilty mind as a condition of a criminal offence, the guilty mind of the directors or the managers will render the company themselves guilty. This is shown by *R v ICR Haulage Ltd* ... .[31]

5.32 However, at the time of *ICR Haulage*, the identification doctrine was arguably not so well established, nor so explicit, as Lord Denning claimed. None of the earlier cases, including *ICR Haulage,* to which Lord Denning referred, made explicit mention of the directing mind theory. One commentator has described Lord Denning's statement as "arguably a bold attempt ... to redefine and unify the law in terms of a simple pervasive theory, rather than to merely reiterate what already existed".[32]

5.33 In other words, it is unclear whether, in the final sentence of the passage just cited, Lord Denning was right to treat the law as having already established an identification doctrine in the terms that he sets out.

Tesco Supermarkets Ltd v Nattrass[33]

5.34 The decision of the House of Lords in *Tesco Supermarkets Ltd v Nattrass* is widely recognised as the leading authority on the identification doctrine in corporate criminal liability. The decision established that the identification principle applied to all offences not based on vicarious liability. All of their Lordships relied on the passage from *Lennard's,*[34] and endorsed the use of the directing mind theory for establishing criminal liability of corporations. One commentator identifies it as the point at which the directing mind test "finally triumphed" in cases relating to the criminal liability of companies.[35]

---

[30] *H L Bolton (Engineering) Co Ltd v T J Graham & Sons Ltd* [1957] 1 QB 159, 172 (emphasis added).

[31] Above, (emphasis in original).

[32] R J Wickins, "Confusion worse confounded: the end of the directing mind theory?" [1997] *Journal of Business Law* 524, 530.

[33] [1972] AC 153. A discussion of this decision, and of corporate liability in the area of consumer protection more generally, can be found in Professor Cartwright's paper at Appendix B.

[34] See para 5.14 above.

[35] R J Wickins, "Confusion worse confounded: the end of the directing mind theory?" [1997] *Journal of Business Law* 524, 535.

THE FACTS

5.35 Tesco Supermarkets Ltd had been charged with an offence under section 11(2) of the Trade Descriptions Act 1968 of indicating that goods (namely washing powder) would be sold at a price lower than that at which they were in fact sold.

5.36 The Tesco store in Northwich had advertised the washing powder for a certain price, both on posters in the window of their store and in the local newspapers. However a customer was unable to find the product for sale at the advertised price. When he enquired, he was told that the product was not in stock for that price. An inspector of weights and measures then interviewed the manager and was told that his assistant had failed to notify him of the lack of stock at the advertised price and had instead refilled the shelves with the higher priced stock. The store manager was responsible for the display of the posters and the marking of prices on goods in the store. The manager received instruction, training and supervision from the defendants.

5.37 The main issue was whether the defendants, Tesco, could rely on the due diligence defence in section 24(1) of the Trade Descriptions Act 1968 by showing that the offence was due to the act or default of "another person". The company argued that the commission of the offence was due to the act or default of another person, namely the branch manager, who had failed to supervise the assistant who actually committed the offence.

THE DECISION

5.38 The magistrates convicted the appellants, finding that the defendants had exercised all due diligence in devising a proper system for the operation of the store and in ensuring as far as was reasonably practicable that it was fully implemented. However, they believed that the requirements of section 24(1) had not been met because the store manager was not "another person" for the purposes of that provision.

5.39 On appeal, the House of Lords held that the defence was available because the branch manager was not part of the directing mind of the company.

5.40 In his speech, Lord Reid set out the limits of liability under the identification doctrine. He stated that the company may be criminally liable only for the acts of "the board of directors, the managing director and perhaps other superior officers of a company who carry out functions of management and speak and act as the company".[36] Lord Reid also emphasised the distinction between liability under the identification doctrine and vicarious liability:

---

[36] *Tesco Supermarkets Ltd v Nattrass* [1972] AC 153, 171.

> [A corporation] must act through living persons, though not always one or the same person. Then the person who acts is not speaking or acting for the company. He is acting as the company. There is no question of the company being vicariously liable … . He is an embodiment of the company … and his mind is the mind of the company. If it is a guilty mind then that guilt is the guilt of the company.[37]

5.41 Lord Morris also made this distinction from vicarious liability, stating that principles of vicarious liability were not generally applicable to criminal matters because criminal liability should be based only on personal fault. As such, the issue for the court was whether "the company itself" took all reasonable precautions and exercised all due diligence.[38]

5.42 Whilst all the law lords agreed on the application of the identification doctrine in this case, their Lordships all espoused slightly tests for determining which individuals were to be identified with the company for this purpose. Viscount Dilhourne described the directing mind as:

> A person who is in actual control of the operations of a company or of part of them and who is not responsible to another person in the company for the manner in which he discharges his duties in the sense of being under his orders … .[39]

5.43 Lord Diplock placed more emphasis on the formal position of individuals rather than actual control. He stated that it was a case of:

> Identifying those natural persons who by the memorandum and articles of association or as a result of action taken by directors, or by the company in general meeting pursuant to the articles, are entrusted with the exercise of the powers of the company.[40]

5.44 Lord Pearson agreed on the importance of the constitution of the particular company concerned, but also looked at the relevant statutory provisions for guidance:

> The reference in section 20 of the Trade Descriptions Act 1968 to "any director, manager, secretary or other similar officer of the body corporate" affords a useful indication of the grades of officers who may for some purposes be identifiable with the company, although in any particular case the constitution of the company concerned should be taken into account.[41]

---

[37] *Tesco Supermarkets Ltd v Nattrass* [1972] AC 153, 170.

[38] Above, 179.

[39] Above, 187.

[40] Above, 200.

[41] Above, 190 to 191.

COMMENTARY

5.45   The decision of the House of Lords in *Nattrass* is widely viewed as the leading authority on the use of the identification doctrine in the criminal law. It certainly provides some of the most explicit references to the doctrine and consideration of its extent. However it is apparent from the extracts above that there were differences between their Lordships' interpretations of directing mind. Lord Reid provided perhaps the most restrictive test, limiting it to the board of directors, managing director and *perhaps* other superior officers.

5.46   What is clear is that these tests could certainly produce different results if and when applied to different sets of facts. Indeed an examination of the subsequent cases shows that the application of the identification doctrine by the courts has been far from consistent following *Nattrass*.[42] One commentator regards it as an inherent weakness of the *Nattrass* judgment that "it could be easily distinguished by future courts, if so desired, on the ground that it really embodied nothing more than the interpretation of a specific, and perhaps exceptional piece of legislation".[43]

5.47   The test for corporate criminal liability espoused by the House of Lords in *Nattrass* has also been criticised for the effect that it has in practice. It makes it far easier to attribute criminal liability to smaller businesses than to larger ones. In this respect, Professor Gobert explains its shortcomings well when he states that the doctrine is:

>   both over- and under-inclusive. It is over-inclusive in that it holds the company liable for crimes of directors, officers and senior management even when the individual in question many have been acting contrary to company policy ... . [It] is under-inclusive in that the range of persons within a large company who will possess the relevant characteristics to render the company liable will inevitably be a rather small percentage of those who work for the company.[44]

After *Nattrass*

5.48   Following this well known decision, there are further examples of the courts applying the doctrine and tackling the issue of whose acts could be attributed to the company.

***R v Andrews Weatherfoil Ltd*[45]**

5.49   This case concerned a conviction for offences of bribery and corruption in relation to council building contracts, under section 1 of the Public Bodies Corrupt Practices Act 1889.

---

[42]   See paras 5.48 to 5.79 below.

[43]   R J Wickins, "Confusion worse confounded: the end of the directing mind theory?" [1997] *Journal of Business Law* 524, 537.

[44]   J Gobert, "Corporate criminality: four models of fault" (1994) 14(3) *Legal Studies* 393, 400.

[45]   (1972) 56 Cr App R 31.

5.50 This offence was not an absolute statutory offence but rather one involving proof of a guilty mind. As such, the case concerned the application of the identification doctrine rather than vicarious liability. The company appealed to the Court of Appeal on two grounds. First, the company claimed that the judge failed properly to direct the jury as to the criminal responsibility of a limited liability company for the act of a servant. Secondly, the company said the judge failed to deal with the correct factors that in law determine the question whether a criminal intention of an employee is also that of the company.

5.51 The prosecution alleged that the managing director, a technical director and the manager of the housing division all had the requisite status and authority to involve the company itself in criminal liability for corruption. The Court of Appeal disagreed. In allowing the appeal and quashing the conviction of the company, Mr Justice Eveleigh stated that:

> It is not every "responsible agent" or "high executive" or "manager of the housing department" or "agent acting on behalf of the company" who can by his actions make the company criminally responsible. It is necessary to establish whether the natural person or persons in question have the status and authority which in law makes their acts in the matter under consideration the acts of the company so that the natural person is to be treated as the company itself.[46]

5.52 This suggests that the court had in mind the restrictive directing mind and will category from *Nattrass*. The judgment establishes that liability for a corporation, for offences involving a guilty state of mind, cannot be established without first determining that the individual did, as a finding of fact, belong to such a category. Mr Justice Eveleigh considered it necessary that the judge in such cases "invite the jury to consider whether or not there are established those facts which the judge decides as a matter of law are necessary to identify the person concerned with the company".[47]

RECENT CASES

5.53 A study of more recent cases concerning the application of corporate criminal liability to fault-based offences shows that, since *Nattrass,* the application and scope of the identification doctrine has become less certain. In several cases the doctrine has not been applied, or not applied in the way one might expect. One commentator has suggested that, "it was not until more than twenty years after the Tesco Supermarkets decision that a crack began to appear in the whole edifice of the directing mind theory, ironically in the case of *Tesco Stores v Brent London Borough Council*".[48]

---

[46] *Andrews Weatherfoil Ltd* (1972) 56 Cr App R 31, 37.

[47] Above, 38.

[48] R J Wickins, "Confusion worse confounded: the end of the directing mind theory?" [1997] *Journal of Business Law* 524, 538.

Tesco Stores Ltd v Brent London Borough Council[49]

5.54 This case arose out of the prosecution of the appellants for the offence of selling a video to person under the age of 18 years contrary to section 11(1) of the Video Recordings Act 1984. The defendants relied on the defence available under section 11(2), that they had neither known nor had reasonable grounds to believe that the purchaser was under the age of 18. The court found that the employee at the checkout who sold the video had had reasonable grounds to believe that the purchaser was under the age of 18, and as such that the defence failed.

5.55 The appeal against conviction was dismissed. The court stated that the only issue on appeal was whether section 11(2) was concerned with the knowledge and information of the employee who supplies the video or only with the knowledge and information of those who represent the directing mind and will of the company. Lord Justice Staughton distinguished the present case from *Nattrass*. Whilst acknowledging the general principle that a company could not be guilty of a crime unless the criminal conduct and guilty mind existed in those who truly manage its affairs, he then stated that:

> Statutes may and sometimes do provide otherwise. There are offences for which, in derogation of the general rule, a company may incur liability through the behaviour of its servants.[50]

5.56 The court held that in this case the wording and intent of the legislation was quite different from that in *Nattrass*. The knowledge and belief required was clearly intended to be that of the cashier. The court added that, "were it otherwise, the statute would be wholly ineffective in the case of a large company".[51]

5.57 It is no doubt true that, as Lord Justice Staughton observed, were the statute to allow the defence where one of its senior officers neither knew nor had reasonable grounds to believe that the purchaser was under-age, large corporations could never be convicted. However the defence in section 11(2)(b) refers to the knowledge or reasonable belief of the accused, and in this case the accused was the corporation. It seems therefore strange that in *Nattrass* the store manager was considered too junior for his acts to be attributed to the company, yet in *Tesco v Brent* the acts of a cashier could be attributed to the company.

5.58 In the mid-1990s there were at least three cases in which the courts considered the directing mind and will approach of *Nattrass*, and further reduced its application.[52] The effect of these judgments has been described as:

> With little fanfare reduc[ing] this whole elegant structure to a heap of intellectual rubble, from which it is hard to discern how much – if anything – can be salvaged.[53]

---

[49] [1993] 1 WLR 1037. For further discussion of this case, see Appendix B.

[50] *Tesco Stores v Brent London Borough Council* [1993] 1 WLR 1037, 1041.

[51] Above, 1042 by Saughton LJ.

[52] Although, to keep our discussion shorter, we discuss only three cases, in fact there are others, to the same effect, that we could have considered. See for example, the discussion of *R v British Steel PLC* [1995] 1 WLR 1356, by Professor Cartwright, Appendix B.

El Ajou v Dollar Land Holdings plc[54]

5.59   This was a civil case, with complicated facts, but essentially concerning the tracing of funds by an investor who had been fraudulently divested of them in breach of trust. In the course of determining this, the question arose whether the knowledge of the Chairman of the board of directors could be imputed to the company. The Chairman in this case was in fact a Swiss financial agent appointed by the American owners of the company. He only played a minor and perfunctory role in the actual management of the company, attending to the paperwork and carrying out the instructions of the owners. On these grounds, the trial judge found that his was not a directing mind.

5.60   The Court of Appeal disagreed, and in so doing redefined the directing mind test to cover also those officers of the company who control a certain type or class of transaction. They held that the officers did not have to be at the top level of management, or be in control of the general management of the company. On the facts, the Court of Appeal held that although the Chairman may not have been exercising independent judgment he was still the directing mind for the purpose of obtaining the funds that were in dispute. Lord Justice Nourse stated that:

> This doctrine, sometimes known as the alter ego doctrine, has been developed, with no divergence of approach, in both criminal and civil jurisdictions … . The doctrine attributes to the company the mind and will of the natural person or persons who manage and control its actions.[55]

5.61   It is clear from the judgments in the case that the court took a much broader approach to directing mind and will, stretching it beyond the understanding in *Nattrass*. Lord Justice Nourse stated that "it is necessary to identify the natural person or person having management and control in relation to the act or omission in point".[56] Similarly Lord Justice Rose considered the identification doctrine to encompass a wider group of people, concluding that:

> First, the directors of a company are, prima facie, likely to be regarded as its directing mind and will whereas particular circumstances may confer that status on non-directors. Secondly, a company's directing mind and will may be found in different persons for different activities of the company.[57]

---

[53]   R J Wickins, "Confusion worse confounded: the end of the directing mind theory?" [1997] *Journal of Business Law* 524, 525.

[54]   [1994] BCC 143.

[55]   *El Ajou v Dollar Land Holdings plc* [1994] BCC 143, 150.

[56]   Above, 151.

[57]   Above, 154.

Pioneer Concrete[58]

5.62   In this case the respondents were all engaged in the supply of ready mixed concrete. They were subject to an injunction obtained by the Director General of Fair Trading restraining them from giving effect to or purporting to enforce certain existing unlawful agreements or any other agreements in contravention of section 35(1) of the Restrictive Trade Practices Act 1976.

5.63   Local managers of the companies were found to have made an unlawful arrangement to fix prices and allocate work. This agreement was made contrary to the express instructions and without the knowledge of the respondents. Nonetheless, the House of Lords allowed the appeal of the Director, and restored the original order of the Restrictive Practices Court, holding the respondent companies guilty of contempt of court. In reaching this conclusion the House of Lords expressly distinguished the 'directing mind and will' test of *Nattrass*. The House of Lords said that the test was particular to the statutory defence provided by the Trade Descriptions Act 1968: section 20(1) expressly distinguished between "any director, manager, secretary or other similar officer of a body corporate" and other persons who were merely its servants or agents.

5.64   It is clear from the speeches in the case that the Lords dealt with the case as one of vicarious liability. Lord Nolan stated that:

> The principal significance of this case, and of the cases to which it refers, as it seems to me, lies in the acceptance of the proposition that even in the case of a statute imposing criminal liability, and even without any express words to that effect, Parliament may be taken to have imposed a liability on an employer for the acts of his employees, provided that those acts were carried out in the course of the employment. Further, the liability may be imposed even though the acts in question were prohibited by the employer.[59]

> ...

> The plain purpose of section 35(3) is to deter the implementation of agreements or arrangements by which the public interest is harmed, and the subsection can only achieve that purpose if it is applied to the actions of individuals within the business organisation who make and give effect to the relevant agreement or arrangement on its behalf.[60]

5.65   In a statement which clearly contrasts with the identification doctrine, Lord Templeman stated that:

---

[58]   *Director General of Fair Trading v Pioneer Concrete (UK) Ltd* [1995] 1 AC 456.

[59]   Above, 472 to 473.

[60]   Above, 475.

> An employee who acts for the company within the scope of his employment is the company. Directors may give instructions, top management may exhort, middle management may question and workers may listen attentively. But if a worker makes a defective product or a lower manager accepts or rejects an order, he is the company.[61]

5.66   The court held that the fact that the agreements were made without the knowledge of the employer, and any steps taken by them to prevent it from being made, could count only towards mitigation.

5.67   It would seem that, had a strict interpretation of directing mind and will under the identification doctrine as applied in *Nattrass* been applied to this case, the respondent companies would not have been liable for the acts of their local managers. However, the speech of Lord Nolan in particular would seem to support the approach of the court in *El Ajou*, where it was thought that the directing mind and will could be found in different people for different activities of the company, and liability should arise based on a finding of management responsibility in fact, rather than a finding of management responsibility in law. Applying this expanded concept of directing mind and will to *Pioneer Concrete*, liability could possibly have been established under the identification doctrine on the basis that the local managers had the authority to make the agreements in question, and as such for that purpose were to be identified with the company.

5.68   In distinguishing the *Nattrass* decision as particular to the statutory defence available in that case, *Pioneer Concrete* significantly undermines the identification doctrine. In so doing, the decision is liable to produce even greater uncertainty in determining the criminal liability of corporations.

The Meridian Case[62]

5.69   The decision of the Privy Council in *Meridian* took a different tack, in relation to the version of the identification doctrine espoused *in Nattrass*. The key holding in Lord Hoffmann's speech in *Meridian* is that, where criminal liability is created by a statutory offence, whether an act could be attributed to the corporation would be a matter of statutory interpretation. As we suggested above, that was in all probability also the approach of many of the earlier cases on corporate liability established other than vicariously.

THE FACTS

5.70   In 1990 a group of people in New Zealand, Malaysia and Hong Kong tried to gain control of Euro-National Corp Ltd (ENC), a cash-rich publicly listed company, to use its assets for their own purposes. The scheme was to use bridging finance to purchase a 49% controlling share of the company and to then use the company's own assets to repay the bridging finance once the group was in control.

5.71   The bridging finance was provided by the appellant company Meridian, through the chief investment officer and the senior portfolio manager, and involved an improper use of their authority.

---

[61]   *Director General of Fair Trading v Pioneer Concrete (UK) Ltd* [1995] 1 AC 456, 465.

5.72   The New Zealand Securities Amendment Act 1988 required formal disclosure by any person who became a substantial security holder in a publicly listed company. The aim of the legislation was clearly to enable boards and investors to resist predatory raids by requiring immediate disclosure to the target company and the stock exchange. It was accepted that Meridian had acquired a relevant interest in ENC and had not given the required notice. The existence of the holding had been concealed from the corporation by the fraudulent employees party to the scheme.

5.73   At first instance the judge held that Meridian knew it was a substantial security holder by attributing to the company the knowledge of the fraudulent investment officer and portfolio manger. The Court of Appeal then affirmed the decision, but on the explicit grounds that the knowledge should be attributed to Meridian because their investment manager was the directing mind and will of the company. Meridian appealed to the Privy Council arguing that it did not have knowledge, actual or constructive, that it had acquired a substantial interest. The appellant argued that neither of the employees was identified in its constitutional instruments as being part of the directing mind and will, and as the investment officers performed their duties under the supervision of the managing director, they did not in fact have ultimate responsibility for the investment activity.

THE DECISION OF THE PRIVY COUNCIL

5.74   The court dismissed the appeal. In reaching that conclusion the court looked at the purpose of the statute and concluded that for the purposes of the act in question it was surely the knowledge of the individual who, with the authority of the company, acquired the relevant interest, that should be attributed to the company. The court reasoned that, were it otherwise, companies could allow employees to acquire interests on their behalf and not declare them until the board or senior management knew of it, defeating the purpose of the statute.

5.75   Lord Hoffmann justified this purposive approach to determining corporate criminal liability by examining the previous cases in light of their particular statutory contexts. He sought to show how the courts had fashioned special rules of attribution, particularly emphasising the contrast between *Nattrass* and *Pioneer Concrete*. Lord Hoffmann explained the need for this more flexible approach to attributing corporate liability:

---

[62] [1995] 2 AC 500. See also the discussion of this case in Appendix B.

There will be many cases ... in which the court considers the law was intended to apply to companies and that, although it excludes ordinary vicarious liability, insistence on the primary rules of attribution would in practice defeat that intention. In such a case, the court must fashion a special rule of attribution for the particular substantive rule. This is always a matter of interpretation: given that it was intended to apply to a company, how was it intended to apply? ... One finds the answer to this question by applying the usual canons of interpretation, taking into account the language of the rule (if it is a statute) and its content and policy.[63]

COMMENTARY

5.76 The response to Lord Hoffmann's speech in *Meridian* has been mixed. On the one hand, it introduces a flexibility which would allow for greater sophistication in the approach to the imposition of corporate criminal liability. On the other hand, it has been said to bring uncertainty to this area of the law.

5.77 In suggesting that the restrictive identification doctrine is not always appropriate, Lord Hoffmann's speech has been praised, as it, "appeared to herald a more modern, organisational, concept of liability".[64] It has also been seen by one leading company lawyer as bringing, "a welcome degree of flexibility into a difficult area of the law".[65] In another commentator's view, this creates the potential to allow imposition of corporate criminal liability in a broader range of circumstances.[66]

5.78 However, there have been some concerns expressed about Lord Hoffmann's approach. One commentator has suggested that, "following *Meridian* ... there is no general theory of how to attribute a state of culpability to companies".[67] It has been suggested that, by reclassifying the directing mind and will as merely one of several applicable rules of attribution, *Meridian* creates a situation where, "both the company's own rules of attribution and the particular statute [will be] competing for attention in deciding whose acts can be said to be those of the company".[68]

[63] *The Meridian Case* [1995] 2 AC 300, 507.

[64] C Wells, *Corporations and Criminal Responsibility* (2nd ed 2001) p 103.

[65] L S Sealy, "The Corporate Ego and Agency Untwined" [1995] *Cambridge Law Journal* 507, 509.

[66] *Smith & Hogan, Criminal Law* (12th ed 2008) p 250.

[67] P Cartwright, *Consumer Protection and the Criminal Law* (2001) p 104.

[68] C Wells, *Corporations and Criminal Responsibility* (2nd ed 2001) p 104.

5.79 It is certainly true that there are benefits in terms of certainty to the more constrained approach to the directing mind and will theory, exemplified in *Tesco v Nattrass,* under which liability is limited to those with plenary authority. The question is whether the approach taken in *Meridian,* that allows for a more policy-orientated and purposive exercise of statutory interpretation, in determining the nature and scope of corporate liability, should nonetheless be preferred.[69]

5.80 That leads us to an examination of the weaknesses of the identification doctrine, as a matter of principle.

THE WEAKNESSES OF THE IDENTIFICATION DOCTRINE

Interpreting directing mind and will

5.81 First, it is important to note that directing mind and will is a phrase that has been interpreted in various ways. As Pinto and Evans have suggested, it, "appears to be less a term of art than a matter of construction depending on the context and the meaning of the section under consideration".[70]

5.82 Further recognition of this uncertainty can be seen in the current editions of practitioner texts. For example, Blackstone's Criminal Practice states that:

> Precisely which employees or officers are identified with the company for these purposes is a matter of some debate ... it seems that it will normally only be senior persons at or close to board level who will normally be identified with the company.[71]

5.83 From an examination of the case law on the issue, it seems that the uncertainty over directing mind and will extends beyond merely differences of approach depending on context. *Nattrass* is often seen as the case which unequivocally applied the directing mind and will theory; yet even in that case three of their Lordships described the test in significantly different terms, capable of leading to different results if applied to a different set of facts than the one they faced.[72]

Inappropriate method

5.84 Perhaps of greater concern regarding the identification doctrine is that, quite apart from the difficulties apparent in its application, it may simply be an inappropriate and ineffective method of establishing criminal liability of corporations.[73] This wider concern may be particularly evident when the identification doctrine is applied in its strictest sense, in which case Smith & Hogan note that:

---

[69] See G R Sullivan, "The Attribution of Culpability to Limited Companies" (1996) 55(3) *Cambridge Law Journal* 515, 521 to 524.

[70] A Pinto QC and M Evans, *Corporate Criminal Liability* (2003) p 46.

[71] *Blackstone's* (2010) para A5.17.

[72] See paras 5.42 to 5.44 above.

[73] See further the discussion in Professor Cartwright's paper, Appendix B.

Only the very senior managers will be likely to fit the description as the directing mind and will of the company. This illustrates one of the major shortcomings of the identification doctrine – that it fails to reflect the reality of the modern day large multinational corporation … . it produces what many regard as an unsatisfactorily narrow scope for criminal liability.[74]

5.85 This concern that the doctrine is inappropriate for modern corporations has been widely expressed, Professor Gobert has stated that the doctrine, "fails to capture the complexity of the modern company".[75] By focusing on attributing the acts and state of minds of a limited range of senior people to the corporation, the identification doctrine fails to reflect the fact that, in modern corporations, a good deal of important policy or strategic decision-making may be de-centralised, or regional rather than national.

5.86 Further, Professor Clarkson notes that, "the doctrine ignores the reality of modern corporate decision-making which is often the product of corporate policies and procedures rather than individual decisions".[76] This may be one of the reasons that the courts have in recent cases sought to avoid an application of the identification doctrine, undermining any status it might have had as a general principle. In that regard, one commentator, drawing on an analysis of recent cases, reaches the conclusion that "courts are beginning to recognise the 'corporateness' of corporate conduct, thus acknowledging the limitations inherent in the controlling officer, directing mind, conception of liability".[77] Similarly, another commentator sees the confusion apparent in the latest authorities as indicating that, "a fundamental shift of direction has occurred".[78]

5.87 A related difficulty with the identification doctrine, as a method of establishing corporate liability, is that it necessarily involves applying the same test to corporations of very different sizes, from one-man-bands to multinational corporations. This may create unfairness, as between the two groups. It is more likely that in small companies Directors (or equivalent persons) will have a direct hand in the running of the business at the front line, and hence will have the knowledge required to impute their individual fault to the company itself because they embody the directing mind and will of the company. In a large or multinational corporation, Directors are much less likely to take such an active front line role, and the policies that they set for those at the front line to follow may intentionally give considerable decision-making latitude to employees further down the line.

---

[74] *Smith & Hogan, Criminal Law* (12th ed 2008) p 249.

[75] J Gobert, "Corporate criminality: four models of fault" (1994) 14(3) *Legal Studies* 393, 395.

[76] C M V Clarkson, "Kicking Corporate Bodies and Damning Their Souls" [1996] *Modern Law Review* 557, 561.

[77] C Wells, "Corporate liability for crime: the neglected question" [1995] *International Banking and Financial Law* 42, 44.

[78] R J Wickins, "Confusion worse confounded: the end of the directing mind theory?" [1997] *Journal of Business Law* 524, 555.

5.88 Accordingly, large or multinational corporations with complex multi-level organisational structures will find it easier to deny that individuals who took decisions that led to the commission of fault-based offences had a truly directing mind and will. The result is the company itself avoids liability for what was, in fact, the devolved decision of an employee, even though that employee might have been quite a senior employee.[79] Professor Gobert recognised this weakness when he noted that:

> The identification doctrine propounds a test of corporate liability that works best in cases where it is needed least [small businesses] and works worst in cases where it is needed most [big business].[80]

5.89 This situation can be contrasted with that generated in law by the extended vicarious liability approach adopted by the court in *Pioneer,* where Lord Nolan noted that:

> Liability can only be escaped by completely effective preventative measures. How great a burden the devising of such measures will cast upon individual employers will depend upon the size and nature of a particular organisation.[81]

Conclusion

5.90 It is clear from the examination of the main authorities dealing with the application of the identification doctrine that the law in this area suffers from considerable uncertainty. Professor Cartwright notes that "it is troubling that we are left with a series of cases which do not provide a definite answer to important issues of corporate and vicarious liability".[82] Certainly, it would have been a considerable improvement if Parliament had stepped in long ago to define the nature and scope of the identification doctrine.

5.91 However, it is unlikely that having only one basis on which companies can be found criminally liable, however broadly stated, will prove to be workable or desirable across the board. Recent legislation in fact points in the opposite direction, namely in the direction of specially tailored solutions to fit different contexts in which crimes may come to be committed by, or on behalf of, companies.

---

[79] See *Smith & Hogan, Criminal Law* (12th ed 2008) p 249.

[80] J Gobert, *Rethinking Corporate Crime* (2003) p 63.

[81] [1995] 1 AC 456, 475.

[82] P Cartwright, *Consumer Protection and the Criminal Law* (2001) p 105.

Individually tailored solutions

CORPORATE MANSLAUGHTER AND NEGLIGENCE

5.92   For example, the Corporate Manslaughter and Corporate Homicide Act 2007 makes it possible to impose liability on companies for manslaughter by a form of gross negligence, even though no individual Director may have contributed to a death through his or her gross negligence. The Act achieves this by permitting the aggregation of negligent conduct on the part of directors and employees at all levels of a company, so long as the negligence of Directors (or equivalent persons) played a substantial role in bringing about the unlawful death.[83] It is not necessary, under the 2007 Act, to find that a Director (or equivalent) person made a causal contribution to the death by his or her own gross negligence, irrespective of the fault of lower-level persons involved.

5.93   Such an approach by-passes the identification doctrine by, within limits, permitting aggregation of fault demonstrated by different people at different levels within a company. However, the approach is peculiarly well-suited to liability established on the basis of gross negligence, a fault term used by the common law only in manslaughter cases. Whilst people can share an intention, or knowledge, in criminal law they can be regarded as doing so only by an act of will or consciously. By way of contrast, in principle, (gross) negligence may be inferred or found by putting together discrete pieces of conduct that are not in that same sense part of a shared consciousness.

5.94   It follows that the approach taken by the 2007 Act will not be suitable to all crimes involving proof of fault.

5.95   What is true of gross negligence is also true of simple negligence, in any of its forms. Suppose a criminal offence can only be committed if it is proved that someone had 'reason to believe' that a state of affairs existed. In principle, whether or not a company had reason to believe something could be assessed by putting together pieces of information held by the company in different ways or in different but connected places, especially if there was meant to be a company system by which such information was collated.

5.96   It is true that the strict application of the identification doctrine to such a case would entail asking whether a director (or equivalent officer) had reason to believe in the relevant state of affairs.[84] Even so, we will suggest below that the courts would not necessarily, when interpreting a statute, be bound to apply that doctrine.

---

[83]   On this point, see Professor Cartwright's comments in Appendix B.

[84]   This difficult issue – whose beliefs or reasons to believe something, within a company – are relevant to the extent of liability or to exculpation is discussed briefly by Professor Cartwright in Appendix B.

5.97　A different approach needs to be taken when the fault element for a crime involves intention, knowledge, or an allied term such as dishonesty. Either someone possessed (or two or more people shared) an intention, knowledge or a dishonest state of mind, or they did not. Showing that a director or equivalent person possessed such a state of mind, as required by application of the identification doctrine, can make the criminal liability of companies almost impossible to establish in many instances.

5.98　In order to overcome the problem set for such instances by the identification doctrine, the Bribery Act 2010 takes a different tack.[85] The Act takes the commission of bribery to benefit the company by an employee or agent as the trigger for a possible investigation of corporate liability. The Act then requires the tribunal of fact to ask whether the company itself failed to prevent the act of bribery, and if it did, whether the company has shown that it had adequate procedures in place to avoid such acts taking place.[86]

5.99　This approach, unlike the approach to corporate manslaughter, does not implicate directors or equivalent persons in the commission of the criminal act itself.[87] The 2010 Act creates a kind of second-order form of criminal liability, liability at directorial level for failing to prevent a crime being committed by a lower level employee, on behalf of the company.

5.100　What is of significance about this structure of liability is that an important justification for employing it is the recognition that, where bribery is concerned, middle managers and employees may have substantial incentives to commit the offence for the benefit of the company. Directors may rightly deplore the commission of crimes by their employees. Even so, the fact remains that there may well be substantial incentives for employees to commit some kinds of crime that benefit their company, and corresponding incentives on companies to turn a blind eye to such conduct (even at some risk to their reputation, if the commission of the crime becomes public knowledge). These facts point, in policy terms, in the direction of corporate liability founded on a company's failure to prevent the offending, rather than on the involvement of the company itself in the offending.

5.101　It follows that it is perfectly possible that this approach may not be appropriate in all circumstances. For example, whilst it works well enough when crimes that benefit the company, such as bribery, are in issue, it may not be so appropriate when other crimes that are not acquisitive are in issue. This is because non-acquisitive crimes are unlikely to be committed on behalf of the company even if they take place in the course of company business. Here is an example:

---

[85]　For further exploration of reasons to take a different course with corporate liability for bribery, see Appendix B.

[86]　Bribery Act 2010, s 7(2).

[87]　Although, obviously, a company could, if the identification doctrine was satisfied, be found guilty of bribery.

Company X has an agreement with the National Offender Management Service that it will employ sex offenders in its car cleaning business, to help them re-gain a place in society. A failure adequately to supervise these employees leads to an incident in which one of them commits a sexual assault at a company car wash.

5.102 Of course, it is arguable that the company should be exposed to criminal liability in such cases for a failure to prevent a sexual assault; but the arguments in favour will not be quite the same as those in favour of failure-to-prevent offences when the offences were meant to benefit the company financially. The arguments in favour will be much broader ones about the duties of care owed by all employing organisations respecting the acts of employees, whether those organisations are in the private or the public sector.

The benefits of context-sensitive reform

5.103 In an ideal world, every criminal offence applicable to companies would include a provision indicating on what basis a company can be found liable for the offence. In a world that falls short of that ideal, in our view, the approach of Lord Hoffmann in the *Meridian* case is the right one. It is clear from the decisions in *Pioneer Concrete*[88] and in *Meridian* that the courts now have the latitude to interpret statutes imposing corporate criminal liability as imposing it on different bases, depending on what will best fulfil the statutory purpose in question. Consequently, there is no pressing need for statutory reform or replacement of the identification doctrine. That doctrine should only be applied as the basis for judging corporate conduct in the criminal law if the aims of the statute in question will be best fulfilled by applying it.

5.104 This interpretive freedom is an advantage that must be weighed against the lack of predictability that comes from the absence of a single theory of corporate criminal liability applicable in all cases. No one can categorically assert that the balance must be struck one way rather than the other, even if an alternative model of corporate criminal liability to the identification doctrine could be found that commanded the support of a sufficiently wide range of consultees.

5.105 In their contributions to this CP, Professors Cartwright and Wells explore the strengths and weaknesses of a number of different models of liability.[89] We commend that discussion to the courts, when they are faced with the question of which model to apply to a given statute.[90]

---

[88] Notwithstanding the fact that this was not a straightforward criminal case.

[89] Appendices B and C.

[90] Further discussion of the views of Professor Cartwright and Professor Wells can found at paras 5.106 to 5.109 below.

5.106   For example, Professor Cartwright considers whether the approach to corporate liability adopted by the Corporate Manslaughter and Corporate Homicide Act 2007 would be an appropriate model to apply to consumer protection legislation. We have already seen that there has been uncertainty over the right approach in this field, with different courts taking different approaches to different pieces of legislation, depending on their understanding of the nature and scope of the identification doctrine.[91] Professor Cartwright says of the 2007 Act:

> Whether the Act's approach should be adopted for consumer protection more generally is interesting. Some elements would need to be reconsidered (such as the requirement for a gross breach of a relevant duty of care) and consumer law seldom involves the commission of very serious harm. However, the focus on the way that activities are managed or organised is, perhaps, a better reflection of corporate fault where *mens rea* offences are concerned than any attempt to locate fault within a member of the directing mind and will.[92]

5.107   Professor Wells discusses, amongst other things, the novel approach adopted by the Australian Criminal Code Act 1995.[93] Under this approach the issue in relation to offences requiring proof of fault is whether the fault (intention, knowledge or recklessness) can be attributed to the company; and it will be attributed to the company if the company, "expressly, tacitly or impliedly authorised or permitted the commission of the offence".[94] In proving whether or not there was such authorisation or permission, the prosecution is entitled to rely on, for example, proof that, "the body corporate failed to create and maintain a corporate culture that required compliance with the relevant provision".[95]

5.108   Looking back, one can perhaps detect the influence of this kind of approach in a case such as *Pioneer Concrete*.[96] The company had instructed the local managers not to enter into price-fixing arrangements. However, it may be argued that the company failed to create and maintain a corporate culture in which these instructions would unquestionably be followed by local managers, and that is why the court fixed the company with liability in the way that it did.

5.109   Most importantly, Professor Wells concludes:

---

[91]   See paras 5.48 to 5.78 above.

[92]   Appendix B. We have seen that an approach where the focus was, in effect, the way that the company was managed or organised, was adopted by the courts in the *El Ajou* case, and in the *Pioneer Concrete* case: see paras 5.59 to 5.68 above.

[93]   Appendix C, paras C.60 to C.73.

[94]   Australian Criminal Code Act 1995, s12.3(1).

[95]   Appendix C, para C.68.

[96]   See the discussion at 5.62 to 5.68 above.

Somewhat paradoxically it has been in statutory interpretation rather than in the development of common law principles of attribution, that the courts have been most responsive to the social and economic context of business operations ... the variety in corporate form, reach and activity taken together with the extensive range of criminal laws require a flexible response in terms of corporate liability models.[97]

5.110 We agree. Consequently, we provisionally propose that:

Proposal 13: Legislation should include specific provisions in criminal offences to indicate the basis on which companies may be found liable, but in the absence of such provisions, the courts should treat the question of how corporate criminal liability may be established as a matter of statutory interpretation. We encourage the courts not to presume that the identification doctrine applies when interpreting the scope of statutory criminal offences applicable to companies.

---

[97] Appendix C, para C.100.

PART 6
A JUDICIAL POWER TO APPLY A DUE DILIGENCE DEFENCE?

INTRODUCTION

6.1 In this Part, we make a case for a proposal that the courts should have the power to apply a defence of due diligence in all the circumstances to a statutory provision imposing criminal liability without a requirement for proof of fault. When such a defence is applied to a statutory provision, the burden of proof would be on the defendant to show that he or she exercised due diligence in all the circumstances to avoid committing the offence.[1] Were the power to apply such a defence available, there would cease to be a need to draw on the unwieldy presumption of fault requirements to make ostensibly strict liability offences fairer to defendants.

6.2 In many instances statutes creating criminal offences remain silent as to the fault element required, if any. Very many of these statutes are to be found in regulatory contexts. Such provisions may operate unfairly to the prejudice of accused persons unless some kind of fault element or defence is applied to them. At present, the primary means of ensuring fairness to accused persons in the application of such provisions is the courts' willingness to find that, where the statute has remained silent on the matter, proof of a fault element is an implicit requirement. Ideally, Parliament would always either provide for a fault or defence element in a new criminal offence, or contrariwise, in some way make it clear that fault-based liability is inappropriate for the offence. The importance of this is shown by the fact that the presumption of fault has not proved to be a very effective guarantee of fairness, or of certainty.

6.3 The problem is not just uncertainty over when the presumption applies; it is also uncertainty over the kind of fault that the courts will require the prosecution to prove when the presumption does apply. In general, Mr Glazebrook has described the case law as providing:

> [A] litany of vague, overlapping criteria which from time out of mind has signally failed to compel from the judges predictable answers to the question whether, when Parliament has been silent on the point, a person must, if she is to be convicted of a given offence, be presumed to have been at fault in respect of all, or some, of its external elements.[2]

---

[1] In practice, this would mean that an appeal court finding that the defence should apply would in all probability have to order a re-trial.

[2] P Glazebrook, "How old did you think she was?" (2001) 60(1) *Cambridge Law Journal* 26. See also P Cartwright, *Consumer Protection and the Criminal Law* (2001) p 88, where he says "the courts have found it surprisingly difficult to identify the principles by which they decide that statutory provisions impose strict criminal liability".

6.4 The statutory context will necessarily have a strong influence on whether or not the presumption of fault is displaced, and so in one way such unpredictability is not surprising. Moreover, sharpening up the criteria that determine when the presumption is displaced may not do much to improve the law. It will not improve it if the presumption of fault is not the best way to ensure that the prosecution of criminal offences is undertaken in a fair way in regulatory contexts, so far as both individual and corporate defendants are concerned.

6.5 Of course, if the guidelines for the creation of criminal offences in regulatory contexts that we propose are adopted, there will be few if any criminal offences without fault elements, because the wrongs such offences are aimed at will be dealt with in other ways.[3] However, there will inevitably still be a considerable number of important criminal offences on the statute book that say nothing about the need to prove fault. The courts' approach to these in future must be a concern of equal significance to anyone seeking to ensure that the criminal law is used in a discriminating and fair way in regulatory contexts.

6.6 The problem with the current approach, employing the presumption that proof of fault is required, is that it often involves courts in seeking to answer the wrong question. The issue should not be (at least not normally) whether or not the person charged was individually at fault in committing the wrong or in allowing it to be committed, in that they were aware that wrongdoing might occur. The issue should be whether the defendant made sufficient effort in all the circumstances to try to ensure the wrongdoing did not occur even though they were aware that wrongdoing *might* occur. In other words, did they exercise due diligence?

6.7 In that regard, were the courts to have a power to apply a defence of due diligence in all the circumstances to an offence of strict liability, they would no longer be required to exercise their minds over the question of whether Parliament by necessary implication (if not expressly) requires proof of fault if the offence itself is to be established.[4] Further, such a defence would not come into play by presumption irrespective of statutory context. It applies when, in the court's view, considering the purpose and operation of the statute in context, the application of the defence would lead to use of the criminal law in that context that was fair to defendants without placing unnecessarily obstructive obstacles in the way of prosecuting authorities (this can be called the fairness objective).

6.8 Finally, although the idea that the courts might have be given a power to apply the defence is a significant one, the defence itself is very familiar to courts, to regulators, to prosecutors and to businesses. They all regularly encounter it, in some form, in a wide range of existing regulatory contexts.

---

[3] See the analysis in Part 3 above.

[4] This would be unnecessary, because due diligence is a defence to an admitted offence. No interpretation of the scope of the offence itself is thus in issue.

THE PRESUMPTION OF FAULT

6.9 In dealing with the question of whether a fault element can and should be implied into an offence of ostensibly strict liability there is a strong common law presumption that all criminal offences were intended to have a fault element. This presumption is often cited by the courts, and is expressed in the following well-known statement of Mr Justice Wright in *Sherras v De Rutzen*:[5]

> There is a presumption that mens rea, or evil intention, or knowledge of the wrongfulness of the act, is an essential ingredient in every offence; but that presumption is liable to be displaced either by the words of the statute creating the offence or by the subject matter with which it deals, and both must be considered.[6]

6.10 In this case the court was concerned with the interpretation of section 16(2) of the Licensing Act 1872 which prohibited the supplying of liquor to a police constable whilst on duty. Here, despite the fact that the express requirement of "knowingly" in the offence under subsection (1) was omitted from subsection (2), the court upheld the presumption of fault and quashed the conviction. The conviction was quashed on the grounds that the publican had an honest and reasonable belief that the police constable was off duty.

6.11 *Sherras v De Rutzen* was in some ways an unusual case, because it involved an offence committed in the course of running a business, and the courts have in general lacked much sympathy for businesses when they face prosecution for strict liability offences. By way of contrast, perhaps especially in recent times, they have been much more solicitous of the interests of natural persons charged with such offences.

6.12 For example, in the case of *B (a minor) v Director of Public Prosecutions*,[7] the court was concerned with the application of section 1(1) of the Indecency with Children Act 1960 to a young boy. Section 1(1) made it an offence for any person to commit "an act of gross indecency with a child under the age of 14, or ... [to incite] a child under that age to such an act with him or another". This offence was defined by Parliament solely in terms of the proscribed physical acts, saying nothing of the fault element. B, the young boy, was convicted of an offence against section 1(1). The question on appeal was whether section 1(1) imposed strict liability, or whether a mistaken belief as to the age of the victim could amount to a defence. The House of Lords allowed the appeal, holding that the presumption of fault applied to the section 1 offence under the Children Act 1960. In such cases, the prosecution should have to prove that the defendant did not believe that the victim was under the age of 14. In upholding the presumption the House of Lords had regard to the gravity of the offence:

---

[5]   [1895] 1 QB 918.

[6]   *Sherras v De Rutzen* [1895] 1 QB 918, 921

[7]   [2000] 2 AC 428.

The more serious the offence the greater is the weight to be attached to the presumption, because the more severe is the punishment and the graver the stigma which accompany a conviction.[8]

6.13 In arriving at their decision, the House of Lords also considered the furtherance of the purpose of the statute:

It is far from clear that strict liability regarding the age ingredient of the offence would further the purpose of section 1 more effectively than would be the case if a mental element were read into this ingredient.[9]

6.14 Whether or not the latter claim is true, it demonstrates the importance of statutory context and purpose to the issue of when fault elements should be implied. That importance will remain if our proposal for a defence of due diligence in all the circumstances is adopted. For example, it is perfectly possible that this defence could be applied to a provision, itself silent as to fault, that adjoins a provision to which an all due diligence defence has been applied by Parliament. By analogy with *Sherras v De Rutzen*, whether it would be right to take this course of action would depend entirely on the statutory context.

6.15 More significantly, a crucial aspect of the application of the presumption by their Lordships in *B (a minor) v Director of Public Prosecutions* is its embodiment of a traditional common law fault element: the absence of an honest belief that certain circumstances obtain. In other words, having decided that the presumption of a fault requirement was not displaced in this case, on a proper reading of the statute, their Lordships did not go on to consider what kind of fault requirement would best strike the right balance between the interests of accused persons, and those of the prosecution and of the child victims of gross indecency. Their Lordships did not consider themselves free to decide that, for example, a defendant charged under section 1(1) of the Indecency with Children Act 1960 could escape conviction only if he or she had taken reasonable steps – exercised due diligence – in all the circumstances (making allowance for the defendant's age) to discover the age of the victim. We regard this as an important limitation or flaw in the court's approach.

6.16 This flaw is capable of posing significant problems if the same approach is taken when corporate defendants are prosecuted for serious offences where the identification doctrine applies. For, in such cases, the logic of *B (a minor) v Director of Public Prosecutions* would suggest that a director (or equivalent person) must be shown to have been individually at fault – not to have had the relevant belief – if the company is to be convicted. We saw in Part 5 the kind of problems to which that approach can lead. In that regard, it must be kept in mind that companies can be convicted of sexual offences attracting stigma of the same broad kind as the offence at issue in *B (a minor) v Director of Public Prosecutions*.

---

[8]   *B (a minor) v Director of Public Prosecutions* [2000] 2 AC 428, 464.

[9]   Above, 465.

6.17   An example is the strict liability offence of taking or distributing indecent photographs of children.[10] This offence could be committed by a photographic company employed to take photographs at a children's party. In such a case, the issue in relation to primary liability should not be whether or not the directors (or equivalent officers) had any subjective fault in relation to the commission of the offence, such as a realisation that there was a risk that employees might take indecent photographs.[11] The issue should be whether or not the directors (or equivalent officers) had exercised due diligence in all the circumstances, as through the provision of adequate training, to ensure that the offence of taking or distributing indecent photographs of children was not committed by company employees.

6.18   The central element in the decision in *B (a minor) v Director of Public Prosecutions* – requiring proof of subjective fault when the statute in question was silent as to requirements of fault – may or may not have been correct, in the particular circumstances of that case.[12] Whatever the answer to this question the decision is not a helpful precedent for regulatory contexts in which businesses are more likely to be the defendants. In our view, an approach that allows the application of a due diligence defence is much more preferable in that respect.

DUE DILIGENCE DEFENCES

An overview

6.19   In this Part we consider the possibility that the courts should be given the power, when interpreting the scope of a statutory offence, to apply to the offence a defence of due diligence in all the circumstances. The application of the defence would not rest on a fiction about Parliament's intent. Rather, it would depend on the court's assessment of the strength of the case for its application in the particular context as a basis for promoting fairness to accused persons in the pursuit of regulatory objectives without unduly hindering regulatory prosecutions (the fairness objective).

6.20   In practice, this power would come into play where a statute has created an offence without a fault element or without other defences that are meant to secure the fairness objective. In other words, it would become relevant in broadly the same circumstances in which the presumption of a fault requirement currently applies.

---

[10]   Protection of Children Act 1978, s 1(1).

[11]   Such a realisation might be relevant to the secondary liability of directors (or equivalent persons), namely to their liability for the offence established through their assistance or encouragement of the offence committed by the employee.

[12]   Parliament made great haste to reverse it: see s10 of the Sexual Offences Act 2003.

6.21   It is our provisional view that the question of whose due diligence was relevant would depend simply on who was charged with the offence. So, if a company was charged with the offence, the due diligence of directors (or equivalent persons) is the focus. That would involve an examination, for example, of their systems of management and control over employees. If the person charged was, by contrast, a store manager, the focus would be on the adequacy of his or her management decisions in the discharge of his or her role and so on.

6.22   Consequently, if, for example, a company was charged with the offence, it would not be enough for them to show that someone else – perhaps an employee – had exercised due diligence in seeking to avoid committing the offence. The issue would be whether the company's own system for preventing offences being committed reflected due diligence in all the circumstances, in that regard.

6.23   In our provisional view, the burden of proof (on the balance of probabilities) should be on the person seeking to benefit from the defence to prove that due diligence in all the circumstances had been shown. That is commonly the position when such a defence is made available under existing statutes.

Current use

6.24   There are a number of areas where Parliament has introduced offences that do not require proof of fault by the prosecution in any of the traditional forms (intention, knowledge, recklessness, or negligence). In some instances, the statute instead provides for affirmative defences, such as all due diligence shown, which the defendant must prove on the balance of probabilities. Such defences are particularly common in the regulation of business conduct. The legislation may contain one due diligence defence which applies to all the offences created under the legislation, or alternatively it can contain differing defences for certain provisions in the legislation.

6.25   Professor Wells has commented that offences of this type:

> Are similar to strict liability offences in the sense that the prosecutor does not have to prove knowledge, intention, or recklessness. But for the purposes of corporate liability they have been treated as mens rea offences because they contain a reverse onus of proof defence which allows the defendant to prove that she exercised all due diligence in avoiding the offence, or took all reasonable precautions or some similar formulation.[13]

6.26   In a similar vein, in relation to a more specific context, Deborah Parry has commented that:

---

[13] C Wells, *Corporations and Criminal Responsibility* (2nd ed 2001) pp 101 to 102.

> Modern consumer protection legislation normally depends on the criminal law to ensure compliance. Regulatory offences involving strict liability are the norm. To make these offences more acceptable to the business community, fairly standard "due diligence" defences … are available … . This confirms that liability is "strict" but not "absolute".[14]

6.27 It should be noted that not all due diligence defences come in exactly the same form. There may be subtle linguistic differences that can, at least on the face of it, make some such defences appear tougher to comply with than others. It is useful to examine some examples before going on to consider the proposal for a general power to apply a due diligence defence.

Statutory examples

General due diligence defence

6.28 The most common formulation of a due diligence defence in current statutes is that the accused "took all reasonable precautions and exercised all due diligence to avoid the commission of the offence".

6.29 This exact formulation appears, for example, in section 118(2) of the Environmental Protection Act 1990 which provides for a defence to certain offences under the Act.

6.30 Under section 28(1) of the Weights and Measures Act 1985 it is an offence for a person to deliver less than they purported to sell. To this offence section 34(1) provides a defence where an accused person can show that they "took all reasonable precautions and exercised all due diligence".

6.31 It is an offence under section 7(1) of the Children and Young Persons Act 1933 to sell tobacco or cigarette papers to a person under 18. Section 7(1)(A) now provides the defence of proving that the seller "took all reasonable precautions and exercised all due diligence".

6.32 Section 21 of the Food Safety Act 1990 provides a defence:

> For the person charged to prove that he took all reasonable precautions and exercised all due diligence to avoid the commission of the offence by himself or by a person under his control.

6.33 This defence is available to offences such as rendering food injurious to health,[15] selling food not complying with food safety requirements,[16] and falsely describing or presenting food.[17]

---

[14] D Parry, "Judicial Approaches to Due Diligence" [1995] *Criminal Law Review* 695. We will not be using the distinction between strict and absolute offences because the sense in which it is used here is not the same as that when it is used in other contexts. There is thus a risk of confusion.

[15] Food Safety Act 1990, s 7.

[16] Above, s 8.

6.34   There are also some slight variations in terminology on this common form of due diligence defence which appear to have the same substantive effect. For example, the term "reasonable steps" is used rather than "reasonable precautions" in both section 39 of the Consumer Protection Act 1987 and section 65(11) of the Water Industry Act 1991.

6.35   These are, of course, for the most part offences with which either an individual or a company could be charged.

Restricted due diligence defences

6.36   The common formulation of the due diligence defence is sometimes found in a restricted form, where it is only available in certain situations or if certain other conditions are also met.

6.37   One example of this is section 24(1) of the Trade Descriptions Act 1968 which provides for a defence to offences under the Act where:

> The commission of the offence was due to a mistake or to reliance on information supplied to him or to the act or default of another person … *and* he took all reasonable precautions and exercised all due diligence to avoid the commission of such an offence by himself or any person under his control.[18]

6.38   It is worth noting that the trade descriptions offences under the Trade Description Act 1968 to which this defence applies are by their nature commonly committed by companies. This statutory defence was relied upon in *Tesco v Nattrass*.[19]

6.39   Another example is the offence of making a false or misleading statement about a prescribed matter in the course of an estate agency business or a property development business contrary to section 1 of the Property Misdescriptions Act 1991. There is a defence under section 2(1) to show that the defendant took all reasonable steps and exercised all due diligence to avoid committing the offence. However, this defence is restricted in that it cannot be used where the defendant has relied on information unless he or she shows that it was reasonable in all the circumstances for him to rely on it.

---

[17]   Food Safety Act 1990, s 15.

[18]   Emphasis added.

[19]   [1972] AC 153. See Part 5 above.

6.40   Similarly section 39 of the Consumer Protection Act 1987 provides a defence to offences under the Act for the defendant to show that he or she "took all reasonable steps and exercised all due diligence to avoid committing the offence". This defence is available in relation to offences such as breach of safety regulations and breach of a prohibition notice.[20] However, where the defence involves an allegation that the offence was due to reliance on information given by another, the defendant is required to show that it was reasonable for him or her to rely on that information in all the circumstances.

Lack of fault

6.41   A third category of defences can be identified which are based on proving a lack of fault, or proving a lack of fault combined with proof of the exercise of some element of due diligence.

6.42   Section 24(3) of the Trade Descriptions Act 1968, now repealed, provided for a defence to offences under the Act involving supplying or offering to supply goods to which a false trade description is applied. The defence applied if the defendant proved that, "he did not know, and could not with reasonable diligence have ascertained" that the description was false.

6.43   Section 2(4) of the Clean Air Act 1993 provides a defence to the offence of emitting dark smoke where the alleged emission was inadvertent and the defendant proves that all practicable steps had been taken to prevent or minimise the emission of dark smoke.

6.44   Finally, section 123(5) of the Road Traffic Act 1988 provides a defence to the offence of giving paid instruction in the driving of a motor car by a person not on the register of approved instructors or their employer, if the defendant proves that "he did not know and had no reasonable cause to believe" that his or her name was not on the register.

Are qualifications to due diligence defences necessary?

6.45   Parliament may, of course, add to or modify a due diligence defence in any way that seems appropriate in a particular context. One may question whether or not some modifications make a great deal of difference. For example, in the instances in which Parliament has made special provision for cases in which the defendant relied on information supplied by another,[21] it could be argued that a due diligence defence, properly understood, can itself deal with such instances.

---

[20]   Consumer Protection Act 1987, ss 39(5) and 12 to 13.

[21]   See para 6.37 above.

6.46   For example, a defendant might claim that it was reasonable to rely on information supplied by someone without checking that information because the information was supplied by a Government official. Certainly, blind reliance on information supplied in such circumstances could be reasonable, but that does not mean that a due diligence defence has no application to such cases. By checking that the person supplying the information is indeed a relevant Government official, the defendant could be regarded as having exercised due diligence, whether or not he or she has checked the accuracy of the information itself.

6.47   Of course, it might be said of such an example that the defendant has not exercised all due diligence if he or she has not checked the accuracy of the information, as well as the reliability of its source. However, the due diligence defence that we are provisionally proposing requires the defendant to have shown due diligence in all the circumstances, not *all* due diligence. Broadly speaking, a general defence to a criminal offence should not counsel perfection. Whether or not someone can show that they have exercised due diligence in all the circumstances is a question of fact and degree.

6.48   The importance of this discussion is as follows.

6.49   In our view, first, a due diligence defence will not, in practice, so frequently require extra qualifications and modifications to make it fit different contexts. That would be too difficult for courts to apply as a general defence to particular statutory provisions.

6.50   Secondly, to accommodate the variations on the wording and strictness of the defence, and to give priority to securing the fairness objective, we believe that the defence the courts should have the power to apply should take the form that is most generous to the defendant. This means that the defence should be one of exercising due diligence in all the circumstances, rather than one of taking all reasonable precautions and exercising all due diligence.

6.51   However, we recognise that this is a controversial view, and we will be asking consultees whether the new defence, if introduced, should take a different, stricter form.[22]

OVERSEAS JURISDICTIONS

6.52   A due diligence defence has been used in several other common law jurisdictions, especially to secure the fairness objective in relation to corporate liability. As Jonathan Clough and Carmel Mulhern put it:

> Due diligence is a device by which the harshness of many corporate liability provisions is offset by allowing the corporation or individual to show that the offence occurred despite reasonable steps being taken to ensure compliance.[23]

---

[22]   See para 6.97 below.

[23]   J Clough and C Mulhern, *The Prosecution of Corporations* (2002) p 148.

6.53 Below is a brief outline of how due diligence has been used as a defence in the common law jurisdictions of Australia and Canada.

Australia

6.54 The general rule is that the defence is a creature of statute and as such is only available where it is expressly provided for within the terms of the statute that imposes the criminal liability.[24] Clough and Mulhern have concluded that:

> It would seem that as the law stands in Australia, on the balance of authority and on the basis of principle, the common law defence of due diligence to offences of strict liability is not available, except where specifically provided for by statute or where the criminal code applies.[25]

The Australian Criminal Code

6.55 Where there is no fault element, criminal responsibility under the Australian Criminal Code is governed exclusively by the words of the Code. Thus the defence of due diligence is only available where expressly provided for by the Code.

6.56 The Code provides that a company may rely on a defence of due diligence. The question is whether the conduct of a high managerial agent is not attributable to a company because it exercised due diligence to prevent the conduct at issue.[26]

6.57 The Code also provides for a due diligence defence where an employee had a reasonable but mistaken belief that the conduct was not criminal:

> A body corporate can only rely on the defence of a mistake of fact if the employee, agent or officer of the corporation, who carried out the conduct, had a reasonable, but mistaken, belief that the conduct was not criminal. The corporation also needs to prove it exercised due diligence to prevent such conduct.[27]

6.58 According to Clough and Mulhern, a company must show that it has exercised due diligence through the application of appropriate checks to ensure that it is conducting its business prudently and in compliance with legislation. However, the mere establishment of a checking system may not be enough to establish the defence of due diligence. The system must be "controlled, supervised, and updated".[28]

---

[24] J Clough and C Mulhern, *The Prosecution of Corporations* (2002) p 149.

[25] Above.

[26] Australian Criminal Code Act 1995, s 12.3(3).

[27] Above, s 12.5(1).

[28] J Clough and C Mulhern, *The Prosecution of Corporations* (2002) p 149.

6.59   Such a defence will fail if lack of due diligence is manifested in inadequate
        corporate management, control or supervision of the conduct of its employees,
        agents or officers. The defence will also not succeed if there was a failure to
        provide adequate systems for conveying relevant information to relevant persons
        in the body corporate.[29]

6.60   The relevant provisions of the Criminal Code were drafted in response to findings
        of the Criminal Law Officers Committee of the Standing Committee of Attorneys-
        General. The *Tesco v Nattrass* principle, that criminal liability could be attributed
        to corporations if the corporate officer involved in the commission of an offence
        was sufficiently senior to represent the mind of the corporation, was held by the
        Committee to be no longer appropriate as the touchstone for corporate criminal
        liability. The problem with the principle (as we have seen) was thought to be that
        it enabled larger companies to escape liability by decentralising responsibility
        within their organisation,[30] presenting an "almost insurmountable obstacle in the
        prosecution of larger corporations".[31]

Canada

6.61   The position in Australia can be contrasted to that in Canada, where a due
        diligence defence has developed at common law.[32] This defence is available to
        offences of ostensibly strict liability. It is available either as a separate defence at
        common law or as an extension of the defence of honest and reasonable mistake
        of fact.[33] In *R v City of Sault Ste Marie*[34] the Supreme Court of Canada held that
        for offences of strict liability the accused could rely on a defence of due diligence
        where: (1) he or she reasonably believed in a mistaken set of facts which, if true,
        would have rendered the act or omission innocent; or (2) he or she took all
        reasonable steps to avoid the particular event. It is this second element, the
        general due diligence defence, which is akin to the defence we are now
        considering.

BROADER DISCUSSION OF A DUE DILIGENCE DEFENCE

6.62   There has been some commentary on the merits of due diligence defences, and
        on the possibility of a general due diligence defence in English law. An outline of
        some of the commentary is provided below.

---

[29]   Australian Criminal Code Act 1995, s 12.5(2).

[30]   T Woolf, "The Criminal Code Act 1995 (Cth) – Towards a Realist Vision of Corporate
       Criminal Liability" (1997) *Criminal Law Journal* 257.

[31]   J Clough, "A Realist Model of Corporate Criminal Liability" (2007) 18 *Criminal Law Forum*
       267, 272.

[32]   See *R v City of Sault Ste Marie* (1978) 85 DLR (3d) 161.

[33]   J Clough and C Mulhern, *The Prosecution of Corporations* (2002) p 151.

[34]   (1978) 85 DLR (3d) 161.

6.63   Amanda Pinto QC and Martin Evans have considered the meaning of due diligence as it currently exists in regulatory schemes in England and Wales.[35] They note that it is for the accused to prove on the balance of probabilities that due diligence was exercised. In addition they point out that, under current law, a company cannot rely on the defence if it has delegated its responsibilities to another who does not act with due diligence. The failure of the delegate is the failure of the principal, that is, the company.[36]

6.64   In the paper written for us by Professor Wells, on models of corporate liability, one can see that forms of strict or vicarious liability are commonly accompanied by some form of due diligence defence.[37] For example, the table that Professor Wells provides in Appendix C shows that vicarious liability is often limited by a due diligence defence, not only in the UK but also in other jurisdictions.[38]

6.65   One commentator, writing on the criminal liability of corporations under Scottish law, has suggested the introduction of a general due diligence defence in Scotland. Richard Mays suggests that a due diligence defence should be available to companies in two situations. He suggests that it should be available both to a prosecution for a common law offence, where the defendant can show that they took reasonable precautions and exercised due diligence to avoid the criminal act, and to statutory crimes where the statutory enactment does not make clear provision for a fault element.[39]

6.66   Professor Cartwright, writing on the use of the criminal law in consumer protection legislation, has highlighted the usefulness of due diligence defences in the regulatory context.[40] Professor Cartwright notes that due diligence defences have an important role to play in allowing defendant companies to avoid liability where no one in the organisation was at fault. However, he notes that there is a problem with such defences still being subject to the identification doctrine. Professor Cartwright favours a narrow due diligence defence, proposing that:

> It is submitted that the best solution would be to allow a company to plead that it had taken all reasonable precautions and all due diligence where everyone in the company has fulfilled this requirement. Only where the fault to which the offence is attributable is outside the company should the company be able to plead the defence.[41]

---

[35]   A Pinto QC and M Evans, *Corporate Criminal Liability* (2nd ed 2008) ch 20.

[36]   Above, p 338 and see *R v Mersey Docks and Harbour Company* (1995) 16 Cr App Rep (S) 806.

[37]   See Appendix C.

[38]   See Appendix C, Table 1, p 221 below.

[39]   R Mays, "The Criminal Liability of Corporations and Scots Law" (2000) *Edinburgh Law Review* 46, 72.

[40]   P Cartwright, *Consumer Protection and the Criminal Law* (2001) p 110. See also the paper he has written for us, at Appendix B.

[41]   P Cartwright, *Consumer Protection and the Criminal Law* (2001) p 110.

6.67   In our provisional view, this understanding of a due diligence defence would prove to be too demanding. Whether due diligence in all the circumstances has been shown should depend on who has been charged with the offence. A company should not necessarily be found liable when it is the carelessness of an employee that leads to the commission of an offence if the company itself exercised due diligence in all the circumstances to avoid commission of that offence.

6.68   Arguments in favour of the use of unmitigated no-fault liability, especially in the regulatory context, tend to be focused on claims that it has a highly deterrent effect, that it is justified where the regulated activity has been voluntarily engaged in, and that there is a significant public interest in the prohibition of the particular activity. Professor Genevra Richardson has examined the empirical evidence relating to the use of unmitigated no-fault liability to define offences in regulatory contexts.[42] Professor Richardson casts doubt on the deterrent value of such liability, and suggests that its use may in fact detract from the importance of offences in regulatory contexts, by distinguishing them too sharply from the main body of criminal law.

6.69   This provides further support for the power to apply a due diligence defence in regulatory contexts. It would mean that no-fault liability is not unmitigated, thereby bringing regulatory crime closer to attaining the fairness objective.

FORMS OF DUE DILIGENCE DEFENCE

6.70   An important feature of such a defence of due diligence in all the circumstances is its capacity to secure the fairness objective for both large and small firms alike, as well as for individuals. This is because the question whether due diligence has been exercised in all the circumstances may include consideration of the size and capacity of businesses, and of their resources. Clearly, exercising due diligence in seeking to avoid the commission of offences may involve very different kinds of steps, as between a business consisting of four people playing an equal role, and a multinational corporation.

6.71   In our view the introduction of a power to apply such a defence would not involve the development of a new power for the courts to become back-seat drivers in regulatory enforcement policy development. Increasingly, use of the criminal law should become less central to regulatory policy in any event. However, when it is employed, there is every reason to think that its character as well as its enforcement should, in law, be judged by the fairness objective. That entails consideration of whether it is unfair and disproportionate to permit an offence to operate on the basis of unmitigated no-fault liability. Having said that, we have also stressed that whether or not the defence should be applied to a statutory provision is a matter to be determined by consideration of the statutory context as a whole.

---

[42]   G Richardson, "Strict Liability for Regulatory Crime: the Empirical Research" [1987] *Criminal Law Review* 295.

APPLYING A DUE DILIGENCE DEFENCE TO DECIDED CASES

6.72 The following are examples of cases where it is possible that the fairness objective might have been better secured, had the courts been able to apply a defence of due diligence in all the circumstances. We express no concluded view, so far as any of the cases is concerned, because it would not be possible or desirable here to seek to perform the task that would fall to a court of weighing the competing policy considerations in context. Nonetheless, we believe that discussion of our provisional proposal in relation to some well-known reported cases will be helpful to consultees.

Tesco Stores v Brent London Borough Council[43]

6.73 This case concerned the Video Recordings Act 1984 and the facts are described in Part 5.[44] The appeal against conviction of selling a video to a person under the age of 18 failed. The appellant had argued that the defence under section 11(2) of the Act, under which the defendant could show that they neither knew nor had reasonable grounds to believe that the purchaser was under 18, was available but the court held that this was concerned with the knowledge or belief of the employee who sold the video and not with the knowledge or belief of the company.

6.74 On this interpretation, the defence provides no protection to a corporation prosecuted under this Act, other than when the directors (or equivalent persons) are those actually selling videos. The court might in these circumstances have at least considered applying a defence of due diligence in all the circumstances to section 11(1). This would have allowed *Tesco Stores* to seek to show, on the balance of probabilities, that they had exercised due diligence in seeking to avoid the commission of the criminal act. This would have involved them establishing, for example, that they had adequate procedures and staff training in place, updated, and enforced, to prevent the sale of video recordings to underage persons.

6.75 Naturally, in relation to this particular provision, the court might have concluded that the application of a defence of due diligence in all the circumstances would not further the fairness objective significantly. This is why we are only suggesting that the courts should have a power to apply a due diligence defence. The defence should not be applied where to do so would be contrary to Parliament's intention or would otherwise frustrate the purpose of the legislative provision in question.

---

[43] [1993] 1 WLR 1037.

[44] See paras 5.54 to 5.58 above.

London Borough of Harrow v Shah[45]

6.76   In this case the defendants were prosecuted by the local authority for selling a ticket to a person below the prescribed age, contrary to section 13 of the National Lottery Act 1993. The two defendants were the proprietors of a small newsagent's shop, and were themselves unaware of the transaction having been concluded. The sale had been made by an employee, who sold a ticket to a 13-year-old boy, in the belief that the boy was 16 years old. At trial, the justices acquitted the defendants, on the basis that the defendants lacked knowledge or awareness at the time of the sale that the buyer was or might be under 16.

6.77   However the local authority's appeal was allowed. The court held that section 13 of the National Lottery Act 1993 was phrased so as to imply strict liability. As such, the knowledge or recklessness of the defendants was irrelevant. Mr Justice Mitchell held that:

> The prosecution does not have to prove, for the purposes of establishing the offence, that the defendant or his agent was either aware of the buyer's age or was reckless as to his age.[46]

6.78   The court noted the severity of the punishment in these circumstances,[47] but held that this was not a conclusive factor. The offence was concerned with an issue of social concern – gambling by young people – and it was held that this displaced any presumption that proof of fault was required. The court said:

> [If] strict liability attaches to this offence [it] will unquestionably encourage greater vigilance in preventing the commission of the prohibited act.[48]

6.79   We already noted that the belief that strict liability has a greater deterrent effect has been called into question.[49] In *Shah*, in relation to this provision, there would arguably have been quite a strong case for the application of a defence of due diligence in all the circumstances.

---

[45] [2000] 1 WLR 83.

[46] *London Borough of Harrow v Shah* [2000] 1 WLR 83, 90.

[47] The offence was punishable by up to two years' imprisonment.

[48] [2000] 1 WLR 83, 89.

[49] See para 6.68 above.

6.80   Further, there is a good chance that, had such a defence been made available, it could have been successful. In the judgment, it was acknowledged that the defendants had made their employee aware of the obligation not to sell lottery tickets to underage purchasers, that if in doubt employees should require proof of identification, and that if still in doubt he should refer the matter to the defendants or refuse to sell. The court also acknowledged that the defendants had, in addition to displaying the mandatory public signs regarding the sale of lottery tickets, placed handwritten signs on the counter, till and lottery terminal reminding staff not to sell to those under 16 years of age. It was, further, accepted that the defendants also regularly reminded their staff orally of their obligations. Had the defence been applied, the court would have been able to consider whether these steps were sufficient to amount to a display of due diligence in all the circumstances.

Pioneer Concrete[50]

6.81   In this case, the respondents were all engaged in the supply of ready mixed concrete. At the relevant time, they were subject to an injunction obtained by the Director General of Fair Trading. This restrained them from giving effect to or purporting to enforce certain existing unlawful agreements or any other agreements in contravention of section 35(1) of the Restrictive Trade Practices Act 1976. The case became a criminal case because a breach of that kind of injunction is a criminal offence in that it is a contempt of court.

6.82   Local managers of the companies were found to have made an unlawful arrangement to fix prices and allocate work, but it was the respondent company that was charged with contempt of court, in virtue of having broken the injunction. The House of Lords held that the respondent companies were guilty of contempt of court, despite the agreement made by the local managers being contrary to the express instructions and without the knowledge of the respondents.

6.83   Let us suppose this case was a more straightforward one of criminal liability for the making of an agreement that was unlawful because it was in breach of prohibitions on restrictive trade practices. This might have provided an instance in which the court would *not* have chosen to exercise a power to apply a defence of due diligence in all the circumstances.

6.84   The purpose of the prohibition might have been largely defeated had a company been able to avoid conviction where, as in this case, their local managers had entered into prohibited agreements, by showing that they had taken reasonable steps to prevent the formation of such agreements. Local managers might in general have a great deal of discretion over the terms on which agreements are concluded and very considerable financial incentives to fix prices. It might have been too difficult in practice for any company to police the conduct of local managers with a view to ensuring that offences concerned with restrictive trade practices were not committed. If that were so, the case for a defence of due diligence in all the circumstances would be weak because it would undermine the protection the relevant legislation gives to the public from restrictive trade practices.

---

[50]   *Director General of Fair Trading v Pioneer Concrete (UK) Ltd* [1995] 1 AC 456.

6.85   As Lord Nolan noted, where the statute so intends, "liability may be imposed even though the acts in question were prohibited by the employer".[51] In examples such as *Pioneer Concrete*, the concern is that the company may officially tell managers not to enter into prohibited restrictive agreements and they might yet have an unofficial policy of turning a blind eye to such practices. It may therefore be the case that the application of a due diligence defence in this instance would have unduly weakened the protections. This would of course be a matter for the courts to determine when interpreting the relevant statutory provisions in order to decide whether they ought to exercise their discretion to apply a due diligence defence.

Pharmaceutical Society of Great Britain v Storkwain Ltd[52]

6.86   In *Storkwain* the House of Lords was concerned with section 58(2)(a) of the Medicines Act 1968. This provision restricts the sale or supply of certain medicinal products except in accordance with a prescription given by a doctor. Section 67(2) of the 1968 Act creates an ostensibly strict liability offence where any person contravenes section 58.

6.87   The appellants had been convicted of a section 58 offence when they were found to have sold medicinal products that they reasonably believed to be covered by a doctor's prescription but which, in fact, were not covered by the prescription because it was a forgery. They appealed against their conviction, on the basis that the presumption of fault applied, and they had supplied the medicines believing in good faith and on reasonable grounds that it was a valid prescription.

6.88   The House of Lords dismissed the appeal, Lord Goff stating that it was clear from the Act that:

> Parliament must have intended that the presumption of mens rea should be inapplicable to s 58(2)(a) … it appears from the Act that, where Parliament wished to recognise that mens rea should be an ingredient of an offence created by the Act, it has expressly so provided.

6.89   This may be another case in which the court would have benefited from the power to apply a due diligence defence. The application of the defence would have allowed the appellants an opportunity to establish that they had exercised due diligence in all the circumstances to avoid the commission of the offence. Having said that, the Medicines Act 1968 itself provides a due diligence defence that is available to some offences under the Act, but not the section 58 offence.[53] This would obviously be a factor that the courts would take into account when deciding whether or not to apply the due diligence defence. However, it would not necessarily be a conclusive factor counting against the application of a defence of due diligence in all the circumstances. As Lord Reid noted in *Sweet v Parsley* when speaking of the presumption of fault:

---

[51]   *Director General of Fair Trading v Pioneer Concrete (UK) Ltd* [1995] 1 AC 456, 472.

[52]   [1986] 1 WLR 903.

[53]   Medicine Act 1968, s 121.

> The fact that other sections of the Act expressly require mens rea ...
> is not itself sufficient to justify a decision that a section which is silent
> as to mens rea creates an absolute offence.[54]

NOT APPLYING THE DEFENCE TO CERTAIN STATUTES

6.90 There may be some contexts – the road traffic context may be an example – in which, if our proposal becomes law, too much of the courts' time would be taken up by vain attempts to persuade the courts to apply a due diligence defence to offences under the relevant legislation. It might be better right from the outset to say that the defence simply has no application to some offences, such as those created by road traffic legislation, and possibly other legislation.

6.91 Accordingly we are asking consultees if they agree that the power to apply the defence would be inappropriate in the case of some statutes. If so, the question for consultees will be, which statutes do they think should be exempted from the scope of the defence?

CONCLUSION

6.92 In an ideal world, criminal offences created by statute would always indicate when fault need not be proved, or if it needs to be proved what kind of fault (or defence) is involved. Since there are so many criminal offences under statute that fall short of the ideal, we believe that, subject to some possible exceptions, the courts should be given the power to apply a defence of due diligence in all the circumstances to statutory offences that would otherwise involve strict liability with no adequate defence. This approach has the advantage of leaving the strict basis of liability in the relevant provision intact. That means the courts will no longer need to search for what may be non-existent Parliamentary intention respecting fault requirements and will no longer need to decide whether a presumption that fault must be proved applies, and if so, whether the presumption has been displaced.

6.93 Clearly, the courts would not apply the defence of due diligence where to do so would defeat the purpose of the statute. A related point is that we would expect the courts not to apply it if, despite the absence of a requirement for proof of a positive fault requirement, there are specific defences applicable to the offence that mean the fairness objective has been met.[55] Even where the courts did apply it, the burden of proof, on the balance of probabilities, would be on the defendant to establish that due diligence in the circumstances had been shown.

---

[54] *Sweet v Parsley* [1970] AC 132, 149.

[55] See para 6.7 above for an explanation of the fairness objective. The possibility that an ostensibly strict liability offence could nonetheless be fair to the defendant, because of the presence of an adequate range of context specific defences, was discussed in Part 3.

6.94 We believe that the introduction of the power to apply the defence has the potential to secure the fairness objective in a greater range of cases than at present. Moreover, unlike the presumption that fault must be proved, it can secure the fairness objective in a way that is sensitive to the differences between the capacities and resources of defendants to organise their affairs in such a way that offences are not committed in the course of business.

PROPOSALS AND QUESTIONS

6.95 We provisionally propose that:

> **Proposal 14: The courts should be given a power to apply a due diligence defence to any statutory offence that does not require proof that the defendant was at fault in engaging in the wrongful conduct. The burden of proof should be on the defendant to establish the defence.**

6.96 If proposal 14 is accepted, we also provisionally propose that:

> **Proposal 15: The defence of due diligence should take the form of showing that due diligence was exercised in all the circumstances to avoid the commission of the offence.**

6.97 However, we recognise that consultees may prefer this defence to have the same wording and to impose the same standards as the most commonly encountered statutory form of the defence. Accordingly, we ask following question:

> **Question 1: Were it to be introduced, should the due diligence defence take the stricter form already found in some statutes, namely, did the defendant take all reasonable precautions and exercise all due diligence to avoid commission of the offence?**

6.98 We ask the further question:

> **Question 2: If the power to apply a due diligence defence is introduced, should Parliament prevent or restrict its application to certain statutes, and if so which statutes?**

PART 7
BUSINESSES AND CRIMINAL LIABILITY

THE FOCUS IN THIS PART

7.1 In this Part, we will be considering the following legal issues, as they apply to companies and partnerships:[1]

(1)   Should the doctrine of delegation be abolished?[2]

(2)   Should the consent and connivance doctrine be restricted?[3]

7.2 What we say about these issues should be considered alongside our provisional proposal that the courts should be given the power to apply a due diligence defence to statutes that would otherwise impose strict criminal liability[4] and our suggestion that the courts should regard themselves as free to depart from the identification doctrine when the statute's purpose would be better fulfilled by adopting an alternative theory of corporate liability.[5]

7.3 Taken together, these proposals amount to a reform programme designed to reduce unfairness and arbitrariness in the imposition of liability on (small) businesses and on company directors. Having said that, it is our view that these proposals will not involve any significant disadvantage to police services and prosecutors investigating and pursuing corporate wrongdoing.

7.4 Before we consider these issues, it will help to provide some background or context to business activity in the UK.

INTRODUCTION AND BACKGROUND

The significance of small businesses

7.5 Businesses are more likely than individuals to find themselves the target of regulation (if not of public interest offences) and the target more broadly of governance by statutory instrument.[6] They are also more likely than individuals to find themselves (along with the voluntary sector) subject to legislation initially agreed on a European Union-wide basis in Brussels.[7]

---

[1]   We have already considered the wider application of a due diligence defence in Part 6 above.

[2]   See paras 7.53 to 7.58 below.

[3]   See paras 7.30 to 7.52 below.

[4]   See Part 6 above.

[5]   See Part 5 above.

[6]   See Part 3 above.

[7]   See the statement of Lord Triesman, Written Answer, *Hansard* (HL), 29 June 2006, vol 683, col WA183.

7.6 The significance of this must in part be judged in the light of the typical character of British businesses.[8] According to what was at that time the Department for Business, Enterprise and Regulatory Reform, in July 2008, there were 4.5 million businesses with between 0 and 9 employees (micro businesses). Many such businesses are comprised of family members or relatives. This is 96% of the total number of private business enterprises (4.7 million) in the UK.[9] Micro businesses accounted for 23% of the annual business turnover of £2,800 billion in the UK.[10]

7.7 The following, heavily regulated sectors of the economy and business are very substantially or mainly comprised of micro or small businesses.[11]

Agriculture: 94%

Construction: 75%

Private health and social work: 72%

Real estate: 56%

Hotels and restaurants: 45%[12]

7.8 Amongst other things, smaller businesses are likely to be less well placed than larger ones to make efficient and economic use of professional legal advice in relation to the impact of regulatory obligations on them. Still less are they likely to have individuals within their business whose job it is, in whole or in part, to match these obligations with the firm's structure and practices (an in-house specialist of some kind).[13]

---

[8] BERR, Statistical Press Release URN 08/92, 30 July 2008.

[9] Above.

[10] Small businesses (those with between 10 and 49 employees) accounted for a further 15% of that turnover.

[11] Between 10 and 49 employees.

[12] BERR, Table 4, UK Industry Summary, http://stats.berr.gov.uk/ed/sme/ (last visited 19 July 2010). It should be noted that in the case of the construction industry, in particular, a business may only be micro in size because it contracts out a great deal of its work but there is no reason to think that this fact unduly distorts the figures given.

[13] Memorandum submitted to the Regulatory Reform Committee by the Federation of Small Businesses:
http://www.publications.parliament.uk/pa/cm200809/cmselect/cmdereg/329/9042803.htm (last visited 19 July 2010).

7.9 In that regard, it would be right to point out that a significant proportion of those running micro businesses are relatively young: 71% are 35 years old or under, and 25% are 25 years old or under. Further, 30% have no educational qualifications beyond those gained at secondary school; only 16.5% have a degree; and 5.5% have no educational qualifications at all.[14] Those running micro businesses – businesses that form such a significant part of the British economy – are not especially likely to conform to the stereotypical image, commonly portrayed in scholarly legal textbooks, of tertiary educated "men in grey suits" wedded to ever-increasing profit margins and bonuses.

7.10 On the contrary, individuals owning and running small businesses are much more likely personally to identify themselves with (and to be personally identified with) the business itself. For example, when complaining to an Ombudsman about unfair treatment, small businesses often register their dispute as a personal complaint and not as a business dispute, because "they often see the issues as essentially personal rather than commercial".[15] The value of the business, when it is a small business, commonly lies not in the profit to be made but in the use-value that running it has for the people involved. As Professor Freedman has put it:

> The small business sector ... contains many firms that will never provide much economic growth. [But] this is not a matter for criticism, since these firms have a real value for their owners and users.[16]

7.11 In creating offences, whether of a regulatory or public interest nature, it is essential to have in mind the character and limitations of small businesses. This has, quite rightly, been a matter of concern at Governmental and European level for some time.[17] In the present context, we must consider both whether some of the current principles governing criminal liability work to the disadvantage of small firms and how best to create offences where the likely offenders will be small businesses. This is because when the business of an individual farmer, shop-keeper or other micro-business person is found guilty of a criminal offence, the stigma of conviction may well (depending on the nature of the offence) be just as high as when that individual is convicted in a personal capacity.

---

[14] See generally, the Small Business Service, *Small Firms Big Business: A review of small and medium sized enterprise in the UK* (2003) ch 3.

[15] *Ombudsman News*, Issue 74 (December 08/January 09) p 17.

[16] J Freedman, "Limited Liability: Large Company Theory and Small Firms" [2000] 63 *Modern Law Review* 317, 320 to 321.

[17] The British Government adopted a 'think small first' principle in the mid-1980s: see Department of Trade and Industry, *Burdens on Business* (1985). See also Small Business Service, *Think Small First* (2001). For a European initiative to reduce regulatory burdens, see Communication from the Commission to the Council and the European Parliament: "Better Regulation for Growth and Jobs in the European Union", COM(2005) 97 final, 16 March 2005.

The cost of remaining law-abiding: its impact on business

7.12   An important consideration to mention at the outset is the cost of implementing legislation to secure regulatory initiatives. The British Chamber of Commerce has estimated that the cost to UK businesses of implementing and conforming to new legislation has been some £55 billion since 1998.[18] The Department for Business, Enterprise and Regulatory Reform (now the Department for Business, Innovation and Skills) has estimated the annual cost of compliance at £20 billion. However, incurring these costs and coming to terms with the demands of many regulatory agencies has not necessarily impeded business in an unacceptable way, when considered in a global context. For example, in 2007 the World Bank placed the UK sixth out of 175 countries in terms of the ease with which business may be done.[19] Similarly, in the year 2006 to 2007, the World Economic Forum ranked the UK's public institutions tenth out of 125 countries in their Global Competitiveness Index.[20]

7.13   For some, the trends since 1997 can, as a whole, be explained by the relative success of the better regulation initiatives, such as the establishment in 2005 of a Better Regulation Executive, and the Better Regulation Action Plan[21] (and more recently, regulatory impact assessments[22]). These initiatives are mainly aimed at small businesses, which form the overwhelming majority of businesses in the UK.[23] The Better Regulation Executive has been aiming for a 25% reduction in administrative burdens by 2010, saving £3.3 billion.[24]

---

[18]   British Chamber of Commerce, Burdens Barometer 2007, www.chamberonline.co.uk/policy/pdf/burdens_barometer_2007.pdf (last visited 19 July 2010). The figure was calculated using Government sources of information.

[19]   World Bank, *Doing Business in 2007: How to Reform* (2006).

[20]   World Economic Forum, *Global Competitiveness Report 2006/7* (2006).

[21]   See http://webarchive.nationalarchives.gov.uk/+/http://www.hm-treasury.gov.uk/better_regulation_action_plan.htm (last visited 19 July 2010).

[22]   See www.cabinetoffice.gov.uk/making-legislation-guide/impact_assessment.aspx (last visited 19 July 2010).

[23]   See para 7.6 above.

[24]   HM Government, *Summary of Simplification Plans 2009* (December 2009) p 14: http://www.bis.gov.uk/files/file54013.pdf (last visited 19 July 2010).

7.14   One commentator has suggested that greater regulation, costly though it may be to implement, may actually generate "enabling and motivating tendencies that can bring about improvements in business performance as well as imposing constraints".[25] A simpler explanation may be that, whilst an increasing amount of regulation has imposed increasing costs on businesses, it has proved neither to be a deterrent to new business entrants to markets, nor to have prevented the benefits of doing business in the UK from outweighing the burdens. The relatively low cost of setting up a business in the UK may be a factor in this.[26]

7.15   We will not be taking a stand on these (controversial) issues, because our concern in this CP is not with whether, and to what extent, regulation and regulatory techniques have been successful or not, or how they could be made more successful, other than to the extent that these involve the criminal law. Even when policy initiatives do involve the use of the criminal law, it is impossible for a law reform body that has no specialist experience of what works in particular contexts, to say exactly when it would or would not be appropriate for Government to penalise certain kinds of conduct under certain conditions.

Businesses, Government departments and criminalisation

7.16   A substantial proportion of the large quantity of new criminal (and regulatory) legislation has been targeted at business activity of one kind or another, notably in the commerce and financial services sector.[27] For example, the Financial Services and Markets Act 2000 created a number of new offences connected with, amongst other things, the carrying on of unauthorised investment business, and market rigging.[28] Further, the Companies Act 2006 created some 20 new criminal offences broadly concerned with the way in which companies are established and run, to go with the 69 offences re-enacted from previous legislation (be it primary legislation or statutory instrument).[29]

7.17   Aside from these obvious examples, much modern criminal legislation is in practice likely to have a great deal of its primary impact on small business activity in particular, in a very diverse range of areas. Such legislation often tackles even the smallest of businesses in a very detailed way. For example, consider the following offence under section 11(3) of the Animal Welfare Act 2006:

Subject to subsections (4) to (6), a person commits an offence if—

---

[25]   J Kitching, 'Is Less More? Better Regulation and the Small Enterprise', in S Weatherill (ed) *Better Regulation* (2007), p 173. Certainly, there has been some effort to encourage businesses to see regulation and compliance in certain areas, such as environmental protection and ethical trading, as having the potential to improve efficiency and increase the chances of success: see the 'case studies' at www.businesslink.gov.uk.

[26]   Memorandum submitted to the Regulatory Reform Committee by T Ambler and F Chittenden: http://www.publications.parliament.uk/pa/cm200809/cmselect/cmdereg/329/9042802.htm (last visited 19 July 2010).

[27]   See, for example, the Companies Act 2006 (where, it should be noted, many of the offences were already offences under previous legislation).

[28]   For discussion, see A Pinto QC and M Evans, *Corporate Criminal Liability* (2nd ed 2008) ch 16.

[29]   This figure is taken from the schedule helpfully provided in *Archbold* (2010) para 30-113. A substantially similar number of offences can be found in the Insolvency Act 1986.

(a)   he enters into an arrangement with a person whom he has reasonable cause to believe to be under the age of 16 years, and

(b)   the arrangement is one under which that person has the chance to win an animal as a prize.

7.18   This offence is likely to have its greatest impact on, in effect, small family businesses or those operated by one individual alone making a living by providing entertainment at fairs. It is worth noting that, by virtue of section 32(4) of the Companies Act 2006, this summary offence is punishable by a fine up to level 4 on the standard scale or by imprisonment for up to 51 weeks. That is essentially the same maximum sentence as is available for someone convicted of the summary offence (also likely to have its impact mainly on small businesses) of manufacturing or selling a knuckleduster, stealth knife, or other similar illegal weapon.[30] We offered some criticisms of the use of such low-level criminalisation in Part 3 above.

How successful might an increasingly punitive approach to businesses be?

7.19   In this CP, we have indicated that we will not be considering expanding to any significant extent the scope of criminal liability, as it applies to companies, by, for example, making companies liable generally for failures on their part to prevent the commission of offences by their employees or agents. Indeed, a number of the issues we are addressing would to some extent restrict, rather than expand, the scope of liability in a business context.

7.20   Some might argue that this constitutes a missed opportunity. The argument is that precisely what is needed is greater scope in law, at the level of general principle, to find companies criminally liable for a host of harms or wrongs done that are linked to their business operations.[31] This argument may or may not have some validity but we believe that, when judged in context, there is a need to assess it with caution.

7.21   Professor Robert Baldwin,[32] an acknowledged expert on the effectiveness of regulation, has cast doubt on whether what he calls the strategy of "new punitive regulation" will in fact lead to improved individual and collective behaviour, in a corporate context.[33] His doubts are based on research conducted into firms' attitudes towards punitive risk, and their beliefs about how their company would, or could, respond to such risks.[34]

[30]   Criminal Justice Act 1988, s 141(1).

[31]   See, for example, J Gobert and M Punch, *Rethinking Corporate Crime* (2003) ch 4.

[32]   Department of Law, London School of Economics.

[33]   R Baldwin, "The New Punitive Regulation" (2004) 67(3) *Modern Law Review* 351.

[34]   The research was targeted at board members or at those with close knowledge of board workings.

7.22 On the surface, Professor Baldwin's figures suggest that a punitive approach is likely to pay dividends.[35] Well over 90% of respondents thought that firms' exposure to liability, and the personal exposure of directors to liability, had increased in recent years and was likely to continue to increase. Some 94% of respondents also said that effective management of punitive risks was very important. Further, over 70% of respondents said that direct experience of the imposition of sanctions had had a big impact on their management of punitive risk.

7.23 However, of those who had learned of *others'* experience of sanctions, only 57% said they thought this had had a major impact on their management of the relevant risks. Similarly, although the respondents were either on boards, or had close knowledge of their workings, only 44% claimed that their boards were very aware of company activity that might have punitive consequences (and only 40% claimed that regulatory risk was a board issue).

7.24 Awareness of punitive risk also varied very considerably, depending on the issue at stake. Whereas 60% of respondents said their boards were very aware of the regulatory risk surrounding health and safety issues, this fell to 30% for data protection, bribery and corruption. Over a third of the respondents agreed, or tended to agree, that punitive risks were not discussed in detail at board level, and were seen as operational matters for employees lower down in the organisation. Moreover, Professor Baldwin's research focused on FTSE 250 companies. It is generally acknowledged that smaller companies (the majority) are likely to be even less well-informed and less organised and persistent in their response to punitive risk.[36]

7.25 More broadly, Professor Baldwin's research revealed that there were few staff incentives to engage in risk management, even in firms that were risk-averse. This is perhaps not all that surprising. As Professor Baldwin concludes on this issue, "if [market] analysts and share prices do not advert to quality in risk management, corporate incentives are unlikely to encourage good risk management".[37] Some 76% of respondents thought that there was room for improvement in the implementation of written punitive risk management policies.[38]

7.26 So far as the prospect of individual criminal liability is concerned, this featured surprisingly low on respondents' lists of priority concerns. Whereas 90% put corporate reputation in amongst the four main drivers of activity directed at managing risk, only 36% put fear of personal criminal liability in that group of four, with only 8% including fear for their personal reputation.[39] On this issue, Professor Baldwin concludes that:

---

[35] R Baldwin, "The New Punitive Regulation" (2004) 67(3) *Modern Law Review* 351, 360 to 370.

[36] N Gunningham and R Johnstone, *Regulating Workplace Safety* (1999) pp 3 to 5 and 9 to 94.

[37] R Baldwin, "The New Punitive Regulation" (2004) 67(3) *Modern Law Review* 351, 365.

[38] Above, 366.

[39] Above, 368.

It may not be wise to endorse too wholeheartedly those regulatory approaches that presuppose either that rational deterrence mechanisms operate or that clear distinctions are made between individual and corporate drivers of behaviour.[40]

7.27 In other words, taking an increasingly punitive approach – either to companies or to individuals acting in a corporate capacity – may not have the immediate benefits that those promoting, and those paying for, such an approach would expect to see. Professor Baldwin also identifies other negative factors associated with an increasingly punitive approach. These include too risk-averse a reaction by companies to such an approach (to which some attribute, for example, the growth of an overzealous health and safety culture in the workplace), a worsening relationship with regulators, and an increasing reluctance in part of outsiders to sit as non-executive directors. Professor Baldwin concludes that the dangers of an increasingly punitive approach are:

First, that the punitive stance is too closely aligned to notions of rational deterrence so that it takes the eye off the need to "speak softly" and develop ways to make best use of corporate self-regulatory capacities; second, that directors will be daunted by potential liabilities and will become excessively risk averse; third, that non-executive directors will be increasingly reluctant to sit on boards; fourth, that regulatory tasks will become more difficult as companies increasingly outsource threatening risks and as responsibilities for regulated activities grow more diffused; and fifth, that, on some contexts, compliance will be impeded because relations between companies and regulators will become more distant, more confrontational and less conducive to co-operative methods of reconciling corporate and regulatory objectives.[41]

7.28 There is an additional factor weighing against too aggressive an approach by prosecutors to the imposition of greater liability on individuals at fault for wrongdoing in a corporate context.

7.29 A situation could easily develop in which, to protect their market reputations, companies decide on which individual, within the company, is to take responsibility for the wrongdoing. To that end, the company provides prosecutors with incriminating evidence against the individual in question, making prosecution of that individual much more straightforward than prosecution of the company. In such a situation the successful prosecution of the individual may satisfy the company, the prosecutors and the public (who see a particular person named and shamed). However, it may be that this result is not, in fact, in the public interest, which was – at the very least – in the improvement of the company's procedures for preventing the occurrence of wrongdoing.[42]

---

[40] Above, 370.

[41] R Baldwin, "The New Punitive Regulation" (2004) 67(3) *Modern Law Review* 351, 383.

[42] Of course, prosecutors could counter this, in theory, by developing a practice in such cases of continuing proceedings against the company as well as the individual, unless the company agrees to improve its procedures in a particular way.

THE DOCTRINE OF CONSENT AND CONNIVANCE

Complicity in corporate offending

7.30 At common law, it is possible for individual directors to be complicit in offences committed by their company, if they aid, abet, counsel or procure those offences. In accordance with the normal principles of complicity law, in such instances the individual directors are guilty of the offence itself along with their company. So, if a company commits fraud, with the intentional encouragement or assistance of individual directors, those directors may be (individually) guilty of fraud together with the company.

Consenting to or conniving at corporate offending

7.31 However, statutes creating offences commonly provide for a slightly wider basis on which directors can be found individually liable for offences committed by their company. Such statutes provide that directors can be individually liable if they 'consent or connive' at the commission of the offence by the company. We have explored what may be quite subtle differences between consent and connivance and complicity (though aiding, abetting, counselling or procuring) elsewhere.[43] In essence, consent and connivance provisions ensure that individual directors who are fully aware of, and approve of (or, for example, sign papers consenting to) criminal wrongdoing can themselves be convicted of the crime, even though their approval or consent does not as such encourage or assist the commission of the crime committed, assisted or instigated by other directors or equivalent persons.[44]

7.32 An example can be found in section 18(1) of the Theft Act 1968, which provides:

> Where an offence committed by a body corporate under section 17 of this Act is proved to have been committed with the consent or connivance of any director, manager, secretary or other similar officer of the body corporate … he as well as the body corporate shall be guilty of that offence, and shall be liable to be proceeded against and punished accordingly.

7.33 Similar provisions appear in, for example, section 28 of the Public Order Act 1986, section 12 of the Fraud Act 2006, section 18 of the Terrorism Act 2006, and section 18 of the Safeguarding Vulnerable Groups Act 2006.

---

[43] Reforming Bribery (2007) Law Commission Consultation Paper No 185, at para 9.35.

[44] Although the position is complicated by the fact that there can at common law be duties to intervene to prevent offending, in circumstances where non-intervention will result in a finding that the party who failed to intervene was complicity in the offence: *Tuck v Robson* [1970] 1 WLR 741.

7.34 Very few people would suggest that there can be true consent and connivance without at least a subjective awareness that wrongdoing is or will be taking place. Indeed, it might be argued that even such awareness may not, in and of itself, be sufficient to amount to either consent or to connivance.[45] A requirement for proof of at least such awareness is in keeping with an understanding of the doctrine of consent and connivance as an extension of the complicity doctrine, to fit the reality of corporate decision-making. Moreover, where crimes requiring proof of fault or involving stigma are in issue,[46] a requirement of at least subjective awareness on a director's part would appear to be essential, in point of justice, given that a finding of consent and connivance makes a director (or equivalent person) guilty of the offence itself.

Beyond consent and connivance: corporate offending attributable to directors' neglect

7.35 Unfortunately, the law has paid scant attention to the question of fairness in this context, in the shape of a need to prove subjective fault. The orthodox consent and connivance clause,[47] such as that in section 18(1) of the Theft Act 1968,[48] is frequently extended in some statutes to include instances in which the commission of the offence 'was attributable to any *neglect* on the part of any director [or equivalent person]'. An example can be found in section 18(1) of the Safeguarding Vulnerable Groups Act 2006:

> If an offence under section 9, 10, 11, 23, 27, or 38 or Schedule 6 is committed by a body corporate and is proved to have been committed with the consent or connivance of, *or to be attributable to neglect on the part of—*
>
> (a) a director, manager, secretary or other similar officer of the body, or
>
> (b) a person purporting to act in such a capacity,
>
> he (as well as the body) commits the offence.[49]

7.36 Although we have referred to provisions such as those in section 18(1) of the Theft Act 1968 as the orthodox ones, provisions including a neglect basis for pinning individual liability on directors for offences committed by their companies, may be found in many other offences. For example, they can be found in section 110 of the Agriculture Act 1970, section 9 of the Knives Act 1997, section 400(1) of the Financial Services and Markets Act 2000, and section 20 of the Gangmasters (Licensing) Act 2004.

---

[45] The matter has not been judicially determined.

[46] A crime can involve stigma, on conviction, even if it is an offence of strict liability: see the general discussion in AP Simester, 'Is Strict Liability Always Wrong?', in AP Simester (ed), *Appraising Strict Liability* (2005) pp 21, 31 to 37. An example discussed shortly is the offence of taking indecent photographs of children, contrary to s 45 of the Sexual Offences Act 2003.

[47] By "orthodox" we therefore mean consistent with a slight expansion of the common law doctrine of complicity, and not most common, or longest established.

[48] See para 7.32 above.

7.37   The neglect basis for individual liability is in one way narrower than orthodox consent and connivance. It involves establishing a causal link between the individual director's neglect and the company's commission of the crime, whereas no such link need be established in the orthodox case of consent and connivance. It nonetheless involves a morally significant extension of liability. Yet, we have been unable to discern any rationale behind the imposition of this extended form of liability in some statutes and the imposition of the orthodox form in others.

7.38   In that regard, it is interesting to compare the orthodox (subjective) approach to consent and connivance of section 12(1) the Fraud Act 2006,[50] with the broader (more generously tailored, objective) provision in section 400(1) of the Financial Services and Markets Act 2000 ("the 2000 Act"), that employs the neglect basis for liability. Section 400(1) of the 2000 Act is quite general in its application: it applies to, "an offence committed under this Act committed by a body corporate". Yet the offences under the 2000 Act vary considerably.

7.39   Section 19 of the 2000 Act creates a strict liability offence of carrying on a regulated activity without authorisation. In such a case, neglect, on the part of a director of a company, to which the commission of the offence is attributable, might not seem an inappropriate basis on which to convict the director.

7.40   By way of contrast, section 397(1) of the 2000 Act creates an offence of market rigging, where a high degree of fault is required, in the form of knowledge, dishonesty or recklessness. It is not so easy to see why this offence, which can only be committed by a company upon proof of a subjective fault element, can be committed by a director who has only been guilty of neglect, albeit that the commission of the offence must be attributable to that neglect.

The neglect basis for directorial liability and stigmatic crimes

7.41   The extended, neglect-based form of liability has been employed even when the crimes in question involve not only proof of fault but also social stigma upon conviction.

7.42   Consider the offence of taking indecent photographs of children, contrary to section 1 of the Protection of Children Act 1978. Suppose that a photographic company were to commit this offence. By virtue of section 3 of the Act, the company directors would also be individually liable for the section 1 offence if the commission of the offence was attributable to their neglect.

---

[49]   Emphasis added.

[50]   See para 7.33 above.

7.43   The offence of taking indecent photographs of children is one that carries very considerable stigma. It is an offence which, following conviction, has applied to it the notification requirements of the Sexual Offences Act 2003 in certain circumstances.[51] It must be highly questionable whether an individual should have on his or her record a conviction for taking indecent photographs of children, and potentially be subject to stigmatising notification requirements, when (a) he or she personally did no such thing, and (b) he or she was wholly unaware that his or her company did any such thing. In our view, section 3 of the Protection of Children Act 1978 involves the use of a measure that is both unjustifiable and disproportionate in the circumstances.[52]

7.44   An important contrast can be drawn here with the approach of the Public Order Act 1986 to offences involving stigma. For example, there can be little or no doubt that a conviction for an offence contrary to section 21(1) of the Public Order Act 1986 carries with it very considerable stigma. This is the offence committed when:

> A person who distributes, or shows, or plays, a recording of visual images or sounds which are threatening, abusing or insulting … if—
>
> (a)   he intends thereby to stir up racial hatred, or
>
> (b)   having regard to all the circumstances racial hatred is likely to be stirred up thereby.

7.45   If, for example, a television company that broadcast a controversial programme was found guilty of this offence, by virtue of section 28(1) of the 1986 Act the individual directors could also be found individually liable for committing the offence. However, this could occur only if the company's offence was committed with the consent or connivance of the individual director or directors. That the offence was attributable merely to neglect on the part of the directors would be insufficient. Confining the scope of individual liability of directors in this way, with an offence involving considerable stigma following conviction, arguably makes the legislative response both justifiable and proportionate.

Conclusion

7.46   In our view, when the individual liability of one person depends on the commission of an offence by another person, the individual liability of the first person should not arise unless (at the very least) awareness or assent to wrongdoing engaged in by the other person is proven. This approach is consistent with the Law Commission's recommendations for the law governing complicity and assisting and encouraging crime.[53]

---

[51]   Sexual Offences Act 2003, s 80 and Sch 3.

[52]   The same analysis and conclusion applies to the use of the neglect basis for directorial liability under the Safeguarding Vulnerable Groups Act 2006.

[53]   Inchoate Liability for Assisting and Encouraging Crime (2006) Law Com No 300; Participating in Crime (2007) Law Com No 305.

7.47   It follows that it should not be possible to establish individual directorial liability (or the liability of equivalent persons) for an offence committed by the company, unless there was true, subjective consent or connivance at the offence by the director(s) in question. Such an approach is particularly apposite where crimes requiring fault elements, or crimes involving stigma, are in issue.

7.48   The real harshness of the extended doctrine comes, of course, from the fact that, on the basis of simple neglect, an individual director may be convicted of the offence itself. It follows that some – if not all – of the force of the objection to criminal liability of this kind could be lost, if, in cases where the company's commission of the offence was due to the neglect of an individual director (or equivalent officer), that director was liable for a *separate* offence of, say, negligently failing to prevent the commission of the offence by the company.

7.49   One benefit of having such a separate offence is associated with fairer labelling. To say that a director (or equivalent officer) negligently failed to prevent the commission of an offence for which the company had been convicted more accurately represents the wrong done by the director than conviction for that self same offence. Another benefit of having such an offence in relation, for example, to the offence of taking indecent photographs of children, is that a director convicted of it would not automatically be eligible to have applied to him or her the notification requirements of the Sexual Offences Act 2003.[54] In other words, adverse consequences attached to conviction for certain types of crime such as sexual crimes, would not inevitably follow from conviction for a 'failure to prevent' offence relating to that type of crime.

7.50   The idea that it should be an offence for a company, or for the individual directors of a company, to fail to prevent an offence has proved to be an attractive one to both scholars and legislators.[55] Our understanding is that such an offence would do limited work in this context. It would operate only as a negligence-based substitute for the consent and connivance doctrine. Accordingly, it would have no application unless the company or partnership in question was convicted of the substantive offence in question.

7.51   Accordingly, we provisionally propose that:

> **Proposal 16: When it is appropriate to provide that individual directors (or equivalent officers) can themselves be liable for an offence committed by their company, on the basis that they consented or connived at the company's commission of that offence, the provision in question should not be extended to include instances in which the company's offence is attributable to neglect on the part of an individual director or equivalent person.**

7.52   We also ask:

---

[54]   See paras 7.42 to 7.43 above.

[55]   See, for example, Ministry of Justice, *Bribery: Government Response to the Conclusions and Recommendations of the Joint Committee Report on the Draft Bribery Bill* (November 2009) Cm 7748.

Question 3: When a company is proved to have committed an offence, might it be appropriate in some circumstances to provide that an individual director (or equivalent officer) can be liable for the separate offence of 'negligently failing to prevent' that offence?

THE DOCTRINE OF DELEGATION

7.53 The delegation principle comes into effect when an office-holder (such as a licence-holder) is under a duty, and delegates the performance of that duty to another person, and that other person commits the offence. In such circumstances, the office-holder can be found individually liable for the offence committed by the person to whom he or she delegated the operation of the business. Strictly speaking the principle is not one of corporate liability, but in practice it has its greatest impact on family-run businesses or those operated by one individual alone.

7.54 An example is provided by *Allen v Whitehead*.[56] A café owner employed a manager to run the business and specifically instructed the manager not to permit prostitutes to gather on the premises. The manager ignored the instruction. In consequence, the café owner was found guilty under section 44 of the Metropolitan Police Act 1839, in virtue of which it was an offence, to "knowingly permit or suffer prostitutes or persons of notoriously bad character to meet together and remain" in a place where refreshments are sold and consumed.

7.55 It is obvious that very considerable moral stigma attaches to conviction for such an offence. It does not seem right that the café owner stood to be convicted of knowingly permitting the prohibited activities simply because he delegated the operation of the business to another person. The argument against this form of liability is thus very much like the argument against the neglect-based extension to the doctrine of consent and connivance.

7.56 An important further consideration is that, in practice, larger organisations with an employment structure will much more rarely be caught by the delegation principle than smaller ones with no such structure. This is because an employee – even when he or she has managerial responsibilities – will not be, in Lord Morris's words, "a delegate to whom the company passed on its responsibilities".[57]

7.57 Naturally, we agree with the policy underlying the delegation principle, that someone should not be able to evade their duties as a licence-holder by the simple expedient of appointing someone else whose responsibility it then becomes to perform them. However, that policy would be adequately served by a specific offence of failing to prevent someone to whom a duty has been delegated committing the relevant offence. Such an offence would not carry the same stigma, for the office-holder, as conviction *for the offence itself* and would more fairly reflect the true role of the office-holder in the commission of the offence.

---

[56] [1930] 1 KB 211.

[57] *Tesco Supermarkets Ltd v Nattrass* [1972] AC 153, 180.

7.58   Clearly, there is a close analogy here with what we are proposing with respect to the consent and connivance doctrine. We ask:

Question 4: Should the doctrine of delegation be abolished, and replaced by an offence of failing to prevent an offence being committed by someone to whom the running of the business had been delegated?

PART 8
SUMMARY OF THE PROPOSALS AND QUESTIONS

GENERAL PRINCIPLES: THE LIMITS OF CRIMINALISATION

8.1 PROPOSAL 1: The criminal law should only be employed to deal with wrongdoers who deserve the stigma associated with criminal conviction because they have engaged in seriously reprehensible conduct. It should not be used as the primary means of promoting regulatory objectives.

8.2 PROPOSAL 2: Harm done or risked should be regarded as serious enough to warrant criminalisation only if,

> (a) in some circumstances (not just extreme circumstances), an individual could justifiably be sent to prison for a first offence, or

> (b) an unlimited fine is necessary to address the seriousness of the wrongdoing in issue, and its consequences.[1]

8.3 PROPOSAL 3: Low-level criminal offences should be repealed in any instance where the introduction of a civil penalty (or equivalent measure) is likely to do as much to secure appropriate levels of punishment and deterrence.

GENERAL PRINCIPLES: AVOIDING POINTLESS OVERLAPS BETWEEN OFFENCES

8.4 PROPOSAL 4: The criminal law should not be used to deal with inchoate offending when it is covered by the existing law governing conspiracy, attempt, and assisting or encouraging crime.

8.5 PROPOSAL 5: The criminal law should not be used to deal with fraud when the conduct in question is covered by the Fraud Act 2006.

GENERAL PRINCIPLES: STRUCTURE AND PROCESS

8.6 PROPOSAL 6: Criminal offences should, along with the civil measures that accompany them, form a hierarchy of seriousness.

8.7 PROPOSAL 7: More use should be made of process fairness to increase confidence in the criminal justice system. Duties on regulators formally to warn potential offenders that they are subject to liability should be supplemented by granting the courts power to stay proceedings until non-criminal regulatory steps have been taken first, in appropriate cases.

8.8 PROPOSAL 8: Criminal offences should be created and (other than in relation to minor details) amended only through primary legislation.

---

[1] Putting aside factors such as whether the individual has previous convictions for other offences, and so on.

8.9 PROPOSAL 9: A regulatory scheme that makes provision for the imposition of any civil penalty, or equivalent measure, must also provide for unfettered recourse to the courts to challenge the imposition of that measure, by way of re-hearing or appeal on a point of law.

GENERAL PRINCIPLES: FAULT IN OFFENCES SUPPORTING A REGULATORY STRUCTURE

8.10 PROPOSAL 10: Fault elements in criminal offences that are concerned with unjustified risk-taking should be proportionate. This means that the more remote the conduct criminalised from harm done, and the less grave that harm, the more compelling the case for higher-level fault requirements such as dishonesty, intention, knowledge or recklessness.

8.11 PROPOSAL 11: In relation to wrongdoing bearing on the simple provision of (or failure to provide) information, individuals should not be subject to criminal proceedings – even if they may still face civil penalties – unless their wrongdoing was knowing or reckless.

8.12 PROPOSAL 12: The Ministry of Justice, in collaboration with other departments and agencies, should seek to ensure not only that proportionate fault elements are an essential part of criminal offences created to support regulatory aims, but also that there is consistency and clarity in the use of such elements when the offence in question is to be used by departments and agencies for a similar purpose.

DOCTRINES OF CRIMINAL LIABILITY APPLICABLE TO BUSINESSES

The doctrine of identification

8.13 PROPOSAL 13: Legislation should include specific provisions in criminal offences to indicate the basis on which companies may be found liable, but in the absence of such provisions, the courts should treat the question of how corporate criminal liability may be established as a matter of statutory interpretation. We encourage the courts not to presume that the identification doctrine applies when interpreting the scope of criminal offences applicable to companies.

A general defence of due diligence

8.14 PROPOSAL 14: The courts should be given a power to apply a due diligence defence to any statutory offence that does not require proof that the defendant was at fault in engaging in the wrongful conduct. The burden of proof should be on the defendant to establish the defence.

8.15 PROPOSAL 15: If proposal 14 is accepted, the defence of due diligence should take the form of showing that due diligence was exercised in all the circumstances to avoid the commission of the offence.

8.16 However, we recognise that consultees may prefer this defence to have the same wording and to impose the same standards as the most commonly encountered form of the defence. Accordingly, we ask the following questions:

8.17 QUESTION 1: Were it to be introduced, should the due diligence defence take the stricter form already found in some statutes, namely, did the defendant take all reasonable precautions and exercise all due diligence to avoid commission of the offence?

8.18 QUESTION 2: If the power to apply a due diligence defence is introduced, should Parliament prevent or restrict its application to certain statutes, and if so which statutes?

The consent and connivance doctrine

8.19 PROPOSAL 16: When it is appropriate to provide that individual directors (or equivalent officers) can themselves be liable for an offence committed by their company, on the basis that they consented or connived at the company's commission of that offence, the provision in question should not be extended to include instances in which the company's offence is attributable to neglect on the part of an individual director or equivalent person.

8.20 QUESTION 3: When a company is proved to have committed an offence, might it be appropriate in some circumstances to provide that an individual director (or equivalent officer) can be liable for the separate offence of 'negligently failing to prevent' that offence?

The delegation doctrine

8.21 QUESTION 4: Should the doctrine of delegation be abolished, and replaced by an offence of failing to prevent an offence being committed by someone to whom the running of the business had been delegated?

APPENDIX A
A REVIEW OF ENFORCEMENT TECHNIQUES - PROFESSOR JULIA BLACK[1]

Introduction

A.1 This report reviews the range of enforcement techniques and sanctions available to governmental regulators, focusing principally on the UK. It does not purport to be a comprehensive review of all the enforcement powers of each of the different regulators. Instead, the report provides examples of the different types of enforcement 'tools' that are available, and includes a brief summary of the changes introduced by the Regulatory Enforcement and Sanctions Act 2008 (RESA).

A.2 The report deliberately separates the discussion of the type of sanction that can be used from the legal status that the sanction has, and which body is responsible for imposing it: a court or a regulator. It is important to note that with only a few exceptions, most types of sanction can be imposed by criminal, civil and / or administrative means.

A.3 The first part of the report discusses some of the implications of the policy choice as to whether a sanction should be criminal, imposed by the civil courts, or imposed by the regulator or an administrative body.

A.4 The second part of the report discusses some of the principal enforcement tools which can be or are currently being used in regulatory regimes in the UK and overseas. These can be arranged under seven headings:

    (1)   Investigative tools.

    (2)   Pre-enforcement/warning tools, eg notices.

    (3)   Monetary/financial tools.

    (4)   Tools relating to the terms on which business continues.

    (5)   Restorative tools.

    (6)   Performance disclosing tools.

    (7)   Undertakings and compliance management tools.

A.5 In addition, the report looks briefly at defences.

---

[1] London School of Economics and Political Science, March 2009.

A.6   It is important to stress that inducing compliance is not a matter that can or should be left to the enforcement regime alone. Sanctions are important, but as important is the overall design of the regulatory regime (the regulatory strategy as opposed to the enforcement strategy); the combinations of tools that can be used; and how different regulatory regimes interact. Considering choices of regulatory strategy in this broader sense is necessary, but is beyond the brief of this paper.

General context

A.7   The range of sanctions available to regulators has recently been enhanced, following the recommendations of the Macrory Review of Penalties.[2] The Review found that there was an over-reliance by regulators on criminal sanctions, and that the nature of the sanctioning powers available to them was highly variable. It recommended the introduction of a wider set of powers, extending beyond the traditional reliance on the criminal law, and proposed six Penalties Principles, and a further seven characteristics that should be met by any regulator's enforcement regime.

Macrory Review's Six Penalties Principles

A sanction should:
1. Aim to change the behaviour of the offender;
2. Aim to eliminate any financial gain or benefit from non-compliance;
3. Be responsive and consider what is appropriate for the particular offender and regulatory
issue, which can include punishment and the public stigma that should be associated with
a criminal conviction;
4. Be proportionate to the nature of the offence and the harm caused;
5. Aim to restore the harm caused by regulatory non-compliance, where appropriate; and
6. Aim to deter future non-compliance

Seven characteristics

Regulators should:
1. Publish an enforcement policy;
2. Measure outcomes not just outputs;
3. Justify their choice of enforcement actions year on year to stakeholders, Ministers and
Parliament;
4. Follow-up enforcement actions where appropriate;
5. Enforce in a transparent manner;
6. Be transparent in the way in which they apply and determine administrative penalties; and
7. Avoid perverse incentives that might influence the choice of sanctioning response.

---

[2]   R Macrory, *Regulatory Justice: Making Sanctions Effective* (Better Regulation Executive) (Final Report, November 2006).

A.8 The Macrory Review also made nine specific recommendations, which were accepted by the Government in full. The recommendations were:

(1) That the Government review the drafting and formulation of any criminal offences relating to regulatory non-compliance.

(2) The design of sanctions to be in line with the penalty principles and characteristics outlined in the review.

(3) Giving criminal courts new powers to punish regulatory offences, including new financial penalties as an intermediate sanction.

(4) Improving the system of statutory notices.

(5) Introducing enforceable undertakings and 'undertakings plus' as a sanction for all regulators.

(6) Considering pilot schemes to gain restorative justice for regulatory non-compliance.

(7) Making alternative sentencing options in criminal courts.

(8) Introducing new measures to improve transparency and accountability, including a working group of regulators to share best practice and publishing enforcement activities on a regular basis.

A.9 The Regulatory Enforcement and Sanctions Act 2008 (RESA) adopted some of these recommendations by introducing a new, wider range of sanctions for regulators, notably:

Fixed monetary penalties.

Stop notices.

Enforcement undertakings.

Discretionary requirements including:

Variable monetary penalties

Compliance notices

Restoration notices

Variable monetary penalties with voluntary undertakings

These are discussed further in Section 3 below.

Criminal, Civil or Administrative Processes

A.10   Regulatory sanctions can be imposed by one or more of three different processes: criminal, civil or administrative. These different processes may involve different bodies in triggering actions or imposing sanctions and each set of procedures has its own strengths and weaknesses. The lines between the different types of sanctions have also become slightly blurred by the RESA. Under the Act, a regulator has to believe 'beyond reasonable doubt' that an offence has been committed in order to impose a fixed monetary penalty or a discretionary remedy, whereas the grounds for the issuing of a stop notice or enforcement undertaking are for a 'reasonable belief' and 'reasonable suspicion' respectively.

Criminal Processes

A.11   The standard design of regulatory regimes in the UK prior to RESA was for there to be legally defined requirements with criminal sanctions imposed for their breach. This combination of legal rules and criminal offence is often described as 'command and control' regulation.

A.12   However, while criminal law is used extensively in the design of regulatory systems in the UK, and many agencies have prosecutorial powers,[3] in practice criminal law plays a peripheral and indirect role in the implementation of regulation.[4] This is partly because criminal law is in practice difficult to apply to corporations. As has been famously observed, corporations have 'no soul to damn; no body to kick'.[5] It is also because taking criminal proceedings is extremely resource intensive for a regulator, and can result in only trivial sanctions being imposed.

A.13   For example, prosecution powers, though extensively granted to regulators, are relatively little used. Regulators in the UK do not routinely prosecute firms for breaches of regulatory requirements. Only 25% of local authorities prosecute under the fly tipping legislation (s.33 Environmental Protection Act 1990), for example, due to the difficulties of obtaining a successful outcome.[6]

A.14   Prosecution, though rare, does often result in criminal sanctions being imposed. Regulators select their cases for prosecution with care, and it pays off. Prosecutions for regulatory offences have a high conviction rate, often over 90% for the Environment Agency, the Forestry Commission and the Health and Safety Executive, for example.

---

[3]   See R Baldwin, 'The New Punitive Regulation' (2005) *Modern Law Review* 351.

[4]   See generally, K Hawkins, *Law as Last Resort* (2002).

[5]   JC Coffee, 'No Soul to Damn; No Body to Kick: An Unscandalised Inquiry into the Problem of Corporate Punishment' (1981) 79 *Michigan Law Review* 386.

[6]   Defra, *Fly-Tipping Strategy: A Consultation Document* (London, February 2004).

A.15 The victory is very often hollow, however. For although successful prosecutions can be secured, the average fines imposed for regulatory offences is very low. The Hampton Report found that the average fine imposed by magistrates' courts in 2003-4 for environmental offences was £6,680, and for health and safety offences it was £4,036. The figures were higher in the crown courts (£35,594 and £ 33,036 respectively), but still low. These figures were not out of line with previous years).[7] This contrasts with the £14m fine imposed on Shell by the Financial Services Authority in the same period.

A.16 Such low criminal fines are despite the large profits which can be gained from non-compliance by firms, and the damage that non-compliance can impose.[8] For example, a person who was paid £60,000 to dump toxic waste and which cost the local authority £167,000 to clean up, was fined only £30,000. A waste disposal company which had illegally dumped waste for two years, saving £250,000, was fined only £25,000. A company which illegally dumped several thousand tonnes of waste over a ten year period was fined only £830. As the Hampton Report noted, fines at this low level are no deterrent; in fact the firm makes a profit through not complying with the law.[9]

A.17 Fine levels can also vary significantly across regions, and tend to be lowest in those areas which have the greatest number of cases. Most courts, particularly magistrates' courts, have very little exposure to environmental cases. There is little central collection of sentencing data on environmental cases by the court services, suggesting that when courts do not have the data to enable them to be aware of their own previous sentencing practices or those of other courts. Research has also found there was little awareness of relevant sentencing guidance, including the toolkit, 'Costing the Earth' launched by the Magistrates' Association in 2002.[10]

A.18 Most regulatory offences also carry a prison sentence, but again these sanctions are rarely applied. There were only five jail sentences for breach of health and safety regulations between 1975-2004, for example, although there were six imprisonments for breaches of environmental law in 2004.[11]

A.19 A further issue in regulatory policy is whether criminal liabilities should target individual corporate directors or senior managers/responsible staff in addition to the corporation itself. A number of regulators have expressed faith in the deterrent effects of personal liability but sceptics have cautioned that these deterrent effects can be exaggerated.[12]

---

[7] P Hampton, *Reducing Administrative Burdens: Effective Inspection and Enforcement, Final Report* (London, 2005), para 2.78.

[8] See eg NAO, *Environment Agency: Protecting the Public from Waste*, Report by the Comptroller and Auditor General, HC 156 Session 2002-2003 (London, December 2002); Hampton Report, para 1.55.

[9] Hampton Report, paras 2.80-2.81.

[10] By Dupont and Zakkour (Trends in Environmental Sentencing)

[11] See Hampton Interim Report, p.20.

[12] See eg R. Baldwin above note 2 (2005); B Fisse and J Braithwaite, *Corporations, Crime and Accountability* (1993).

Advantages of criminal sanctions

A.20 There has traditionally been a strong policy makers' adherence to using criminal law as the principal means by which regulatory requirements can be enforced. The main advantages are often seen to be twofold:

(1) Moral disapprobation – criminalising the activity is often said to send a strong signal that the conduct is not to be tolerated.

(2) Deterrence – criminalising the activity may enhance the deterrent effect on firms or individuals who do not want a criminal conviction. However, the low levels of fines imposed are likely to reduce the deterrence effect in practice.

Disadvantages

A.21 Extensive experience and research has revealed the limitations of using criminal law as the main or only tool of enforcement. The main disadvantages include the following:

(1) Criminal prosecution per se, regardless of the sanction imposed, can be seen by both the regulatory and regulated firm as disproportionate to the regulatory breach, discouraging its use.

(2) Most regulatory offences are regarded in criminal law as 'mala prohibita' (acts which are simply prohibited) rather than 'mala in se' (acts which are wrong in themselves). This can undermine the signals of moral condemnation which the use of criminal law is meant to convey.

(3) Strict liability offences can seem inappropriate to regulators and courts as they impose unwarranted criminal liability, i.e. liability where there is no moral blame, leading to low levels of prosecution and low penalties.

(4) Deterrent effects maybe low due to ignorance of liabilities; the motivation of managers by factors other than potential liability (such as profit making); and risk shifting strategies.

(5) Paradoxically, the prospect of criminal sanction may over-deter the conscientious from what is otherwise socially useful conduct.

(6) Criminal law is focused on the individual and as a result is not always easy to apply to corporations, particularly for offences which result in death, though this situation has now changed with the introduction of the Corporate Manslaughter and Corporate Homicide Act 2007.

(7) Prosecutions are highly resource intensive for the regulator.[13]

(8) Procedural requirements of criminal law discourage prosecutions.

(9) Prosecutions involve the risk to the regulator that it will not succeed in court.

---

[13] See Hawkins, *Law as Last Resort.*

(10)   Criminalising all regulatory offences leads to under-enforcement of certain types of offences. Prosecutions tend to be brought only for offences which are clearly defined in law, and which have led to a visible result – death, injury, pollution, rather than which are designed to be preventative. This skews the enforcement activity away from more complex case and lead to partial enforcement (e.g. breaches of clearly defined offences relating to safety are prosecuted more often than those relating to health).[14]

(11)   Even if conviction is obtained, the low fines imposed by courts seriously undermine the effectiveness of prosecution as an enforcement tool in a number of ways. They undermine the utility of prosecution as a deterrent, they trivialise the offence and remove any sense of moral approbation, low fines are disproportionate to the costs of the harm caused, to the financial profits the offender can make by breaching the requirements, to the costs to the regulator of bringing the prosecution.

When to use criminal sanctions

A.22   There is no doubt that criminal law can have a valuable role to play in a regulatory regime. However, current research demonstrates that it is not optimal to rely on criminal conviction as being the principal, or indeed only, route for the enforcement of regulatory provisions. This finding was echoed in the Macrory Review.[15]

A.23   To be effective, at a minimum the following conditions need to exist:

(1)   Criminal sanctions need to be used within a wider set of effective enforcement tools.

(2)   Regulators have to be prepared to use criminal sanctions in order to give credibility to their overall enforcement strategy.

(3)   The criminal sanctions imposed have to be sufficiently severe to act as a real deterrent to unscrupulous operators.

(4)   Regulated parties have to be aware of their potential liabilities and be responsive to them.

Civil Liability Regimes

A.24   Civil liability regimes often co-exist with regulatory regimes, although in some cases the availability of a private civil remedy may be limited by the primary legislation establishing the regime.[16]

---

[14]   See Hawkins, *Law as Last Resort*.

[15]   R Macrory, *Regulatory Justice: Making Sanctions Effective* (Better Regulation Executive) (Final Report, November 2006); R. Macrory, *Regulatory Justice: Sanctioning in a post-Hampton World* (2006).

[16]   For example under the Financial Services and Markets Act 2000, the Financial Services Authority is given the power to nominate those provisions with respect to which civil actions can be brought. Section 50 of the Act further stipulates that the rights of action are to be restricted to private investors.

Public civil law

A.25   It is helpful to distinguish between public civil actions and private civil actions. Public civil actions are those brought to civil law courts by public bodies.[17] Civil actions can be brought by regulatory bodies if they are given the relevant powers in primary legislation.

A.26   The US Environmental Protection Agency has extensive powers to bring civil actions for the breach of environmental legislation and regulations. In Australia, the Australian Securities and Investments Commission, the Australian Competition and Consumer Commission and Environment Australia, the environmental regulator, all have the power to bring civil actions against those that breach regulatory requirements.

ADVANTAGES

A.27   The advantages of public civil actions are that:

They avoid the procedural complications of criminal proceedings.

The burden of proof is lower.

Courts remain involved in the enforcement process, thus improving accountability.

The threat of civil action can provide a real deterrent and be used to induce compliance.

Criminal actions can be reserved for the more serious offences.

They can be combined with a variety of sanctions.

DISADVANTAGES

A.28   The disadvantages, for regulators, are:

Courts are still involved, making the process more protracted.

Procedural complexities are still greater than for administrative/regulatory sanctions.

A.29   Civil penalties have on the whole proved to be a far more useful enforcement tool than criminal law in other countries, and the financial sanctions imposed are often far higher than those imposed through criminal law in the UK.

A.30   If civil regimes are to be effective:

The procedures have to allow for regulators to take actions against firms expeditiously.

Courts must have a wide array of sanctions available to them.

The sanctions imposed must be effective.

Private civil law

A.31   In the UK, civil liability regimes are primarily based in private law, i.e. individuals bringing claims to civil courts for loss, harm or other damage caused. Private civil liability regimes depend on the allocation and recognition of certain rights, for example relating to property and duties of care towards others. These arise in common law (for example the laws of negligence and nuisance), or may be specifically created in statute (for example consumer rights under the unfair contract terms legislation).

A.32   The economic theory supporting civil liability regimes argues that the duty-holder will be deterred from breaching its duties by its potential liability to pay damages. The deterrent effect will be the amount of damages multiplied by the likelihood of those damages being imposed. In terms of economic efficiency, the optimal level of deterrence is that which will ensure that the regulated firm will spend money ensuring compliance up to the point where the cost of doing so exceeds the damage caused by non-compliance. After that point, it is more efficient to pay damages than to increase expenditure on ensuring compliance.

ADVANTAGES OF PRIVATE CIVIL ACTIONS

A.33   The main advantages of private civil actions are that:

Individuals who have been harmed can seek compensation directly from the regulated firm.

The costs of enforcement do not fall on the state (unless the actions are state funded).

Under-enforcement and 'capture' of the regulator by the regulated can be compensated for by individuals bringing actions to enforce the regulatory requirements.

The deterrence effect of private litigation can induce compliance.

DISADVANTAGES

A.34   In practice, there can be considerable weaknesses in civil liability regimes as enforcement tools. Many of these have been highlighted in the reports Defra has commissioned on environmental justice.[18] They include the following:

---

[17]   Note that public law actions in general are those brought with respect to the administration and regulation of activities taken on behalf of and for the benefit of society; they include criminal law and judicial review. For the purposes of this paper, attention is confined to civil actions brought by regulatory bodies.

[18]   See generally Environmental Justice Project, *A Report by the Environmental Justice Project* (London, March 2004); R Macrory and M Woods, *Modernising Environmental Justice: Regulation and the Role of an Environmental Tribunal* (London: UCL, 2003); M Adebowale, Capacity Global, *Using the Law: Access to Environmental Justice: Barriers and Opportunities* (London, 2003); P Stookes, Environmental Law Foundation, *Civil Law Aspects of Environmental Justice* (London 2003).

Enforcement is patchy and *ad hoc* as it is dependent on individual litigants.

Individual litigants can face considerable difficulties in accessing advice about their legal rights under specialist regulatory regimes.

Individuals may not know that they have been harmed either at all, or before the limitation period has expired.

Obtaining sufficient information to mount a claim is problematic.

Establishing a causal link between the actions of the regulated firm and the harm caused can be complex.

The costs of litigation are high which deters potential litigants, and because the cases tend to be complex and have an uncertain outcome, they are rarely taken on a 'no win, no fee' basis.

The rule that loser bears the costs of litigation can act as a significant deterrent to bringing litigation.

Lack of specialist knowledge by the courts, which is a problem common to civil and criminal sanctions.

IMPROVING THE UTILITY OF CIVIL ACTIONS

A.35   A number of proposals have been made to improve the potential for civil liability regimes to be effective in enforcing regulatory requirements.[19] These include:

Improving access to advice and information on legal rights, e.g. by the establishment of an 'e-library' of resources and an environmental advice agency.

Extension of public funding to certain regulatory cases (environmental, health and safety, for example).

Amending the rules relating to the apportionment of legal costs, e.g. pre-emptive costs orders; each side pays its own costs; and presumption against requirements to provide cross-undertakings in damages.

The establishment of specialist courts to hear both private civil law claims, e.g. a specialist environmental court.

---

[19] See references above.

A.36 In addition, legislation could provide for the nomination of 'representative' or 'empowered' litigants to bring actions to enforce regulatory requirements, even where they have not directly suffered harm or loss. In the UK, certain representative organisations such as *Which?* are given rights to enforce provisions under the unfair contract terms legislation, for example. In Australia, the Australian Competition and Consumer Commission has the power to bring representative actions for breaches of the trade practices legislation. Allowing this type of representative action addresses the problems of lack of information, expertise and resources in bringing private actions.

Administrative/Regulatory Sanctioning

A.37 Administrative or regulatory sanctions are those imposed directly by the regulator itself without recourse to court. These have not traditionally been a major feature in UK regulation. However, the introduction of RESA has considerably expanded the scope of administrative sanctions available to regulators.

A.38 Prior to RESA, the most widely available regulatory sanction was the ability to impose financial penalties. These may involve either fixed penalties (such as for parking offences) or variable penalties. In the UK, the Office of Fair Trading, the Financial Services Authority, the Pensions Regulator, and HM Revenue and Customs all have the power under their own legislation to impose variable financial penalties. These powers can be considerable. The OFT has the power to impose fines of up to 10% of turnover for breach of competition law, and the Financial Services Authority has the power to impose unlimited fines. These fines can be significant. In 2007 the OFT imposed a fine of £121.5m on British Airways.[20] The FSA's highest fine, £17m, was imposed against Shell for market abuse in 2004.[21]

Advantages

A.39 Administrative sanctions (including but not limited to financial penalties) bring a number of advantages:

They are easier to administer and less resource-intensive than civil or criminal sanctions.

They enable a speedy response to regulatory breaches.

They can be flexible and targeted in their design and implementation.

They can supplement more formal, criminal or civil actions.

They avoid the moral disapprobation on the firm/individual that is imposed by criminal law whilst providing for effective enforcement.

[20] OFT Annual Report 2007-8 p.99.

[21] FSA, Fines Table, available at http://www.fsa.gov.uk/Pages/About/Media/Facts/Fines/index.shtml.

They allow criminal prosecutions and court time to be reserved for the most serious offences (The White Paper *Respect and Responsibility* of 2003 reported that only 2% of fixed penalty notices it reviewed had ended in court).

Their ease of application may produce higher probabilities of sanctioning and, in turn, higher levels of deterrence.

Some offenders may respond best to a rapid, straightforward face to face approach to control.

Fixing penalty levels can limit the dangers of abuse of discretion.

Discounts for early payment (or penalties for late payment) can help to keep contests out of court.

Disadvantages

A.40   The main disadvantages relate to procedural and accountability issues. The Financial Services Authority, for example, has been criticised by the Financial Services and Markets Tribunal for the way in which it conducted its disciplinary proceedings with respect to Legal and General, leading to an overhaul of their enforcement procedures.[22] The weaknesses are principally:

They involve the grants of considerable degrees of discretionary powers to regulators – who may act as investigators, prosecutors, judges and juries – and so accountability mechanisms need accordingly to be strengthened.

In the absence of appropriate procedural protections, they can be contrary to human rights legislation.

They breach the principle of separation of powers between the executive, the legislature and the judiciary.

If used in relation to non-trivial offending there may be a loss of the public condemnation that flows from use of normal court processes.

Accused persons may not always appreciate their rights to contest sanctions and this may produce unfairness.

Using administrative sanctions effectively

A.41   On balance the advantages of regulatory or administrative sanctions outweigh their disadvantages as enforcement tools, as long as appropriate procedures are in place for their implementation. This was also the recommendation of the Macrory Review, and has been adopted in RESA.

---

[22]   See FSA, *Enforcement Process Review: Report and Recommendations* (London: July 2005).

A.42   Part 3 of RESA imposes a number of procedural requirements on regulators with respect to each of the sanctioning powers which it introduces, and makes provision for rights of appeal on specified grounds. In addition, those regulators who are afforded the RESA sanctioning powers are required to issue guidance stating how those powers will be used, to which they are required to adhere. They are also required to observe the principles set out in RESA s.5(2), viz

(a)   regulatory activities should be carried out in a way which is transparent, accountable, proportionate and consistent

(b)   regulatory activities should be targeted only at cases in which action is needed'.[23]

A.43   Moreover, they may only be given the powers if the relevant authority (Minister in England or Welsh Assembly in Wales) considers that the regulator will observe these principles.[24] The relevant authority has to review the exercise of the powers on a three yearly basis.[25] It also has the power to intervene in particular cases to prevent the imposition of a sanction if the regulator has not complied with the statutory requirements relating to the imposition of the sanction, or has not complied with its own guidance, or has not complied with the regulatory principles.[26]

Enforcement tools

A.44   As noted at the outset of this report, most enforcement tools, with the obvious exception of imprisonment, can be applied either through the criminal courts, the civil courts or by administrative bodies, including regulators. Traditionally, criminal offences led principally, in legal terms, to criminal sanctions imposed by criminal courts. Increasingly, regulators have been given a wider range of powers to impose sanctions directly themselves, culminating in RESA. The result is that although breach of regulatory requirements is still frequently a criminal offence, the allocation of powers for imposing sanctions has broadened from being the sole preserve of the criminal courts and now includes regulators, who also now have a far wider range of enforcement options.

A.45   This section provides a brief discussion of a number of different types of enforcement tool, giving examples of current use. These tools can be arranged into six main groups, and will be discussed in this order:

Pre-prosecution or disciplinary notices.

Monetary penalties

Statutory notices imposing conditions on the terms on which business continues.

Restorative & compensatory sanctions.

[23] RESA, ss 64 and 65.

[24] RESA, s 66.

[25] RESA, s 67.

[26] RESA, s 68.

'Naming and shaming'.

Undertakings and compliance management tools

Exclusion powers: disqualifications, licence revocations, imprisonment.

A.46   In addition, this section will look briefly at defences.

Pre-prosecution or disciplinary notices/warning tools

A.47   All regulators use a range of pre-enforcement notices or other warning devices as part of the enforcement process. These range from formal cautions to informal, oral warnings.

A.48   In short, they offer considerable advantages to regulators as they can be effective in promoting compliance and yet do not require extensive administrative resources to administer. For those regulators whose only other enforcement powers are prosecutions, pre-prosecution notices are often the main enforcement tool used.

A.49   However, to be effective, warnings have to be followed by a sufficient number of formal actions to be credible. If firms know that the most likely consequence of continued non-compliance is another warning, this is unlikely to have a positive effect on its behaviour.

A.50   The most common tool is the written statutory notice. Written notices are warnings or requirements to take action, and failure to do so may lead to the use of formal disciplinary powers or prosecution. These are widely used, particularly where the regulator's only real enforcement tool is prosecution.[27]

A.51   Regulators may also be under an obligation to issue warnings before formal disciplinary processes are commenced: for example the Financial Services Authority is required to issue a series of notices or warnings before formal disciplinary action can be taken.

Monetary/financial penalties

A.52   Monetary or financial sanctions are widely used in regulatory systems. These can be either simply fines, or less frequently, can include disgorgement of profits orders.[28]

A.53   Most systems use criminal law to impose fines. However, as noted above, there is an increasing move towards the imposition of civil fines by courts, or increasingly, regulatory or administrative penalties imposed by regulatory bodies themselves.

---

[27] NAO Sea Fisheries, p 3.

[28] For example the FSA has powers to order firms to disgorge profits.

A.54   The trend had been for those regulators established from 2000 onwards to have the powers to impose fixed or variable fines, and this power has been extended to more regulators under RESA. The penalties imposed can be substantial, and are often far higher than those imposed by the criminal courts. Regulatory fines can:

> Act as an effective deterrent.

> Prove procedurally simpler than criminal fines.

> Involve less commitment of regulatory resources.

> Recapture economic harm imposed and financial profits gained by firm from the breach, unlike other administrative actions (such as notices or cautions).

> Recover the costs associated with inspections and enforcement action (if the fines are hypothecated).

> Variable fines can be flexible and targeted at particular circumstances, including reductions for co-operation.

A.55   Regulators' discretion to impose fines is currently managed to a degree by imposing binding or non-binding principles or other requirements on the regulator for how to use their powers, or requiring the regulator to develop and publish its own set of principles. For example the Financial Services Authority is required by statute to publish a policy statement on the use of its powers, and has done so. Similarly the Consumer Credit Act requires the Office of Fair Trading to publish a policy statement on its powers to impose fines under the consumer credit provisions.[29]

A.56   It is also desirable that the regulator publish a record of fines imposed with details of the parties and the types of non-compliance involved, for example the Fines Table published by the Financial Services Authority. This gives transparency; can be an effective 'naming and shaming' device; and helps to make the fine a powerful deterrent to others. Publication of sanctions is required under RESA.[30] Rights of appeal to an independent tribunal (not Ministers) should also be available. This situation has been improved following the Tribunals, Courts and Enforcement Act 2007.

Optimal level of fines

A.57   A key issue in using fines, regardless of who imposes them (court or regulator), is what should be the optimal level of the fine. The optimal level depends in part on what the imposition of the fine is aiming to achieve.[31] This is usually one or more of the following:

---

[29] Consumer Credit Act 2006, s 54.

[30] RESA, s 65.

[31] For general discussion of the deterrence and pricing models, see A Ogus, 'Corrective Taxes and Financial Impositions as Regulatory Tools' (1998) 61 *Modern Law Review* 767.

To deter future non-compliance by the operator or other operators: in strict economic terms, the fine should be set by the formula pD > *U*, where p = probability of detection; D = disutility of the sanction (including reputation effects) and U = utility from non-compliance.

To 'price' the non-compliant behaviour in relation to the harm caused: the 'polluter-pays' principle.

To recover profits made through non-compliance.

A.58　However, a fine does not have to cover all those objectives. It is possible to separate these objectives out, and have different types of financial sanctions targeted at each one. Thus orders for the firm to carry out remedial work, or to pay for remediation work carried out by the agency, can in effect 'price' the non-compliant behaviour. Profits can be recovered through restitution and disgorgement of profits orders.

A.59　Even if the fine is simply to act as a deterrent, there is a complicated issue as to the level at which it should be set. In economic terms, the optimal level of the fine should be a function of the benefit to the regulated firm of non-compliance and the probability of detection. Where the benefit from the unlawful activity is high but the probability of detection is low, however, the economically defined optimal level of the fine may be so high that an average firm cannot afford to pay it (the 'deterrence-trap'). Even if the fine is pitched at a lower level, paying the fine can weaken the financial position of small and medium enterprises and may reduce the enterprise's ability to institute remedial steps for the purposes to compliance. In addition, some firms may have the capacity to do damage (e.g. to the environment) that greatly exceeds their own resources – they will accordingly be under-deterred by the threat of a fine.

A.60　To address this issue, some regulators look to develop models which can calculate the profits made from non-compliance and the damage caused. In the US, for example, the Environmental Protection Agency has developed complex formula to calculate the violator's economic savings from non-compliance to evaluate the company's claim that it cannot afford to pay financial penalties, and to calculate clean up costs. Such models can provide a sophisticated and targeted approach to setting financial penalties, enabling the debate to move beyond issues of ability to pay.

A.61　Further, fines can impose a deterrent, but any deterrent effect only operates if firms behave rationally – if they know the levels of fines that are likely to be imposed and their reasons for non-compliance are economically driven (i.e. it is cheaper not to comply than to comply and/or the firm can profit from non-compliance in other ways). This will not be the case when non-compliance arises from ignorance irrationality or lack of organisational or technological capacity to comply, irrespective of the level of the fine.

A.62   Finally, there are particular issues relating to regulators having the powers to impose fines which are in addition to the generic issues which arise with respect to regulators having any independent enforcement powers, such as transparency, consistency and accountability. The specific issue when the fine is imposed by the regulator is to whom the money is paid. Some regulators, such as the FSA, retain the fine and are required to use it for the benefit of the regulated community, i.e. by reducing the fees firms have to pay. Issues can then arise of whether there is a conflict of interest between the regulator and the regulated firm when the regulator sets the level of the fine. To address this issue, some regulators, such as the securities regulator in Quebec, are allowed to retain the fine but have to pay it into a separate fund, out of which they are required to fund public education programmes and academic research. In Columbia, the electricity regulator retains the fines but has to use the money to subsidise the provision of electricity to rural areas. In the UK, the OFT, and those regulators gaining fining powers under RESA, are required to pay the fine into the Consolidated Fund, a less imaginative solution but one which serves the same purpose as mandatory hypothecation.

A.63   Disgorgement of profits orders, though less frequently used, can avoid a number of the difficulties associated with fines, as they can avoid the 'deterrence trap', can target the gains of non-compliance effectively, and can be independently assessed, avoiding the problem of conflicts of interest.

Restorative tools

A.64   There are four main restorative tools: compensation orders, restitution orders, remediation plans and reparation orders, and restorative conferences.

COMPENSATION ORDERS

A.65   Compensation orders are intended to compensate a person for a harm or loss caused. Both magistrates and crown courts have a discretionary power to make an order requiring a convicted defendant to pay compensation for any personal injury, loss or damage resulting from an offence.[32] The maximum sum that can be awarded by magistrates is £5,000 in respect of each offence; the Crown Court can order an unlimited sum to be paid as compensation. An order can be made in favour of the relatives and dependants of a deceased person, in respect of bereavement and funeral expenses. The amount of compensation should be such as the court considers appropriate. In making the order the court must have regard to the defendant's means, and the defendant and the prosecutor can make representations to the court as to the loss suffered by the victim. If the court does not make a compensation order when it is empowered to do so, it must give reasons for its decision.

A.66   A compensation order can be imposed alongside a separate sentence or as a penalty in its own right. Where both a fine and a compensation order are appropriate but the offender lacks the means to pay both, the compensation order payments must take priority.

---

[32] Powers of Criminal Courts Sentencing Act 1990, ss 130 to 134.

A.67 The advantages of compensation orders are that they give increased recognition of the need for those who have suffered because of a breach of regulatory requirements to be integrated into the regulatory system and to receive adequate reparation. They can also avoid the need for individuals to have to pursue separate, and costly, civil actions.

A.68 There are two potential disadvantages:

Compensation orders, particularly if low, can prove to be a token gesture which neither changes the firms' behaviour nor gives adequate reparation to the individual.

The compensation required may be more than the firm can afford to pay; or the firm may have gone out of business.

A.69 Balancing the need for effective compensation with ability to pay is critical. In some areas compensation funds have been established to address the latter issue. Those who have suffered loss as a result of a breach of regulatory requirements are able to pursue their claim for compensation on the general compensation fund. These are often funded by the regulated industry, for example the Financial Services Compensation Scheme.[33]

RESTITUTION ORDERS

A.70 Restitution orders are designed to put a person in the position that they would have been in had the offence not occurred. In contrast to compensation orders, they are aimed at restoring the position that existed prior to the offence, rather than giving compensation for loss or harm that has resulted. Restitution orders are often associated with theft offences.[34] However they also have a role in regulatory systems, where they can be used to ensure that losses that a person has suffered can be redressed by the party responsible. Powers to order restitution usually lie with the courts. Restitution orders can be given by the courts for breach of the regulatory provisions under the Financial Services and Markets Act 2000 and the Pensions Act 2004 for example.[35] However, in a few cases regulators have the power to impose them directly: the Financial Services Authority, for example, has the power to impose restitution orders in cases of market abuse.[36]

A.71 Restitution orders have a number of advantages. They recognise that breaches of regulatory provisions are not 'victimless' crimes, and that firms can gain considerably through non-compliance. If effectively calculated and calibrated, there are no obvious disadvantages, other than those which attend monetary penalties generally relating to ability to pay.

---

[33] See www.fscs.org.uk.

[34] Powers to order restitution are given to magistrates and the crown court under section 28 of the Theft Act 1968.

[35] Financial Services and Markets Act 2000, ss 382 to 384; Pensions Act 2004 ss 16 and 19.

[36] FSMA, s 384.

RECOVERY OF COSTS FOR REMEDIAL ACTIONS CARRIED OUT BY THIRD PARTIES

A.72 In many cases, remedial work is necessary to restore the status quo ante, particularly in environmental cases. Often, remedial orders can be imposed by the courts. However, in cases where the offender is unwilling or unable to carry out the remedial work, the agency may have powers to arrange for this work to be done, and the costs recovered from the offender. For example, the Environment Agency carries out remedial work with the intention of recovering costs from the offender, often with respect to waste management. The Forestry Commission has similar powers.[37]

A.73 The main advantages are that remediation is achieved, and paid for by the offender. The sanction therefore serves the dual purpose of emphasising the 'polluter pays' principle, by ensuring that the costs of remediation are met in full – something which rarely happens under the current regime of criminal fines, and that remediation is effected.

A.74 The disadvantages are that the damage and consequent costs of remediation can be so significant that the offender cannot pay for them, leaving the taxpayer to foot the bill. The Environment Agency, for example, estimates that there are in total 50,000 cases of fly-tipping incidents (illegal dumping of waste) each year, costing local authorities between £50 million and £150 million to clean up.

A.75 The issue of the ability to pay can be partly addressed by bonding or other arrangements that require operators to make financial provision to cover any future liabilities. For example, under the Environmental Protection Act 1990 there is a requirement for operators to make suitable financial provision to meet the continuing costs of managing waste disposal sites. These obligations can continue for 30 years or more after the end of the licence. With respect to landfill sites, the Agency requires firms to enter into formal financial arrangements to meet these prospective liabilities. Initially these were to cover liabilities were the firm to go insolvent; however in 2004 the requirements changed to cover liabilities during the course of the licence and a significant period thereafter in all circumstances, to reflect changes in EU law. These are mainly performance bonds: a guarantee by a financial institution to pay an agreed sum to the EA if the operator defaults on its licence obligations or becomes insolvent (in 2002 there were 761 bonds to a value of £165.3m). Also used are escrow accounts (where cash is deposited in an account and both parties must agree to withdrawals), and cash deposits. More generally for non-landfill sites, since 2003 the Agency has required firms to show that they have sufficient financial resources to meet future liabilities when the firm applies for a licence as part of meeting the 'fit and proper' licensing criteria.[38] Cash deposit-refund schemes have also been widely used on a much smaller scale to encourage recycling: for example the system of paying a deposit when buying a bottled drink, with the deposit being returned when the purchaser returns the bottle.

---

[37] Forestry Act 1967, ss17A, 24 and 26.

[38] Environment Agency, *Policy on Financial Provision for non-landfill site waste management licences*, September 2003, and accompanying *Guide for Assessment* (Environment Agency, 2003).

A.76   Requiring finances to be put aside to cover the costs of remedial work based on sound principles, upholding both the precautionary and the polluter-pays principles. However, requirements have to be carefully calculated to ensure that they guarantee that those costs will be met. At present, this is not the case, at least as operated in the context of waste disposal. Bonds are typically only for 3 years at a time; and escrow accounts and cash deposits can be too low, because raising them to provide a meaningful insurance against liabilities can have significant effects on the liquidity of an operation. As a result, they may not cover the actual costs of making the sites safe. Of the 15 instances in which financial provisions were called upon between 1996-June 2002, there was insufficient funds to cover the actual costs in making the sites safe in 6 of those instances.[39] Further, on insolvency, the licence can be disclaimed as 'onerous property', in effect negating the duty to bear financial responsibility for the site after the cessation of the licence.

A.77   Even with the complications of insolvency, performance bonds, if appropriately designed, can be a good way to ensure that firms are required to internalise the costs of their activities prior to them carrying them out. The firm knows that in the event of it breaching its obligations it will be required to pay the costs of remediation, at least as long as it remains a going concern. On that basis, they could beneficially be extended to other areas. If necessary, primary legislation could provide that financial provisions for remedial work which have been made consequent on regulatory requirements cannot be disclaimed in the event of insolvency.

A.78   It may still be the case that the financial provisions made are too small to cover the costs of remedial work, for example because the firm responsible was a small operator and / or the remedial work was more extensive than was foreseen when the financial provision was made and the firm does not have sufficient current funds to supplement the financial provision. One way to address this circumstance would be to have an industry-funded remediation fund to cover the costs of remediation. Such a fund was at one point proposed by the Environmental Services Association to pay the costs of clean up for waste disposal firms who have gone out of business or otherwise cannot afford to pay.[40] Such initiatives could be revived and expanded to other areas.

---

[39] NAO, *Protecting the Public From Waste*, p 37.

[40] Above, p 38.

REMEDIATION PLANS/RESTITUTIVE ORDERS

A.79 Remediation plans and restitutive orders are common in environmental and health and safety regulation. The Environment Agency and the Forestry Commission have the power to issue remediation notices. In health and safety regulation, the court has the power to issue a remediation order.[41] The HSE finds this a particularly effective sanction where a firm has failed to comply with an enforcement notice.[42] The Hampton Report advised that they should be used more extensively.[43] Others have recommended that companies should be required to draft their own remedial plans, to ensure that they become fully involved in the process.[44]

A.80 Under RESA, regulators now have the powers to issue discretionary remedies, one of which is the power to impose a requirement on firms to take such steps as the regulator specifies, and within the time it specifies, to secure that the position is restored to its former situation as far as possible.[45] This can include an undertaking to take action to benefit any person affected by the offence, either by providing compensation or otherwise. Regulators can impose a fine for failure to comply with the notice or undertaking.[46]

A.81 The advantages of remedial or restoration orders are that the sanction is not limited to a fine but requires the firm to restore the circumstances to the position they were in before the misconduct occurred. The disadvantage of remediation orders that are not accompanied by a recovery of costs order is that the firm may simply not comply. Whilst this will result in a further sanction, it will not result in the remedial work being performed. Thus to be effective the firm has to be in the financial position to be able to carry out the remedial work (which may mean that it should be required to take out compulsory insurance or make some other financial provision), and there has to be an effective sanction for non-compliance. As noted, RESA provides regulators with powers to impose a fine for non-compliance with the notice. An alternative would have been to provide a power for the regulator to conduct the remedial work and recover costs, subject to the provisos above.

---

[41] HSWA 1974, s 42.

[42] HSE, Enforcement Guidelines.

[43] Hampton Report, paras 2.87 to 2.88.

[44] Fisse and Braithwaite, 1988.

[45] RESA s 42(3)(c).

[46] RESA s 45.

RESTORATIVE CONFERENCES

A.82   Restorative justice processes, notably restorative conferences, are relative newcomers to criminal justice and regulatory processes. Nonetheless, they have been discussed by the Health and Safety Commission,[47] and the Hampton Report advised that more use be made of them, recommending that the Better Regulation Executive should consider how this could be achieved.[48] The Macrory Review also recommended their development and use in the regulatory context, and found overwhelming support for them amongst respondents.[49] They were not included in the reforms introduced by RESA, however.

A.83   Restorative processes are concerned with restoring victims, offenders and communities through a deliberative process in which these 'stakeholders' in the offence come together to resolve collectively and deliberatively how to deal with the consequences and implications of the offence, and where what is to be restored is whatever matters to the victims, offenders and communities affected by the crime. Restorative justice is a group process of polycentric problem solving. It often requires the definition of the issues to be broadened well beyond the offence itself, which can lead to wide-ranging remedial and other actions on the part of the firm and others involved.[50]

A.84   Restorative conferences can be informal or formal. An extensive study of nursing home regulation in the US and Australia found that involving both the nursing home managers and the residents in discussions as to what actions the nursing home could take to remedy non-compliance and ensure future compliance were more effective in promoting compliance than the application of formal sanctions.[51]

---

[47]   HSC, *An Update on the Evaluation of the HSC's Enforcement Policy Statement*, HSC 04/74, available at www.hse.gov.uk/aboutus/hsc/meetings/2004/080604/c74.pdf.

[48]   Hampton Report, para 2.88, Recommendation 10.

[49]   R Macrory, *Regulatory Justice: Making Sanctions Effective* (Better Regulation Executive) (Final Report, November 2006). pp 69 to 72.

[50]   See generally J Braithwaite, *Restorative Justice and Responsive Regulation* (2001).

[51]   J Braithwaite, T Makkai, 'Trust and Compliance' (1994) 4 *Policing and Society* 1.

A.85   The ACCC in Australia has also used restorative conferences to good effect. In one example, which concerned the mis-selling of insurance policies to Aboriginal communities, the restorative process involved senior managers conducting extensive visits to the communities, involving meetings with victims, local Aboriginal community council, the regulators, and local officials at the social security offices where the premiums were being deducted from social security payments. This was followed by meetings with insurance regulators, industry associations and ministers about follow up regulatory reforms. The insurance company agreed to compensate policy holders, establish an education fund for financial literacy, Education Fund to 'harden targets' for future attempts to rip off illiterate people and conduct an internal investigation into its compliance programme and identify those responsible. Over 80 individuals were sacked in the firm, including some senior managers, and one large corporate agent was dismissed. Procedures relating to social security payments were changed, and there were legal and self-regulatory changes to the licensing of insurance agents.[52]

A.86   The advantages or strengths of restorative conferences are that:

> They incorporate the principles and practices of reintegrative shaming: naming and shaming the non-compliant firm, but in a context which promotes redress by the firm and remedial action which can turn a non-complier into a complier.

> They make the firm aware of the consequences of non-compliance for others.

> They can be most effective where the main reason for non-compliance is failure by the regulated person to accept the legitimacy of the regulatory requirements, i.e. where the reaction is that the regulation is 'red tape' and that non-compliance will have no effect on anyone (e.g. fishermen).[53]

> They can promote active responsibility for compliance by the regulated person, going beyond merely writing a cheque for the fine.

> They can instil long term cultural change in the firm away from non-compliant conduct.

> They involve wider range of participants in identifying and addressing the causes of non-compliance.

> They are both restorative and preventative in their effects.

> They can be used in conjunction with other enforcement tools, e.g. enforceable undertakings.

A.87   There are disadvantages or weaknesses:

---

[52] Fisse and Braithwaite 1993, p 235.

[53] See NAO, *Fisheries Enforcement in England*.

One party (the regulated person, the regulator or another) may inappropriately dominate the process.

The regulated person may not commit to the process, and fail to comply with any outcomes agreed.

The process may result only in superficial actions.

Restorative conferences are most appropriate where there has been some clear harm to a third party (pollution, financial loss, personal injury).

A.88   Research suggests that for restorative conferences to be effective, they need to be run by those with appropriate qualifications and experience, they should be 'nested' within a range of more severe and credible sanctions, and participants must include those harmed by the non-compliance or their representatives.[54]

Disclosing performance

A.89   Increasingly, regulators are using disclosure and publicity as an enforcement tool. This can either be through 'naming and shaming' offenders, or by publishing the performance of all businesses, both compliant and non-compliant, through schemes such as the 'Scores on the Doors' used in food standards regulation.

Naming and shaming; entry on an 'offenders' register

A.90   Publication of the names of those who have breached regulatory requirements can in certain cases be an effective enforcement tool.[55] It is a technique which is being used more and more. For example, regulatory bodies are increasingly issuing press releases giving the outcome of enforcement actions. More specific strategies of naming and shaming include the FSA's Fines Table, and the Environment Agency's annual publication, *Spotlight on the Environment*, which highlights the worst environmental offenders and also describes good environmental practice in individual sectors. The DTI has also used 'name and shame' campaigns in the past against directors of 'phoenix companies', i.e. those who repeatedly start a company, then put it into insolvency, often leaving significant numbers of creditors unpaid, only to start another company often with a similar name.[56]Another example is the Food Standards Agency which publishes its surveillance data and identifies where food samples were purchased.

A.91   Some registers may only have limited disclosures, however. For example, the identity of people on the sex offenders register is not generally publicly disclosable. Certain organisations can check who is on the register, for example schools, and in extreme cases the identity of offenders can be revealed when public safety is at risk.

---

[54]   Braithwaite, Restorative Justice and Responsive Regulation.

[55]   See generally J Braithwaite, *Crime, Shame and Reintegration* (1989).

[56]   See G Wilson, 'Business, State and the Community: Responsible Risk Takers, New Labour and the Governance of Corporate Business' (2000) 27(1) *Journal of Law and Society* 151.

A.92   Naming and shaming can be effective for firms who are anxious to protect their reputations. This clearly includes large firms with strong brand names to protect. However, smaller firms are often keen to protect their local reputation, and press releases of enforcement action which are taken up in the local or the trade press can have an impact.

A.93   The disadvantages, or at least limitations on its use, are that:

> Publication of certain types of breaches may affect public confidence, with adverse effects on the system as a whole. This is particularly the case in banking regulation, where publication that a bank has breached its capital requirements may cause loss of confidence in the bank, leading to a bank run. It may also apply in other areas in some cases.

> Naming and shaming only works if firms have reputations they want to protect. It is therefore not useful against itinerant, fly-by-night operators.

> It only publicises bad practices, therefore does not provide positive models to help firms improve their compliance practices.

> The effects can be easily avoided by firms changing their names, or going into voluntary liquidation and re-forming under a different name.

> Publication can have market distorting effects if not all regulatees are subject to the same scrutiny (e.g. only test carrots at Sainsbury's but not at Tesco).

> It can take time for data to be published, so that data may be out of date.

> Published data can be subject to intense scrutiny by regulatees leading to resource intensive disputes with the regulator.

A.94   The research which has been conducted on the 'naming and shaming' of individual offenders emphasizes the importance of the sanction in the context of a framework of educative and remedial enforcement activity. Some regulators, such as the Environment Agency, complement 'naming and shaming' with statements of best practice.

Publication of individual compliance records

A.95   Alternatively, the policy could be one of naming all, not just the non-compliant. Examples of this technique are prevalent in food standards regulation. In Denmark, food safety inspectors put up 'happy faces' on those restaurants that they inspect which have good compliance records. This policy has been widely adopted by local authorities in the UK, and the Food Standards Agency is seeking to coordinate this activity in its 'Scores on the Doors' initiative. Other regulators also use publicity as an enforcement tool. For example, the Office of Water Services (OFWAT) uses data from the EA and the Drinking Water Inspectorate to publish an annual league table of water companies' performance in providing high standards of drinking water and sewage treatment.

A.96   Publication of the compliance records of firms are intended to affect both the reputation of the firm, and can help to harness market forces in enforcing the regulation by giving consumers and investors more information on which to base their decisions. In this regard, the 'happy faces' signs, for example, are very effective: they are a clear and immediately recognisable indicator of whether the restaurant complies with the relevant requirements.

A.97   Publication of a firm's compliance record can also be used as a regulatory technique to enforce standards which are entirely voluntary. For example, compliance with the voluntary Combined Code on Corporate Governance takes the form of publication of the firm's compliance, with a requirement to state the reasons for non-compliance. Firms also use environmental and other audits in an attempt to demonstrate their compliance with other standards of conduct which are not legally binding. These are discussed further below.

A.98   The disadvantages, or rather weaknesses, are that if publication of the past compliance record is to be effective, it must be clearly disclosed, consumers and investors must be able to rely on it, and they must care about a firm's compliance record sufficiently to alter their behaviour as a result. For example, research has found that FTSE companies that do not comply with the requirements of the Combined Code on dividing the roles of chairman and chief executive suffer no depreciation in their share price as a result.

A.99   For it to be effective, publication of a firm's compliance record requires:

A formal system for recording past compliance.

Clear, easily visible and comprehensible publication of the compliance record.

Understanding and recognition on the part of consumers and investors as to what publication of the compliance record means.

Willingness on the part of consumers and investors to adjust their behaviour in the light of the compliance record.

A clear agreement on when infractions can be deemed to have been 'spent'.

Statutory notices relating to the continuation of the business activity

A.100   In addition to monetary penalties, compensation and restorative remedies, and publicity, there is a range of enforcement tools which relate to the terms and manner in which businesses must conduct their activity in the future, and ultimately, to requiring the cessation of business through withdrawal of a licence, or disqualification of individuals. These can be imposed through licence conditions, where licences are an integral part of the regulatory regime, or independently through other means such as stop notices, prohibitions, or undertakings.

Licence related sanctions:

A.101 Licensing regimes are a very common way of structuring a regulatory regime. The general principle is that an activity is prohibited unless a person obtains a licence to perform it from a designated body. Licensing regimes are used in regulatory regimes ranging from environmental and financial services regulation to the regulation of gangmasters and MOT testing centres. Waste management, animal health and fisheries are all covered by licensing or permitting regimes.

A.102 Using licences to enforce the regulatory regime has a number of advantages:

> It facilitates targeted, proportionate and flexible regulation: the licence conditions can impose particular requirements or restrictions on activities which are tailored to fit the particular circumstances of the operator.

> Relatively low-cost enforcement tool for the regulator once licence is in place.

> The periodic imposition of requirements to renew licences can encourage compliance.

> The threatened loss of access to the market can be a potentially effective deterrent, but only if the operator knows that powers of revocation are likely to be invoked.

A.103 The ultimate sanction under a licensing regime is revocation of the licence (see also below). However revocation of the licence of significant market operators can have a destabilising effect on the market, or may be contractually complex, making the sanction the regulatory equivalent of the nuclear deterrent – something a regulator is rarely, if ever, going to use because of its wider implications. In addition, revocation absolves the licence holder from further responsibilities under the licence. This can mean that further sanctions or requirements for remediation are not effective. It also raises the possibility that the person will continue the activity illegally. For these reasons, regulators can be reluctant to invoke revocation as a sanction: for example the Environment Agency is reluctant to revoke waste management licences, preferring to take some other enforcement action.[57]

Statutory notices

A.104 Powers to issue statutory notices such as improvement notices, stop notices, prohibitions and injunctions with respect to individual firms are frequently found in environmental, food and health and safety legislation. In some cases, there can also be powers to issue orders that are generally applicable across a section of the industry or to certain types of operators, for example, Ministerial powers to introduce emergency control orders relating to the sale of food.

---

[57] NAO, *Protecting the Public From Waste*, p 27.

A.105   Statutory notices are frequently used by regulators and can be an effective way of preventing further harm from occurring whilst further investigative or other enforcement action is taken. The Macrory Review recommended an extension of their use, and as noted above, under RESA, a far wider range of regulators now has the power to issue stop notices, and a general power to impose a requirement 'to take such steps as a regulator may specify, within such period as it may specify, to secure that the offence does not continue or recur.'[58]

A.106   The disadvantage to the operator is that they can impose significant costs without there having been a clear determination of a breach through the normal enforcement processes. Presumably for this reason, s.42 notices can only be issued where the regulator believes 'beyond reasonable doubt' than an offence has occurred. The requirement for the issuing of stop notices is arguably lower: stop notices can only be issued under RESA powers if the regulator 'reasonably believes' that the activity as carried on by that person is causing, or presents a significant risk of causing, serious harm to human health, the environment or the financial interests of consumers. Once the action specified in the stop notice has been carried out, the regulator is required to issue a completion notice. There is a right of appeal against the stop notice.[59]

Seizure, loss of access to, or forfeiture of equipment/goods; confiscation of assets

A.107   There are several examples of sanctions which involve the seizure of goods or prevention of access to goods or equipment, or to confiscation of assets. For example, after successful prosecution under fisheries regulations, a fisherman may lose his catch or its equivalent in value, and their equipment, as noted above. Further, where a person is convicted of an offence of acquisition or use of an explosive article or substance in breach of any of the relevant statutory provisions,[60] the court may order that the explosive article or substance in question shall be forfeited to be destroyed or dealt with in any other way the court orders.

A.108   Other examples include seizure and forfeiture of unauthorised pesticides or unidentifiable bovines. In some cases, for example the condemnation of animals, a court order is also required, for example the seizure and extermination of dangerous dogs.

A.109   The sanction can provide an effective remedy, requiring operators either to hand over what they have gained in breach of the regulations (as in fisheries), or to allow for the removal of a persistent risk to health and safety or the environment (as in pesticides, food, or the condemnation of infected animals).

[58]   RESA s 42(3)(b).

[59]   RESA ss 46 to 49.

[60]   HSWA 1974, s 33(4)(1).

A.110 The disadvantages relate primarily to whether the sanction is criminal or regulatory. If it is criminal, then it is in practice of limited use, given the difficulties of mounting a successful prosecution and the time delay involved. In instances where there is a risk to health, safety or the environment, the sanction is arguably too cumbersome and slow to be effective; regulatory penalties such as stop orders or prohibition orders are likely to be superior. Controversial cases include dogs that have been on death row for two or more years while legal arguments were resolved, creating significant adverse media comment.

Imposition of restrictions on activities

A.111 Impositions of restrictions on activities are usually administered through license provisions, but can be imposed independently of the licence as well. These can include, for example, requirements to submit to inspection or record keeping, e.g. in fisheries, boats are required to notify fishery officers to inspect catches, or loss of access to equipment or goods, or confiscation of assets, e.g. again in fisheries, after successful prosecution, fisherman may lose their catch or its equivalent in value, and their equipment. Under RESA, regulators have been given wider powers to impose these types of restrictions through issuing s.42 notices.

Undertakings and Compliance Management Tools

Enforceable undertakings

A.112 Enforceable undertakings are agreements reached between the regulated and regulator as to certain actions that need to be taken. Breach of an undertaking will itself lead to further enforcement action. This gives the undertaking some formal 'bite'; although in practice voluntary undertakings may be taken just as seriously by both firm and regulator.

A.113 A number of regulators have the formal power to enter into enforceable undertakings, for example the Australian Securities and Investments Commission and the Australian Competition and Consumer Commission. In the UK, the OFT was given a similar power with respect to the exercise of its competition powers in the Enterprise Act 2000. Directors' disqualifications can also be handled by DBERR by means of undertakings.

A.114 The Macrory Review was in favour of the extension of the ability of regulators to enter into enforceable undertakings, and this power was introduced in RESA. The Act enables regulators to accept undertakings from a person where the regulator has reasonable grounds to suspect that the person has committed an offence. The action specified in an enforcement undertaking must be—

(a) action to secure that the offence does not continue or recur,

(b) action to secure that the position is, so far as possible, restored to what it would have been if the offence had not been committed,

(c) action (including the payment of a sum of money) to benefit any person affected by the offence, or

(d) action of a prescribed description.[61]

A.115   Whilst the undertaking is in place, the regulator cannot impose a fine or discretionary remedy against the person, nor can they be convicted of the offence to which the undertaking relates.

A.116   Enforceable undertakings are an extremely flexible enforcement tool, and can be tailored to fit the exact circumstances of each case. The regulator is usually given the discretion to determine what the content of the undertaking should be. The undertaking is then published (the OFT, for example, posts them on its website). They usually include a commitment from the firm not to cease the non-compliant conduct and not to repeat it, and provision for compensation, reimbursement or redress, and any other corrective action that the regulator considers appropriate. Examples of what can be required by an enforceable undertaking in addition to compensation are commitments for re-training/additional training, corrective advertising, and funding of consumer education programmes. The ACCC have also included a third element, which is the requirement to undertake a compliance review and implement an independently audited compliance programme.[62]

A.117   There is an increasing body of research on the effectiveness of enforceable undertakings in Australia,[63] and while there is a debate as to the manner in which they are negotiated, they have been shown to be a useful enforcement tool. The OFT has also made active use of its power to issue enforceable undertakings.

A.118   The advantages of enforceable undertakings are:

> They are highly flexible tools which can extend beyond the formal sanctions available to courts.
>
> They allow for innovative and expansive solutions to be developed to meet the particular case.
>
> They can be tailored to address the underlying causes of non-compliance.
>
> They can include preventative measures to forestall future non-compliance.
>
> They can include restorative and remedial actions.
>
> They can involve regulators, regulated firms and other stakeholders to participate in their development and fulfilment.

A.119   The disadvantages are:

---

[61]   RESA, s 50.

[62]   See Parker, *Restorative Justice in Business Regulation.*

[63]   C Parker, 'Restorative Justice in Business Regulation? The Australian Competition and Consumer Commission's Use of Enforceable Undertakings' (2004) 67(2*) Modern Law Review* 209.

The processes by which they are agreed may be unfair and lacking transparency.

They allow for firms to negotiate 'soft' enforcement options, though there is little empirical evidence supporting this claim.[64]

A.120   To be effective, enforceable undertakings have to meet both substantive and procedural requirements. Substantively, they have to identify the causes of the regulatory breach correctly and must demand actions that will be effective in giving compensation and remediation, and in preventing such actions from recurring.

A.121   In procedural terms, the process for negotiating the undertaking has to ensure both against 'bias' or 'capture' by the regulator, and undue coercion of the regulated firm. Involvement of third parties, such as consumer representatives, representatives of those harmed, or members of the consumer panel attached to the regulatory agency on the one hand, and industry representatives on the other, could serve to meet these concerns.

A.122   If breached, enforceable undertakings will be the subject of court action, allowing for judicial oversight of the undertaking in these circumstances.

Voluntary Undertakings

A.123   Voluntary undertakings are undertakings by the regulated firm to engage in actions specified by, and agreed with, the regulatory agency, but which are do not have the force of law, in that breach of them is not itself actionable. However, the undertaking may be entered into on the basis that if it is breached, the agency will pursue formal enforcement action for the initial non-compliant conduct.

A.124   Undertakings, by nature, depend on the consent of the regulated firm, rather than the use of coercive powers by the regulator, and they are often entered into without the use of formal powers. However, some regulators do have formal powers to enter into voluntary undertakings. For example the US Environmental Protection Agency makes extensive use of its powers to enter into Supplemental Environmental Projects (SEPS) in conjunction with civil penalties. Firms enter into voluntary agreements with the Agency to undertake projects which will benefit the environment which they are not otherwise under a legal obligation to perform.

A.125   Voluntary undertakings have all the advantages of enforceable undertakings, viz.: flexibility, ability to require corrective, remedial, preventative and restorative action extending beyond that which would be possible using formal powers using innovative strategies.

---

[64]   C Parker, 'Restorative Justice in Business Regulation? The Australian Competition and Consumer Commission's Use of Enforceable Undertakings' (2004) 67(2) *Modern Law Review* 209.

A.126   By their nature they are not enforceable per se. It may be that breach of the voluntary undertaking will in practice lead to formal enforcement action being taken, and indeed it is the credible threat of such enforcement action which can incentivise the firm to enter into a voluntary undertaking. However, the range of sanctions available under formal enforcement actions may not provide the same types of tailored responses to non-compliance behaviour that can be reached in a voluntary undertaking. In some circumstances regulators may feel unable to use the voluntary route unless they are confident of being able to bring a good case if undertakings are not fulfilled. Collecting the evidence for such a case may inhibit the use of undertakings.

A.127   Further, depending on whether any admission of liability by the firm has to be a precondition of entering into an undertaking, entering into formal enforcement action can be more costly for a regulator, particularly if the firm will then contest any claim of misconduct.

A.128   Voluntary undertakings can be a valuable enforcement tool, but they need to be nested in a range of credible and effective formal sanctions, so that it is clear that any defection from the undertaking by the firm will be met by formal enforcement action.

Compliance programmes & compliance audits

A.129   It is increasingly common for firms to be required to undertake reviews of their compliance processes as part of the enforcement process. This is often done informally, but it may be done through use of formal powers: compliance audits are frequently part of the enforceable undertakings imposed by ASIC and the ACCC, for example.[65] A compliance audit could also form part of an enforceable undertaking entered into under RESA, as an 'action of prescribed description'.

A.130   The advantages of compliance programmes and audits are that:

> They are forward looking and preventative: aiming to ensure that the misconduct does not re-occur.

> They require the firm to review its own internal processes and consider ways of improving compliance.

> The programme is then verified by an independent third party.

A.131   Compliance programmes and audits need to be carefully managed, for they have a number of potential weaknesses if poorly implemented.

> Regulators may not give sufficient guidance as to their expectations regarding the elements of the compliance programme.

---

[65]   See e.g. C Parker, 'Regulator-Required Compliance Programme Audits' (2003) 25(3) *Law and Policy* 221.

The reviews and audits may focus more on processes rather than underlying systems of work.[66]

Auditors often have no clear guidelines in performing the audit, for example as to what aspects of a firm's systems to review, and what criteria against which to assess the compliance programme. They have to devise their own, leading to inconsistencies, lack of transparency, inability of the regulator to compare the results of different programmes and audits, and potential for capture by management.

There can be a significant expectations gap between what compliance audits can and do deliver and expectations that regulators, investors and consumers may have of them.[67]

Auditors often rely on a very narrow set of information, provided principally by the firm, to review and assess the compliance programme, and do not always seek information from informed third parties: e.g. investors, consumers, those living in the locality of factories etc.

A.132 Compliance reviews and audits have the potential to be a very effective enforcement tool. However, for this potential to be realised:

Regulators need to give clear guidance as to what they expect from firms and auditors.

Auditors need to maintain and demonstrate their independence from the company and include a wider range of parties in the review process.

Compliance reviews and audits have to be able to ensure that the compliance is embedded in the firm's strategy and operations, and not simply focussed on processes and paper audit trails.

Exclusionary powers

A.133 Powers also exist to exclude persons from conducting particular activities, either as individuals or as firms. The possibilities for licence revocation were discussed above (section 3.4.1). In addition, breach of some regulatory offences can lead to the winding up of a company, or a disqualification order with respect to individuals, or ultimately imprisonment.

Bankruptcy/liquidation/winding up

A.134 Breach of some regulatory offences can lead to bankruptcy or liquidation proceedings being commenced. This has been reportedly used successfully in the fisheries sector, for example.[68]

---

[66] For general critique of audits see M Power, *The Audit Society: Rituals of Verification* (1997).

[67] Parker, 'Regulator-Required Compliance Audits'.

A.135   However, its use is not widespread, and is attended by a number of weaknesses. Given the ease with which companies can be incorporated, there is nothing to prevent owners or directors starting up another company doing a similar trade: so-called 'phoenix' companies. Moreover, insolvency is likely to leave small and involuntary creditors unpaid (banks usually will have required personal guarantees from directors). Finally, although undischarged bankrupts are prohibited in law from becoming directors, in practice this has been easy to avoid in the past, as Companies' House did not cross-check the names of company directors against the register of undischarged bankrupts.[69]

Disqualification of directors or other specified personnel

A.136   Directors may be disqualified if their conduct makes them unfit to be a director.[70] A court is also empowered to make a disqualification order against a director convicted of indictable offences in connection with the promotion, formation, management, liquidation or striking off of a company or with the management of a company's property.[71] Disqualification can now be carried out by means of administrative undertakings.

A.137   Disqualified directors must not, without the leave of the court, be a director, liquidator or administrator of a company, or manager of company property or in any way, directly or indirectly, be concerned or take part in the promotion, formation or management of a company for a specified period. The minimum period of disqualification is two years. The maximum period is five years by a magistrates' court and fifteen years by a Crown Court.

A.138   Disqualification disables the director from being involved in the management of a company as an appointed or de facto director. It also avoids the problems of unpaid creditors and 'phoenix' companies.

A.139   However, although disqualification is most commonly used against the directors of small, often 'one man' companies, it is least effective against such individuals as they are the most able to find work or set up in business again as sole traders, in contrast to 'professional' directors of large companies.[72] Further, infringements of disqualification orders which occur where an individual in fact takes an active role in management but is not appointed a director (e.g. in family companies where other family members are appointed) are difficult to detect, particularly in small companies.

A.140   The prospect of disqualification may deter responsible individuals from being directors. This is most likely to apply to 'professional' directors of large companies, although the deterrent effect has not been found to be high.[73]

---

[68]   Defra, *Regulation Taskforce Report*, Annex H.

[69]   Hicks, *Disqualification of Directors: No Place to Hide for the Unfit?*, ACCA Research Report No.59 (London, 1998), available at www.accaglobal.com.

[70]   Company Directors' Disqualification Act 1986.

[71]   CDDA s.2(1).

[72]   Hicks, *Disqualification of Directors.*

[73]   Hicks. *Disqualification of Directors.*

A.141 In addition, regulators may have powers to disqualify individuals from conducting the licensed activity. For example the FSA can bar people from being an 'approved person' under the approved person's regime, and can prohibit them from participating in regulated investment business.

Imprisonment

A.142 Many regulatory offences carry a prison sentence, but as noted above, these sanctions are rarely applied. There were only five jail sentences for breach of health and safety regulations between 1975-2004, for example. However, the Environment Agency has found this effective against fly-tippers, for example, who are sole operators,[74] and there were six imprisonments for breaches of environmental law in 2004.[75]

Defences available to regulated persons/leniency policies

A.143 It may seem out of place to treat defences to enforcement as an enforcement tool, but there has over time been the repeated suggestion that firms should be able to offer a defence of self-reporting and/or due diligence. Alternatively, or in addition, regulators administering regulatory penalties may be empowered to have formal leniency policies, under which the sanction imposed would be negated had the firm reported the offence or otherwise assisted in the enforcement process, or could demonstrate that notwithstanding the breach, the firm had acted with due diligence in trying to prevent it.[76]

A.144 Under a self-reporting defence, the firm receives a lower penalty if it has in fact reported the non-compliance to the regulator. In some circumstances self-reporting may confer immunity from prosecution.

A.145 Under a due diligence defence, sanctions, including individual liability for directors, are reduced if the firm can show it had otherwise effective compliance systems in place.

A.146 Leniency policies are policies operated by regulators to reduce the amount of financial penalty imposed, for example, and are often operated informally simply by not prosecuting firms which have taken steps to prevent the breach occurring.[77]

---

[74] NAO, *Protecting The Public from Waste.*

[75] See Hampton Report, p.20.

[76] For discussion see G Sullivan, 'The attribution of criminality to limited companies' (1996) *Cambridge Law Journal* 575; J Gobert, 'Corporate Criminality: New Crimes for the Times' (1994) *Criminal Law Review* 722; C Parker, *The Open Corporation* (2002), pp 257 to 261.

[77] On the circumstances in which regulators will prosecute, see generally Hawkins, *Law as Last Resort* and see Defra's *Enforcement Policy Statement* (June, 2005).

A.147   An example of a formal leniency policy is the powers of the OFT to issue 'no-action letters' conferring immunity from prosecution to individuals who are the first to inform the OFT that they participate in a cartel.[78] The OFT can also operate a leniency policy which offers immunity under the Competition Act to companies that are the first to inform the OFT of breach of the provisions prior to the OFT commencing an investigation and provided it did not already have sufficient information to establish the existence of a cartel, or reduction of the fine otherwise payable in certain circumstances.[79]

A.148   Courts can also operate similar defences. In Australia, the courts have regularly discounted damages for trade practices legislation where effective compliance systems exist.[80] In the US, the US Sentencing Commission's Federal Sentencing Guidelines for organisations provide that the existence of an effective compliance and ethics programmes system will provide companies or individuals with a reduction in penalty if they are found to have breached the law.[81]

A.149   Due diligence and self-reporting defences and related leniency policies have two main advantages:

> They provide incentives to regulated operators to have effective compliance systems.

> They provide incentives to report misconduct to the relevant regulatory body.

A.150   However, they may be open to misuse by regulators if they are not transparent in their operation. Thus to ensure both transparency and certainty, and to provide the incentives sought, the basis for assessing the compliance programme or other conditions on which the defences or leniency policy operates have to be clearly set out either by the courts or the regulatory agency as appropriate. The US Sentencing Guidelines, for example, provide detailed guidance on what is considered to be an 'effective' compliance and ethics programme in both small and large organisations.

---

[78]   Enterprise Act 2002.

[79]   OFT, *Leniency in Cartel Cases: A Guide to the Leniency Programme for Cartels* (London, 2005).

[80]   Parker, *The Open Corporation*, pp.247-252.

[81]   US Sentencing Commission, Federal Sentencing Guidelines, Chapter 8, Part B, section 2.1 (available at www.uss.gov/2004guid/8b1_1.htm).

Conclusion

A.151 There is thus a wide variety of enforcement tools and sanctions that can be imposed on regulated persons. These include financial penalties, restorative and remedial orders, enforceable undertakings, and ultimately exclusion. Sanctions may be imposed by criminal courts, civil courts or directly by regulators themselves. Increasingly in the UK the trend has been to move away from the assumption that the legal nature of the offence had to determine which body could impose a sanction. The traditional model of regulatory offences was one in which the legal nature of the offence (criminal) was closely aligned to the allocation of powers to impose a sanction for that offence (criminal courts). Increasingly, regulators had been given powers to impose sanctions themselves, even though the breach of the regulatory requirement was still characterised in legal terms as a criminal offence. What has happened under RESA is that this trend of decoupling of the criminal offence from the criminal courts has reached a culmination. The criminal offences remain, but the criminal conviction is now clearly the last resort as a matter of regulatory design, not just the last resort as a matter of regulatory practice. Instead, a tiered system of sanctions has been introduced, giving regulators more scope to impose sanctions in circumstances that would not meet the requirements of criminal procedures in the criminal courts. A criminal conviction remains as the ultimate sanction that can be used against regulated persons, but regulators now have many more options to take other forms of enforcement action with respect to persons when they have cause to believe (on varying grounds of presumption) that a criminal offence has been or is about to be committed.

APPENDIX B
CORPORATE CRIMINAL LIABILITY: MODELS OF INTERVENTION AND LIABILITY IN CONSUMER LAW – PROFESSOR PETER CARTWRIGHT[1]

INTRODUCTION

B.1 Criminal law has been used to protect consumers since the Nineteenth Century.[2] The 1960s saw the proliferation of consumer protection statutes with many, including the Trade Descriptions Act 1968 (TDA), Food Safety Act 1990 (FSA) and Property Misdescriptions Act 1991 (PMA) having had criminal offences at their heart. More recently, the UK Government has chosen to use criminal law when implementing the Directive on General Product Safety and the Unfair Commercial Practices Directive.

B.2 Consumer protection statutes usually require defendants to have acted in the course of a trade or business, or similar. Frequently, the defendant will be a corporation. Most consumer protection offences impose strict liability (although some require proof of fault) and virtually all are subject to due diligence defences. Parliament has taken a variety of approaches when deciding who should be a potential defendant, and under what circumstances. The courts have taken a number of approaches when deciding how liability can, and cannot, be established against such a defendant.

B.3 The principal purpose of this report is to examine the models of corporate liability that have been used in consumer protection offences. This involves an examination of the doctrine of identification, and how it operates in the cases of due diligence defences and *mens rea* offences. The report also considers the extent to which alternative models of liability might be utilised. Because there is little case law on current legislation, it is necessary to consider some statutes that have been repealed. Reference will also be made to how current legislation is expected to be interpreted.

STRICT AND VICARIOUS LIABILITY AND IDENTIFICATION

B.4 Most consumer protection offences have imposed strict liability on defendants in that the prosecution has not been obliged to prove *mens rea* as to all (or, in most cases, any) elements of the *actus reus*. Some statutes provide explicitly for vicarious liability. For example, s.1(1) of the PMA stated that:

> Where a false or misleading statement about a prescribed matter is made in the course of an estate agency business or a property development business...the person by whom the business is carried on shall be guilty of an offence under this section.

---

[1] Professor of Consumer Protection Law, University of Nottingham. The author would like to thank Richard Hyde for comments on an earlier draft. The usual disclaimer applies.

[2] See, for example, the Adulteration of Food and Drugs Act 1872.

B.5 More commonly, vicarious liability arises as a matter of statutory construction. For example, a company supplies goods which its employee supplies.[3] Some degree of vicarious liability is found in nearly all strict liability consumer protection offences.

Strict liability and due diligence defences

B.6 Vicarious liability is, however, restricted by due diligence defences. For example, s.24(1) of the TDA stated:

> ...it shall...be a defence for the person charged to prove-
>
> (a) that the commission of the offence was due to a mistake or to reliance on some information supplied to him or to the act of default of another person, an accident or some other cause beyond his control; and
>
> (b) that he took all reasonable precautions and exercised all due diligence to avoid the commission of the offence by himself or by any person under his control.

B.7 *Tesco Supermarkets Ltd* v *Nattrass*[4] demonstrated the implications of these defences for corporations. Tesco advertised washing powder in a store for a particular price when a customer was charged a higher price by mistake. Tesco claimed that the fault was that of their manager, that he was "another person" for the purposes of section 24(1), and that the company had taken all reasonable precautions and exercised all due diligence. The House of Lords found that Tesco could escape liability by showing that the person at fault did not represent the directing mind and will of the corporation, and that the corporation at a senior level had taken all reasonable precaution and exercised all due diligence.[5] This would be shown:

> if the principal has taken all reasonable precautions in the selection and training of servants to perform supervisory duties and has laid down an effective system of supervision and used due diligence to see that it is observed.[6]

---

[3]   Trade Descriptions Act 1968, s 1.

[4]   [1972] AC 153.

[5]   See *Bolton v TJ Graham* [1957] 1 QB 159 (HL).

[6]   *Tesco Supermarkets Ltd v Nattrass* [1972] AC 153, 198 by Lord Diplock.

B.8   The "directing mind and will" constitutes a very small group, with even employees possessing some relatively senior management responsibilities being merely "a cog in the machine which was devised"[7]. Due diligence defences therefore limit the vicarious liability of corporations. The employee acts in the course of a trade or business, but is another person – separate from the company – for the purpose of the defence. It would be possible for enforcement authorities to prosecute the employee, either under a by-pass procedure such as that found in section 23 of the Act or (it is submitted) directly.[8] However, there are strong policy reasons against doing this.

MENS REA CONSUMER PROTECTION OFFENCES AND IDENTIFICATION

B.9   The principal focus of this paper is on the liability of corporations for consumer protection offences with a fault requirement. There are a number of models to consider.

Mens rea and delegation

B.10   An employer will not normally be vicariously responsible for a *mens rea* offence committed by an employee, but may sometimes be by the doctrine of delegation. Here, the *mens rea* of an employee will be imputed to his or her employer where the employer has delegated full responsibility to the employee.[9] The doctrine was important principally, and probably only, when a statute provided that only a particular class of person can be prosecuted, for example, a licensee under the Licensing Acts. Under such legislation, an employee lacked the status to be prosecuted and the licensee lacked the requisite knowledge. Although there is a case to the contrary[10], it is generally thought that the delegation principle should apply only in such cases and not where the employee is a potential defendant.

Mens rea and identification

B.11   The traditional method by which liability is attached to corporations for *mens rea* offences is through the doctrine of identification. This is the technique used in *Tesco v Nattrass* to distinguish between different classes of employee. The courts identify a class of senior individuals within a corporation whose guilty acts and guilty minds could be said to be the acts and mind of the company. Those individuals are the company's *alter ego*, its "directing mind and will"[11]. Companies can be convicted of *mens rea* offences provided that the *mens rea* required for the offence can be shown on the part of such an individual. The distinction between different classes of employee was famously made by Denning LJ as follows:

---

[7]   *Tesco Supermarkets Ltd v Nattrass* [1972] AC 153, 181 by Lord Morris.

[8]   It is customary for those consumer protection statutes which create criminal offences also to contain by pass procedures. Examples include section 20 of the FSA, and section 16 of the CPRs.

[9]   *Vane v Yiannopoullos* [1965] AC 486.

[10] See *Howker v Robinson* [1973] 1 QB 178.

[11] *Bolton (Engineering) Co Ltd v TJ Graham & Sons Ltd* [1957] 1 QB 159 (HL).

Some of the people in the company are mere servants and agents who are nothing more than hands to do the work and cannot be said to represent the mind or will. Others are directors and managers who represent the directing mind and will of the company and control what it does. The state of mind of the managers is the state of mind of the company and is treated by the law as such.[12]

B.12 There are difficulties with identification where *mens rea* offences are concerned. The first concerns finding someone sufficiently senior who has the requisite fault.[13] Relatively senior employees, including those with supervisory responsibility such as store managers will not be classed as part of the company's directing mind and will.[14] This difficulty has even led to creative prosecutions. In *Formula One Autocentres Ltd* v *Birmingham City Council*[15] a company which might have expected to have been prosecuted under s.14 of the TDA (where knowledge or recklessness was required) was prosecuted under s.1 to avoid the need to prove *mens rea*. Enforcers have estimated that *mens rea* offences take twice the time of strict liability offences to investigate.[16]

B.13 Another difficulty where consumer protection is concerned involves the wording of the offences in question. The forms of *mens rea* most commonly found in consumer protection statutes are knowledge and recklessness. For example, s.14 of the TDA stated:

> It shall be an offence for any person in the course of any trade or business (a) to make a statement which he knows to be false or (b) recklessly to make a statement which is false as to any of the following matters.

B.14 The section then listed matters relating to services, accommodation and facilities. The TDA, along with much consumer protection legislation, was replaced by the Consumer Protection from Unfair Trading Regulations (CPRs) in 2008. While most of the provisions in the CPRs impose strict liability, regulation 8(1) states:

> A trader is guilty of an offence if—
>
> he knowingly or recklessly engages in a commercial practice which contravenes the requirements of professional diligence under regulation 3(3)(a); and the practice materially distorts or is likely to materially distort the economic behaviour of the average consumer with regard to the product under regulation 3(3)(b).

B.15 It is worth examining these fault elements further.

[12] *Bolton (Engineering) Co Ltd v TJ Graham & Sons Ltd* [1957] 1 QB 159 (HL).

[13] See DTI *Consultation on Framing and Enforcing Criminal Sanctions in the Regulations Implementing the Unfair Commercial Practices Directive* (URN 06/2123 (December 2006), para 18.

[14] *Tesco Supermarkets Ltd v Nattrass* [1972] AC 153.

[15] (1999) 163 JP 234.

[16] See DTI *Consultation on Framing and Enforcing Criminal Sanctions in the Regulations Implementing the Unfair Commercial Practices Directive* (URN 06/2123 (December 2006), para 15.

Recklessness

B.16   Recklessness includes subjective recklessness, but encompasses more.[17] Section 14(2)(b) of the TDA stated that a statement made "regardless of whether it is true or false" is deemed to be made recklessly "whether or not the person making it had reasons for believing that it might be false." Similarly, regulation 8(2) of the CPRs states that:

> a trader who engages in a commercial practice without regard to whether the practice contravenes the requirements of professional diligence shall be deemed recklessly to engage in the practice, whether or not the trader has reason for believing that the practice might contravene those requirements.

B.17   There is therefore a duty to have regard to the matters in question. In the s.14 case of *MFI Warehouses Ltd* v *Nattrass*, the Divisional Court found evidence of recklessness where the company chairman "did not have regard to the falsity or otherwise of what was written on his behalf" (he did not appreciate how an advertisement might be interpreted).[18] This suggests that recklessness for the purposes of these provisions includes (at least) subjective and objective recklessness. It is not clear whether it is wide enough to cover the "Caldwell lacuna".[19] In regulation 8, this might be where the trader thinks about whether the practice contravenes the requirements of professional diligence and concludes, unreasonably, that it does not. The trader has not realised there is a risk and taken it, (subjective recklessness) nor has he failed to have regard to the risk (which is classed as recklessness by s.14 and regulation 8(2) and might be described as recklessness by inadvertence). It seems arguable that such a trader is not reckless for the purposes of regulation 8.

Knowledge

B.18   Regulation 8(1) uses the word "knowingly" as an alternative to "recklessly", and s.14 covered D who makes a statement that "he knows to be false". In relation to regulation 8, the DTI has stated that knowledge: "requires an accurate belief on the part of the defendant that relevant circumstances exist."[20] The DTI further stated that "knowledge can be imputed where the defendant deliberately closes his mind to what he suspects and does not make enquiries because he does not want his fears confirmed."[21] Knowledge is defined in neither the TDA nor the CPRs, and there is very little case law on its meaning in consumer protection law.

---

[17]   Para 5.2 of the DTI Consultation (above n.10) mentions subjective recklessness and recklessness by inadvertence. In their responses to one of the Government's consultations, trading standards officers asked for the provision to be based on s.14(2)(b). See BERR Government Response to the consultation on draft *Consumer Protection from Unfair Trading Regulations* (Feb 2008) URN 08/554 para 27

[18]   [1973] 1 WLR 307.

[19]   This lacuna was recognised as existing by the House of Lords in *Reid* [1992] 3 All ER 673.

[20]   See DTI *Consultation on Framing and Enforcing Criminal Sanctions in the Regulations Implementing the Unfair Commercial Practices Directive* (URN 06/2123 (December 2006), para 5.2.

[21]   This echoes *Westminster City Council* v *Croyalgrange* [1986] 2 All ER 353 at 359. Ashworth prefers to see the latter "wilful blindness" as a form of reckless knowledge. See Ashworth *Principles of Criminal Law* (5th ed 2006), p 191.

Identification and fault elements: practical difficulties

B.19 Where fault elements such as recklessness and knowledge are concerned, there are practical difficulties with using identification. With recklessness, the duty to have regard to relevant matters is imposed on the trader (for our purposes, the company). *MFI Warehouses* v *Nattrass* appears to envisage a duty upon the directing mind and will of the company to consider this. This might be difficult to prove, although the courts might infer it in the absence of evidence of such consideration.

B.20 In regulation 8 knowingly appears at the start of the provision, and therefore applies to the whole of the *actus reus*.[22] It must be proved that D knew that he was engaging in a particular commercial practice, and knew that the commercial practice contravened the requirements of professional diligence. The latter might particularly be problematic. According to regulation 2(1), "professional diligence" means:

> the standard of special skill and care which a trader may reasonably be expected to exercise towards consumers which is commensurate with either
>
> (a) honest market practice in the trader's field of activity; or
>
> (b) the general principle of good faith in the trader's field of activity.

B.21 It will therefore be necessary for the court to establish what the honest market practice, and/or the general principle of good faith, in the trader's field of activity are. A trader who is mistaken as to what standards of professional diligence are in his field might be acquitted. Because the question of whether specific conduct contravenes the requirements of professional diligence is a matter of judgement there appears to be room for companies to escape liability through an ignorance of what their business or profession expects of them.[23] In cases that are not clear cut, enforcement authorities might need to rely heavily upon putting firms on notice.

B.22 Section 14(1)(a) of the TDA made it an offence to make a statement which D knew to be false. In *Wings* v *Ellis*, the House of Lords held that this was not the same as knowingly making a false statement, and that D could be guilty where he knew the information [included in a travel brochure] was false, even though he thought that he had corrected the statement and, therefore, did not knowingly make a false statement. This was always a questionable decision, Lord Scarman justifying it apparently on the basis that the TDA "is not a truly criminal statute. Its purpose is not the enforcement of the criminal law but the maintenance of trading standards."[24]

---

[22] See Ashworth *Principles of Criminal Law* (5th ed 2006), p 191.

[23] The Office of Fair Trading's Guidance recognises that "if the practice was well known to be unfair or unprofessional then it would be easier to demonstrate that the trader engaged in it knowingly or recklessly" (Office of Fair Trading, *Consumer Protection from Unfair Trading Guidance* (May 2008) para 12.15).

[24] [1985] AC 272, 293 by Lord Scarman.

Alternatives to identification

B.23 Identification is the principal model used to attach liability to corporations for consumer protection offences with a fault element, and is also relevant where due diligence defences are concerned. However, a number of other models deserve attention.

Extended identification and defences

B.24 The doctrine of identification as explained in *Tesco v Nattrass* was questioned in *Tesco Stores Ltd v Brent LBC*.[25] Tesco was charged with supplying a video to a person under age under the Video Recordings Act 1984. The sale was undertaken by one of D's employees. Section 11(2)(b) provided that it was an defence for D to show that he neither knew, nor had reasonable grounds to believe, that the purchaser was under 18. It was found that the employee who supplied the video did have reasonable grounds to believe that the purchaser was under 18. The question for the Court was whether the knowledge or belief of the employee could be attributed to the defendant for the purposes of the statutory defence.

B.25 On the basis of *Tesco v Nattrass*, it might have been thought that the knowledge or belief in question would have to be that of someone who constituted the directing mind and will of the corporation. Indeed, Lord Justice Staughton accepted that "what mattered in terms of section 11(2)b was whether the accused (Tesco Stores Ltd.) neither knew nor had reasonable grounds to believe that Stuart [the purchaser] was under 18". However, he concluded that:

> it is her [the shop assistant's] knowledge or reasonable grounds that are relevant. Were it otherwise, the statute would be wholly ineffective in the case of a large company.[26]

As Wells observes, Mr Justice Staughton's task "was made easier by the different wording, with its emphasis on knowledge of a circumstance rather than diligence in avoiding a result."[27] But could the same logic apply to due diligence or similarly worded defences? In *R v British Steel plc*[28] some sub-contractors working for British Steel failed to secure a platform properly and a man died as a result. British Steel were charged with an offence under the Health and Safety at Work Act 1974. Section 3(1) of that Act states:

> It shall be the duty of every employer to conduct his undertaking in such a way as to ensure, so far as is reasonably practicable, that persons not in his employment who may be affected thereby are not thereby exposed to risks to their health and safety.

---

[25] [1993] 1 WLR 1037.

[26] Above, 1042.

[27] C Wells "Corporate Liability and Consumer Protection: *Tesco v Nattrass* Revisited" (1994) 57 Modern Law Review 817.

[28] [1995] 1 WLR 1356.

B.26 It was accepted that British Steel had to prove that it was not reasonably practicable to do more than was in fact done. The Court of Appeal decided that Tesco v Nattrass "[did] not provide the answer"[29]. They rejected the argument put forward by counsel for British Steel that section 3(1) permitted an employer to escape criminal liability if the company had taken all reasonable care at the level of its "directing mind". Mr Justice Steyn argued that it would:

> drive a juggernaut through the legislative scheme if corporate employers could avoid criminal liability where the potentially harmful event is committed by someone who is not the directing mind of the company[30].

B.27 There is some difficulty in reconciling the decision with traditional views of corporate criminality, just as there had been in *Brent*. Under the Health and Safety at Work Act the obligation is on the employer to take all such precautions as are reasonably practicable. While this is not the same as having to take all reasonable precautions and exercise all due diligence (the wording usually found in consumer protection statutes), the wordings are analogous.

Extended identification and mens rea

B.28 The courts have also departed from identification as understood in *Tesco* v *Nattrass* where *mens rea* offences are concerned, although there is no such example from consumer protection law. In *Meridian Global Funds* v *Management Asia Ltd*[31] it was asked whether a company "knew" that it had acquired a shareholding in a target company when two employees used funds to acquire shares in the target. The Privy Council decided that the company has such knowledge "when that is known to the person who had authority to do the deal".[32] The question was one of construction "rather than metaphysics". According to Lord Hoffmann:

> It is a question of construction in each case as to whether the particular rule requires that the knowledge that an act has been done, or the state of mind with which it was done, should be attributed to the company... . Each [decision] is an example of an attribution rule for a particular purpose, tailored as it must be to the terms and policies of the substantive rule.[33]

B.29 It seems that the courts will recognise an extended form of identification, both in relation to defences and to fault elements, where to adhere to identification in its traditional (strict) form, would defeat the purpose of the provision. Where this applies, it might even be viewed as a form of vicarious liability.

---

[29] *British Steel plc* [1995] 1 WLR 1356,1361 by Steyn LJ.

[30] Above, 1362 to1363.

[31] [1995] 2 AC 500.

[32] *Meridian Global Funds* v *Management Asia Ltd* [1995] 2 AC 500, 511.

[33] Above, 511 to 512.

Organisational fault 1: corporate manslaughter and homicide

B.30 Much of the academic literature calls for greater attention to be paid to what might be called "organisational fault".[34] A form of such fault is found in the Corporate Manslaughter and Homicide Act 2007, which holds that an organisation (such as a company) is guilty of an offence if "the way in which its activities are managed or organised – (a) causes a person's death, and (b) amounts to a gross breach of a relevant duty of care owed by the organisation to the deceased."[35] It goes on to say that the organisation will be guilty "only if the way in which its activities are managed or organised by its senior management is a substantial element in the breach referred to in subsection (1)."[36]

B.31 This demonstrates a move away from the doctrine of identification. Several factors need to be proved. First, there must be a relevant duty owed to the victim. For the purpose of consumer protection, the most obvious duty would be "a duty owed in connection with...the supply by the organisation of goods or services".[37] Secondly, there must be a gross breach of that duty. In deciding if the breach is gross, the jury can have regard to any matters they consider relevant, but are pointed to a number of matters. They *must* consider whether the evidence shows the organisation failed to comply with any health and safety legislation that relates to the alleged breach and, if so, how serious the failure was and how much of a risk of death it posed. They also may consider a variety of other factors, including evidence of attitudes, policies, systems or accepted practices in the organisation which are likely to encourage or tolerate the failure. Next, it must be shown that the way in which the organisation's activities are managed or organised by its senior management is a substantial element in the breach. Rather than focusing solely on the fault of an individual (as identification does) the Act requires proof of what might loosely be described as "management failure", and whether that failure can be said to be a "substantial element" in the breach. Ormerod notes that the definition of senior management in the Act, reflecting as it does those who play significant roles in making "decisions about how the whole or a substantial part of its activities are to be managed or organised, or the actual managing or organising of the whole or a substantial part of those activities", extends beyond those who might be said to form the directing mind and will for the purposes of identification.[38] Furthermore, he observes that "it will now be possible to combine the shortcomings of a wide number of individuals within the organisation to prove a failure of management by the organisation."[39] By so doing, the offence allows a form of aggregation, which English law had traditionally avoided.[40] Finally, causation must be established.

---

[34] See for example C Wells *Corporations and Criminal Responsibility* (2nd ed 2001) chapter 8; J Gobert and M Punch, *Rethinking Corporate Crime* (2003) chapter 3.

[35] Corporate Manslaughter and Homicide Act 2007, s 1(1).

[36] Corporate Manslaughter and Homicide Act 2007, s 1(3).

[37] Corporate Manslaughter and Homicide Act 2007, s 2(1)(c)(i).

[38] D Ormerod, *Smith and Hogan Criminal Law* (12th ed 2008), p 543.

[39] Above, p 542.

[40] See *A-G's Reference (No.2 of 1999)* [2000] QB 796.

B.32   By focusing on the way in which the organisation's activities are managed or organised by its senior management, the test attempts to get to the heart of corporate failure. However, it has been criticised for retaining a link with individual fault. Gobert, for example, sees the reference to senior management in the Act as being more focused on individual fault than the concept of management failure as a systemic failing that was championed by the Law Commission.[41]

B.33   As noted above, it is possible to envisage a conviction for corporate manslaughter following from a breach of consumer protection law. An obvious example might be where death results from the sale of dangerous goods, and there was a substantial failure to manage the manufacturing process. As Freeman observes "[the Act's] intended scope very much includes manufacturers whose products cause a person's death."[42] Whether the Act's approach should be adopted for consumer protection offences more generally is interesting. Some elements would need to be reconsidered (such as the requirement for a gross breach of a relevant duty of care) and consumer law seldom involves the commission of very serious harm. However, the focus on the way that activities are managed or organised is, perhaps, a better reflection of corporate fault where *mens rea* offences are concerned than any attempt to locate fault within a member of the directing mind and will.

Organisational fault 2: reforming bribery

B.34   The final alternative to identification considered here is that found in the Law Commission's report on *Reforming Bribery*.[43] The Commission recommends that it should be an offence for a company negligently to fail to prevent bribery, with a model that would work as follows. First, the prosecution would prove that an individual connected with the company who had the responsibility to prevent bribery was negligent, and that that negligence led to the failure to prevent bribery. The company would, however, escape liability if it showed that it had adequate systems in place to prevent the commission of bribery on its behalf. As an alternative, the prosecution could show that the negligent failure to prevent bribery was attributable to the company's directors. Where this was the case, the "adequate systems" defence would not be available. Under the proposed scheme, a company might (subject to the defence) be held liable for the negligent failure to prevent bribery which is committed by anyone acting on behalf of the company (therefore including agents, third parties and subsidiaries as well as employees).

---

[41]   J Gobert "The Corporate Manslaughter and Corporate Homicide Act – Thirteen years in the making but was it worth the wait?" (2008) 71(3) Modern Law Review 413, 417 to 418.

[42]   R Freeman, "Corporate Manslaughter Act finally becomes law in the UK" (2007) 28 *European Product Liability Review* 9, 9.

[43]   Reforming Bribery (2008) Law Com No 313.

B.35   The proposed scheme involves a form of organisational, rather than direct liability. The focus is on the company's liability for failing to prevent bribery, rather than for the bribery offence itself. Indeed, the Law Commission has recommended that any extension of direct liability should form part of a general review.[44] Like the Corporate Manslaughter and Homicide Act, the Scheme anticipates a combination of individual fault and wider corporate, or systemic fault. The defence of "adequate systems" (a variation of due diligence) should ensure that companies who can demonstrate that they have appropriate processes in place will not be convicted. Again, a variation of this might be utilised where consumer protection is concerned, although it would take a different form. The Law Commission notes that bribery is "an ordinary criminal offence" and "a serious criminal wrong".[45] By contrast, consumer protection offences tend to be regarded as regulatory, even where *mens rea* is required, and so the question of holding a company responsible for failure to supervise an employee who has committed a serious criminal wrong tends not to arise. [46]

Conclusions

B.36   Where consumer protection offences are concerned, the following difficulties arise from the operation of the doctrine of identification. First, in the context of due diligence defences, it is not always clear when a person's act will be the act of the company, or the act of another person. Following *Tesco* v *Nattrass*, employees who fall outside the small group who constitute the directing mind and will be another person for the purposes of the defence. Provided the directing mind and will have taken all reasonable precautions and exercised all due diligence, the company will be acquitted. Secondly, it is not always clear whose *mens rea* is the *mens rea* of the corporation. The traditional approach holds that only the mens rea of those who constitute the directing mind and will is enough. This poses considerable difficulties of proof for enforcement authorities. The "new approach" cases could potentially make the prosecution's role easier. But there is no evidence that *Tesco* v *Brent* will be followed for due diligence defences, nor that *Meridian* will be followed for *mens rea* offences. The third difficulty is that the meanings of the *mens rea* terms found in consumer protection statutes (chiefly, recklessness and knowledge) are not clear and, to the extent that they are defined, they do not sit comfortably with traditional notions of identification.

B.37   The alternatives outlined have obvious advantages. As noted, extended identification makes it easier to attribute *mens rea* to corporation, and more difficult for the company to escape liability by pleading a statutory defence, by extending the range of people with whom the company is identified. But it still focuses heavily on the *mens rea* of an individual. Organisational fault is perhaps more successful at encapsulating corporate fault, as well as providing strong incentives for companies to pay attention to how their activities are organised and whether their systems are adequate. Detailed consideration of how this might be worded in the context of consumer protection would be beneficial, although beyond the scope of this paper.

---

[44]   Reforming Bribery (2008) Law Com No313, para 6.38.

[45]   Above, paras 6.19 and 6.20.

[46]   See *Wings Ltd* v *Ellis* [1985] AC 272.

APPENDIX C
CORPORATE CRIMINAL LIABILITY: EXPLORING SOME MODELS – PROFESSOR CELIA WELLS[1]

Introduction

C.1 In spite of a large literature on the subject, corporate criminal liability is still much misunderstood, with a shifting vocabulary that often obscures and complicates the relevant questions on which it is or might be based. One of those questions is the role or purpose of criminal law and criminal sanctions. I assume here without being definitive that deterrence plays a role. If a system seeks to deter then it will fail if it is under enforced. Under enforcement could arise from a number of causes: inefficient or corrupt enforcement agencies, unclear or poorly targeted offence provisions, and restrictive liability doctrines. There is evidence that some of these factors have hindered the development of corporate criminal liability in England and Wales. This has led to the perception that corporate criminal liability is a novel idea and one that needs justification, despite the fact that it has been recognised in a number of contexts and in a number of forms since the 19th century.

C.2 The three main forms of corporate criminal liability that are recognised in common law (and in some civil law) jurisdictions are:

   (1)   Agency/Vicarious/strict

   (2)   Identification/direct

   (3)   Organisational/corporate culture

C.3 Not only are the lines between these blurred but the labels are uncertain and descriptively misleading. In particular I am not convinced that the term 'direct' liability is helpful, and I discuss this in section C.39 below. Some jurisdictions opt for the same model to apply to all offences while others (as in England and Wales) use different forms for different offence groups.

C.4 In addition to the three main forms or pillars there are two cross-cutting concepts, one inculpatory, the other exculpatory: they are respectively, failure to supervise and the defence of due diligence. The different forms of liability are explained in greater detail in Section IV below but it may be helpful to give a brief account of what is covered by the three forms here.

C.5 Agency or vicarious liability describes the situation where a company is liable for any offences committed by any of its employees. It is thus a broad principle. It is used for regulatory offences in England and Wales which do not require proof of mens rea, including those which have due diligence defences. It is used in some jurisdictions, notably for federal offences in the USA and in South Africa, for all offences.

---

[1]   The author is grateful to Jonathan Clough, Alice Morgan and Oliver Quick for their helpful comments on this paper.

C.6 Identification liability applies to all mens rea offences in England and Wales (except manslaughter).[2] Under it the corporation will be liable only when the offence has been committed by one of its directors or officers. It is thus very narrow.

C.7 Organisational/corporate culture principles are those which do not require proof of fault by an individual human actor. The leading example is found in the Australian Criminal Code Act (C'th) 1995 which applies to federal offences.[3]

C.8 Manslaughter (and homicide in Scotland) by corporations is now governed by the Corporate Manslaughter and Homicide Act 2007. This introduces the principle of 'senior management failure'. It has some affinity with identification liability because the definition of senior management is those persons who play a significant role in managing or organising a substantial part of the organisation's activities. It also has elements of 'organisational' liability in allowing the jury, when it decides whether there has been a gross breach of duty of care, to consider whether elements of corporate culture – attitudes, policies, systems or accepted practices- contributed to the failure to comply with health and safety legislation.[4]

Theoretical Considerations

Back to Basics

C.9 My aim in this section is to identify the key features that recur in any discussion of corporate criminal liability: corporate personality, corporate responsibility and corporate culture.

C.10 Corporate liability proceeds from the assumption that a corporation is a separate legal entity from its owners, or members, in other words that it is a *legal* (as opposed to human) person. The term 'legal person' includes but is not limited to business corporations or companies. It is used to cover any entity that is legally recognised as separate from its owners or members, and can include for example States, local authorities, and universities. Whether which or any should be subject to criminal law is a different question. Here I am concerned to clarify what it means to say that an entity is a legal person.

---

[2] With some exceptions. One way of putting is that identification liability applies where vicarious does not.

[3] Pt 2.5 This applies generally unless specifically exempted. For a list of statutes that have been amended in order to exempt offences - see J Hill 'Corporate Criminal Liability in Australia: an Evolving Corporate Governance Technique?' (2003) *Journal of Business Law* 1, fn 13

[4] Corporate Manslaughter and Corporate Homicide Act 2007, ss 1 and 8.

C.11   Hart opened his inaugural lecture with these words: "in law as elsewhere, we can know and yet not understand".[5] We use the word corporation but we find it hard to say what it means. It does not correspond with a known fact, or possess a useful synonym. Lying behind the question 'what is a corporation' is often the question 'should they be recognised in law'. It is the context in which we use words that matters. Even if we cannot find a satisfactory synonym, we can explain what the term means and this in its own way can be a definition.

C.12   Sometimes we want to describe (and therefore ascribe responsibility to) a corporation as a collection or aggregation of individuals and sometimes as a unified whole. Thus Hart suggests the better question is not 'what is a corporation?' but "Under what conditions do we refer to numbers and sequences of men as aggregates of individuals and under what conditions do we adopt instead unifying phrases extended by analogy from individuals?"[6]

C.13   This then leads to the conclusion that we cannot deduce whether, why or how, to hold a corporation liable for criminal conduct by defining what a company is. If we state that it is a mere fiction, or that it has no mind, and therefore cannot intend, we 'confuse the issue.'[7]

C.14   For present purposes the issue is *how* to hold a corporation responsible for an offence rather than *whether* to or *when* to. But Hart shows us that any or each of these issues is better approached unencumbered by the clutches of a simple – what is x? - definitional question.

A person or a thing

C.15   Legal personality confers on corporations in their own name the capacity to own property, to make contracts, sue and be sued in tort, and in some circumstances to be liable to criminal liability. It also enables the corporation to outlive its individual members, officers and employees, a characteristic that facilitates commerce but possibly hinders responsibility.

C.16   A corporation is, however, neither exclusively a 'person' nor a 'thing'.[8] The importance of this insight is, as Katsuhito Iwai argues, that there are two forms of ownership relation: the shareholders own the corporation, while the corporation in turn owns the corporate assets.[9] The corporation is both a *subject* holder of a property right – its assets- and an *object* of property rights – the interests of its shareholders, its owners. And it is the 'person/thing duality' that accounts for most of the confusion about the essence of a corporation.[10]

---

[5]   HLA. Hart 'Definition and Theory in Jurisprudence' (1954) 70 *Law Quarterly Review* 37. See also Hoffmann, Foreword in A Pinto and M Evans, *Corporate Criminal Liability* (2003), xiv.

[6]   HLA. Hart 'Definition and Theory in Jurisprudence' (1954) 70 *Law Quarterly Review* 37, 56.

[7]   HLA. Hart 'Definition and Theory in Jurisprudence' (1954) 70 *Law Quarterly Review* 37, 57.

[8]   Katsuhito Iwai 'Persons, Things and Corporations: the Corporate Personality Controversy and Comparative Corporate Governance. (1999) 47 *American Journal of Comparative Law* 583.

[9]   Katsuhito Iwai, "Persons, Things and Corporations: the Corporate Personality Controversy and Comparative Corporate Governance" (1999) 47 *American Journal of Comparative Law* 583, 592.

C.17 Organisations - of which corporations are an example - usually begin with a single instrumental purpose, that is they are the means to an end.[11] That end might be to further some political aim, to protect workers, or to make money from a particular activity. But they often become more like an end in themselves, preserving their existence in order to survive, and importantly acquiring an autonomous character, or as some have put it taking on a social reality. This is important because it shows us the error in seeing all corporations, or organisations, in the same light. It does not help to say that a corporation is 'only' a shell, a nominalism, any more than that the opposite is true, to say that a corporation is necessarily 'real'. Sometimes they are one, sometimes the other.

C.18 This discussion paves the way to the next step in the argument, that of responsibility.

Responsibility

C.19 So far, I have argued that we should try (although it is difficult) to shed preconceptions and assumptions that limit or in some way predetermine the very question that we seek to answer. That question is: by what methods can we attribute responsibility to corporations? It assists us in this to clarify that corporations are not always the same thing or the same type of person. This varies and cannot be pinned down without reference to context.

C.20 Responsibility is multi layered too. Harding, in his recent authoritative monograph, reminds us that responsibility means accountability or answerability.[12] He notes that:

> In so far as norms and standards necessarily impose obligations, responsibility is the allocating device which attaches such obligations to particular persons or subjects of the order in question.[13]

C.21 Responsibility is however an umbrella term under which shelter four different senses or meanings: role-responsibility, capacity–responsibility, causal-responsibility, and liability-responsibility.[14]

---

[10] Above, 593.

[11] C Harding, *Criminal Enterprise: Individuals, Organisations and Criminal Responsibility* (2007), ch 2. Harding distinguishes organisations of governance and representation from organisations of enterprise, although the categories may overlap. Here I am talking more of organisations of enterprise.

[12] C Harding *Criminal Enterprise: Individuals, Organisations and Criminal Responsibility* (2007) ch 5, quoting HLA Hart, *Punishment and Responsibility: Essays in the Philosophy of Law* (1968) p 265

[13] C Harding *Criminal Enterprise: Individuals, Organisations and Criminal Responsibility* (2007) p 103

[14] C Harding *Criminal Enterprise: Individuals, Organisations and Criminal Responsibility* (2007) ch 5, quoting HLA Hart *Punishment and Responsibility: Essays in the Philosophy of Law* (1968) ch IX. The discussion here is taken from C Harding *Criminal Enterprise: Individuals, Organisations and Criminal Responsibility* (2007) ch 5.

C.22   Role responsibility is a useful concept in the context of corporate liability. Not only do some individuals within organisations have specific roles or duties but organisations themselves may bear responsibility for an activity. An example here would be the owner of a ship or of an aeroplane. Owners of ships, planes and trains have responsibilities. Employers have responsibilities. Shipowners and employers can be individuals but they can also be corporations.

C.23   Capacity responsibility refers to the necessary attributes, rationality and awareness, to qualify as a responsible agent. This is often seen as the stumbling block to corporate or organisational liability for it appears to assume human cognition and volition. If we are to accept *the idea* of corporate responsibility, we must necessarily find a different way of expressing capacity than one that immediately precludes anything other than an individual human. While this is an argument that has underpinned the work of the increasing number of scholars in the field,[15] it is raised here in headline terms in order that it can be seen for what it is – an argument about one sort of thing – (human individuals) applied to another thing (corporate 'persons'). For a corporate person to be liable, a form of capacity that is relevant to the corporate person is required. The fact that the capacities relevant to humans are inappropriate is neither here nor there.

C.24   The third dimension, causal responsibility, is on one view merely the link between role and capacity responsibility and liability.[16] Thus if car driver X (role) has capacity (she is not attacked by a swarm of bees) and crashes into Y's property, she has caused damage, and she may be liable for causing damage. But on another view cause responsibility is more blurred, crossing into and affecting the assessment of capacity or role.[17] Car park attendant P negligently directs X to reverse into a parking place, causing her to damage another car. Has X caused that damage? Or was her role responsibility affected by the supervision of the attendant? As Harding states, such 'causal complexity can be seen very clearly in a situation involving both individual and organisational actors.'[18]

C.25   Liability responsibility is the culmination of the three senses of responsibility outlined above. Because establishing liability is the allocating device referred to earlier, it provides the raison d'être for, and is the purpose behind, establishing role, capacity and causal responsibility.

---

[15] LH Leigh, *The Criminal Liability of Corporations* (1969); B Fisse and J Braithwaite, *Corporations, Crime and Accountability* (1993); J Gobert and M Punch *Rethinking Corporate Crime* (2003); C Wells, *Corporations and Criminal Responsibility* (2001).

[16] Broadly the Hart and Honore view HLA Hart and T Honore, *Causation in the Law* (1968), see C Harding, *Criminal Enterprise: Individuals, Organisations and Criminal Responsibility* (2007) p 111.

[17] Broadly the Norrie view, A Norrie, "A Critique of Criminal Causation" (1991) 54 *Modern Law Review* 685.

[18] C Harding, *Criminal Enterprise: Individuals, Organisations and Criminal Responsibility* (2007) p 111.

Corporate Actors and Corporate Culture

C.26 The third key feature is that of the organisation as an autonomous actor, one that 'transcends specific individual contributions'.[19]

> Theories of organizations tend to confirm that it is right to think of the corporation as a real entity; they tell us something about how decisions are made and the relationship between the individual, the organization, and wider social structures. [20]

C.27 Acceptance of the corporation as an organisational actor in its own right is similar to that of the State in international law.[21] Harding suggests four conditions for autonomous action: an organisational rationality (decision-making); an irrelevance of persons (that human actors occupy roles and can be replaced in those roles); a structure and capacity for autonomous action (physical infrastructure and a recognisable identity); and a representative role (that it exists for a purpose, the pursuit of common goals).[22]

C.28 As Clough explains, the personality or culture of a corporation is unique, and arises from a number of identifiable characteristics which include the corporation's structure, goals, training provisions, compliance systems, reactions to past violations, incentives and remedial steps: 'These are all matters which are under the control of those who manage the organisation.'[23]

Models of Liability – Preliminary matters

C.29 I have devoted some space to a discussion of the corporate entity, of the meanings of responsibility and the concept of corporate culture, in order to lay the foundations for the central task of this paper, to explore models of liability that can be applied to corporations.

C.30 We have seen that corporations are not readily definable other than through an explanation of their context. This explains why they have often been subjected to metaphorical flights, likened to the functioning of human beings. The dangers with this arise if we then begin to treat them *as if* they were human beings. In order to work out the ways in which a corporation, or organisation, can be said to be responsible, to have capacity, to have intention or be reckless or negligent, we need stipulative definitions. We do not need to be driven by some unattainable idea of what a corporation actually *is* for that, as Hart showed, is the wrong question.

---

[19] C Harding, *Criminal Enterprise: Individuals, Organisations and Criminal Responsibility* (2007) pp 226 to 227; C Wells, *Corporations and Criminal Responsibility* (2001) ch 4.

[20] C Wells, *Corporations and Criminal Responsibility* (2001) p 151.

[21] C Wells and J Elias, "Catching the Conscience of the King: Corporate Players on the International Stage", in P Alston (ed), *Non State Actors and Human Rights* (2005) p 155.

[22] C Harding, *Criminal Enterprise: Individuals, Organisations and Criminal Responsibility* (2007) ch 9

23 J Clough, "Bridging the Theoretical Gap: The Search for a Realist Model of Corporate Criminal Liability" (2007) 18 *Criminal Law Forum* 267, 275 to 276 and accompanying notes.

C.31   The models are routes to liability for offences – they are not the offences themselves. Corporate liability does not create offences where there were none before; it provides tracks that enable legal actors that are not human beings to be answerable for criminal offences.

C.32   The Allens Arthur Robinson Report[24] identifies a number of 'design issues' that any scheme should address. These include:

        (a)   Is liability generic or specific?

        (b)   What is the relationship between the physical actor and the corporation?

        (c)   On whose fault is corporate liability based?

        (d)   What is the relationship between the prosecution of corporation and the/any individual?

C.33   Design issue (a) is addressed in the following section; (b), (c), and (d) in section IV below.

Schemes

C.34   Before describing in more detail the current approach to corporate liability in England and Wales in paragraphs C.47 to C.59 below, it is useful to consider the *scope* of liability schemes adopted, both in common law jurisdictions and others.[25] By scheme I mean whether corporate liability operates as a general principle across offences or whether it is developed offence by offence. General liability schemes then sub-divide into those which have the same model whatever the type of offence and those that employ different models depending on the fault element of the offence. It is worth emphasising that there is a range of different schemes across common law jurisdictions.

C.35   The following schemes can be identified:

    (1)   General liability scheme

    (2)   Generic- applies to all offences

    (3)   Different models apply to different offence types

    (4)   Offence specific scheme

---

[24] Allens Arthur Robinson (for the United Nations Special Representative of the Secretary-General on Human Rights and Business), *'Corporate Culture' as a basis for the criminal liability of corporations* (February 2008) p 62.

[25] The most comprehensive survey I have found is in Allens Arthur Robinson (for the United Nations Special Representative of the Secretary-General on Human Rights and Business), *'Corporate Culture' as a basis for the criminal liability of corporations* (February 2008). See also S Adam, N Colette-Basecqz and M Nihoul (eds), *Corporate Criminal Liability in Europe* (2008).

C.36 Most jurisdictions adopt a general liability scheme. Many have a generic – one size fits all – model that applies to all types of offence. So for example the USA, Austria, Belgium, France, and South Africa apply the same model whatever the type of offence. (Scheme type a. i). Australia (C'th) and Canada on the other hand have a general liability scheme but apply different models according to the fault element of the offence (Scheme type a. ii).[26] It is thus possible to develop a relatively simple scheme which caters for the full range of types of offences within it (as in Australia and Canada). This has the advantage that the jurisprudence in relation to corporate liability can develop independently of other principles of criminal liability.

C.37 England and Wales has a complex scheme combining both different liability models applying to types of offence (a. ii) together with some exempt offences to which specific rules apply (b.).[27] Examples of b. are the stand alone offence of corporate manslaughter and the Law Commission proposal in relation to bribery.

Typology

C.38 Typology here refers to the different types of corporate liability models that can be adopted within any of these schemes, whether a general scheme, or one developed for specific offences. The three broad approaches to corporate liability were briefly outlined in paragraphs C.5 to C.7 above. The labels commonly attached to them are sometimes unhelpful if taken too literally. Because their meaning is generally understood I have continued to use labels 'vicarious/strict' and 'identification' in what follows but they should be seen as labels rather than descriptively accurate terms.

C.39 But first it is worth considering whether 'direct', which is often attached to the identification principle, is a helpful qualification. It is useful to distinguish between derivative models that require proof of an individual's wrongful conduct and those which are 'corporate' or holistic. But 'direct' liability is sometimes used to describe identification liability or even to explain the basis of employers' liability. Whether the corporation is liable though a doctrine of vicarious agency, or failure to supervise, or identification with senior officers or a corporate culture, it is the corporation that is being held liable. All organisational liability presupposes an organisational agent or actor (see paragraphs C.26 to C.28 above). Holding a corporation liable is separate and distinguishable from any liability for the human actions that have contributed to the realisation of the organisational liability. Different corporate liability models produce different outcomes but these differences are not to do with 'directness.'

---

[26] Switzerland is also an example: Penal Code Art 1 covers all offences, while Art 2 addresses specified offences- criminal organisation, financing terrorism, money laundering, and corruption. See Heine 'Criminal Liability of Enterprises in Switzerland' in S Adam, N Colette-Basecqz and M Nihoul (eds), *Corporate Criminal Liability in Europe* (2008).

[27] It could be argued that this is so in Australia too since the Australian Criminal Code Act's application has been exempted from a number of key federal statutes which have their own models of liability, see J Hill, "Corporate Criminal Liability in Australia: an Evolving Corporate Governance Technique?" (2003) *Journal of Business Law* 1. However, the Australian Code does provide a broad unifying starting point for non exempt federal offences.

Attribution Models

Conduct attribution

C.40   The second design issue drawn from the Allens Arthur Robinson Report - what is the relationship between the physical actor and the corporation? - highlights the importance of establishing a link between the corporation and the physical element of any offence.[28] Depending on the offence definition the physical element can be an act or an omission. Large organisations, including corporations, implement their activities through individual employees. In anticipation of the potential difficulties in showing how an organisation causes a result the Law Commission in its proposals for corporate manslaughter included an explanatory provision that a management failure 'may be regarded as a cause of a person's death notwithstanding that the immediate cause is the act of omission of an individual.' [29]

C.41   The government argued during the scrutiny of the draft Corporate Manslaughter Bill in 2005 that causation is no longer a difficult issue in criminal law. However, both in civil and in criminal law causation is fraught with problems. The House of Lords, in quashing a conviction for manslaughter, recently commented that "Causation is not a single unvarying concept to be mechanically applied without regard to the context in which the question arises".[30]

C.42   Similarly, for offences that are conduct rather than result based, the person whose physical act or conduct led to the commission of an offence may be quite different from the person, or persons, at fault. The person at fault may indeed be the legal person. That is the question that liability models seek to answer- should the route be derived from individuals or is there an organisational or corporate culture?

C.43   The solution to this is both simple and uncontroversial. It is simple because a provision such as that proposed by the Law Commission for causation can be provided.

C.44   A more general provision, as in the Australian Criminal Code Act 1995 would cover all situations:

> If a physical element of an offence is committed by an employee, agent or officer of a body corporate acting within the actual or apparent scope of his employment, or within his or her actual or apparent authority, the physical act must also be attributed to the body corporate.[31]

---

[28] The UN Report is ambiguous here between the physical (ie human) *actor* and the physical *act*. Here my emphasis is on the latter.

[29] Involuntary Manslaughter (1996) Law Com No 237, para 8.39.

[30] *R v Kennedy* [2007] UKHL 38, [2007] 3 WLR 612.

[31] Australian Criminal Code Act 1995, Part 2.5, s 12.2.

C.45 The Canadian Criminal Code incorporates equivalent provisions in the sections dealing with, respectively, negligence and fault offences by corporations.[32]

C.46 It is uncontroversial because it was implicit in the early vicarious/agency cases that the physical act was attributed to the corporation. It was also implicit in the anthropomorphic metaphor that underlay the identification doctrine which saw the 'directing mind and will' as the brains of the company and the workers as the body and hands.[33]

Fault Attribution

VICARIOUS ROUTE

C.47 While I have argued above that a provision in relation to the physical element of the offence will avoid any doubt, the real stumbling block to corporate liability has been the perceived difficulty in releasing the fault element from its individualistic anchor.

C.48 Developed from the master's civil responsibility for his servant (*respondeat superior*), vicarious liability imputes to the corporation the wrongs committed by employees in the course of their employment and for the intended benefit of the employer. As a matter of statutory interpretation in England and Wales, strict liability offences generally give rise to the application of this principle, including those that have a reverse burden defence. It has in rare cases been held to include offences requiring proof of knowledge.

C.49 The Health and Safety at Work Act 1974 provides an interesting example. Section 3 imposes a duty "to ensure, so far as is reasonably practicable, the health, safety and welfare at work of all his employees". It is an offence under section 33 "to fail to discharge" this duty.[34] As recently explained in the House of Lords, the duty to ensure health and safety of employees is not absolute. It describes "a result which the employer must achieve or prevent... . If that result is not achieved the employer will be in breach of his statutory duty, unless he can show that it was not reasonably practicable for him to do more than was done to satisfy it."[35]

C.50 In *R v British Steel*[36] the Court of Appeal held that section 3 imposed a strict, or vicarious, liability. The company could not escape liability by showing that, at a senior level, it had taken steps to ensure safety if, at the operating level, all reasonably practicable steps had not been taken. The company, in other words, falls to be judged not on its words but its actions, including the actions of all its employees.

---

[32] Canadian Criminal Code, s 22.1(a) and s 22.2.

[33] *HL Bolton (Engineering) Co Ltd v TJ Graham and Sons Ltd* [1957] 1 QB 159, 172 by Lord Denning.

[34] Section 40 of the Health and Safety at Work Act 1974 provides that the onus in on the employer to show that all reasonably practicable steps have been taken.

[35] *R v Chargot* [2008] UKHL 73, [2009] 1 WLR 1 at [17] by Lord Hope.

[36] [1995] 1 WLR 1356.

C.51   A number of other cases have taken a similar line.[37] [There is some debate about the appropriateness of the term 'vicarious' liability for the liability is a personal one owed by the employer. However, this is largely a distinction without a difference. Whether it is a personal or a vicarious liability, (that is, whether the company is liable because it has breached its duty personally or because an employee has done a wrongful act), the breach has to come about through human agency. "The difference seems highly formalistic: one did not impute liability from agent to principal; rather, one decided that agent and principal were the same person."[38]]

C.52   Although the vicarious/agency principle is usually confined to strict liability or hybrid offences, exceptions are found. In particular, following the Privy Council decision in *Meridian,* analysis of the language of the provisions, their content and policy, should be undertaken to establish the persons whose state of mind can be attributed to the corporation in statutory offences requiring proof of knowledge.[39] This echoes a long line of 19th and early 20th century cases saying much the same thing.[40]

IDENTIFICATION ROUTE

C.53   This assumes a layer of senior officers within the company who are seen as its 'brains' and whose acts are identified as those of the company; the corporation both acts and thinks only through their human agency.[41]

C.54   The identification doctrine has been described as

> highly unsatisfactory, mainly because it fails to reflect corporate blameworthiness. To prove fault on the part of one managerial representative of a company is not to show that the company was at fault as a company but merely that one representative was at fault.[42]

C.55   In many large organisations, task specialisation means that, even amongst officers senior enough to count for alter ego purposes, one individual director will not have access to all the information on which to base a finding of knowledge or negligence. The drawbacks have been well rehearsed in Law Commission and other reports.[43]

---

[37] *R v Associated Octel* [1996] 1 WLR 1543; *R v Gateway Foodmarkets* [1997] IRLR 189 (a case under section 2 of the Health and Safety at Work Act 1974.)

[38] JC Coffee, "Corporate Criminal Liability" in A Eser, G Heine and B Huber (eds) *Criminal Responsibility of Legal and Collective Entities* (1999) p 15.

[39] *Meridian Global Funds Management Asia Ltd v Security Commission* [1995] 2 AC 500.

[40] C Wells, *Corporations and Criminal Responsibility* (2001) p 90.

[41] *Tesco Supermarkets v Nattrass* [1972] AC 153, *Attorney-General's Reference (no 2 of 1999)* [2000] QB 796.

[42] B Fisse and J Braithwaite, *Corporations, Crime and Accountability* (1993) p 47.

[43] Involuntary Manslaughter (1994) Law Commission Consultation Paper, Involuntary Manslaughter (1996) Law Com No 237; Home Office, *Corporate Manslaughter: The Government's Draft Bill for Reform* (March 2005) Cm 6497; House of Commons Home Affairs and Work and Pensions Committees, *Draft Corporate Manslaughter Bill* Vol 1 Report HC 540-1, p 7.

C.56   This continues to have a firm hold on non- regulatory offences requiring proof of fault (including negligence) in the UK.[44] Identification generally applies to offences needing proof of a mental element, but regulatory offences are sometimes treated differently as explained in paragraph C.52 above.

C.57   The continued application of this flawed doctrine to manslaughter led to the introduction of a separate, stand alone offence of corporate manslaughter. The Corporate Manslaughter and Corporate Homicide Act 2007 (CMCH Act) introduces a broader form of liability than identification. How broad, and how distinct from identification is open to debate, see paragraphs C.77 to C.81 below.

C.58   The CMCH Act specifically precludes individual liability. If the only way that a corporation can be liable is when those who manifestly direct its affairs have the role, capacity and causal responsibility for the offence, then their individual liability is as useful as that of the corporation.

C.59   The identification principle has been a major influence in common law and civil law developments.[45]

Organisational model

AUSTRALIA: CRIMINAL CODE ACT (C'TH) 1995

C.60   The recognition that corporations are autonomous actors, albeit operating through human interaction, has led to the search for organisational models of liability. We need now to put some flesh on these ideas.

C.61   The Australian federal Criminal Code Act 1995 is both the best known but also the most comprehensive example. I will use it as the template against which to compare reforms in other jurisdictions, including Finland, France, Switzerland, Canada, and the UK (corporate manslaughter).

C.62   It is described by the OECD Bribery Group as

> ambitious and progressive … in particular liability based on a corporate culture conducive to the criminal conduct in question. The lead examiners regard section 12 as a commendable development, and well-suited to prosecutions for foreign bribery.[46]

C.63   This should not be taken to mean that it is unsuitable for other offences, the comment merely reflects the terms of reference of the Bribery group.

---

[44]   Scotland and Northern Ireland adopt the same approach as England and Wales. Canada captures a wider range of personnel using the term 'senior officers'. Criminal Code 2003 s 2.

[45]   M Pieth, "Article 2: The Responsibility of Legal Persons" in M Pieth, LA Low and PJ Cullen (eds) *The OECD Convention on Bribery: A Commentary* (2007).

[46]   OECD (Directorate for Financial and Enterprise Affairs), *Australia: Phase 2: Report on the Application of the Convention on Combating Bribery of Foreign Public Officials in International Business Transactions and the 1997 Recommendations on Combating Bribery in International Business Transactions* (4 January 2006), para 148.

OFFENCES OF INTENTION, KNOWLEDGE, RECKLESSNESS

C.64 The relevant sections are set out in full in the Appendix but this summary by the OECD is a useful starting point:

> It provides that "bodies corporate" are liable for offences committed by "an employee, agent or officer of a body corporate acting within the actual or apparent scope of his or her employment, or within his or her actual or apparent authority" where the body corporate "expressly, tacitly, or impliedly authorised or permitted the commission of the offence".:

> Section 12 is generally detailed enough to enable companies to know with adequate precision what conduct is prohibited.[47]

C.65 The headline principle in the Australian scheme is 'authorisation or permission'. This can be express or tacit.

C.66 Authorisation or permission by the body corporate may be established in four different ways.

(1) The board of directors intentionally, knowingly or recklessly carried out the conduct, or expressly, tacitly or impliedly authorised or permitted it to occur;[48] or

(2) A high managerial agent intentionally, knowingly or recklessly carried out the conduct, or expressly, tacitly or impliedly authorised or permitted it to occur;[49]

C.67 These first two modes build on the identification principle including both its narrow (UK) and its broader form (the term 'high managerial agent' echoes, inter alia, those US States that have adopted the Model Penal Code,[50] and the Canadian Criminal Code Act).[51]

C.68 It is in the third and fourth modes of proving authorisation or permission that the ambition of the Code is realised.

(3) iii. 'proving that a corporate culture existed within the body corporate that directed, encouraged, tolerated or led to non-compliance with the relevant provision';[52] or

---

[47] OECD (Directorate for Financial and Enterprise Affairs), *Australia: Phase 2: Report on the Application of the Convention on Combating Bribery of Foreign Public Officials in International Business Transactions and the 1997 Recommendations on Combating Bribery in International Business Transactions* (4 January 2006).

[48] s. 12.3 (2) (a)

[49] s. 12.3 (2) (b)

[50] A.L.I. Model Penal Code, para. 2.07 (Proposed Official Draft 1962), see JC Coffee, "Corporate Criminal Liability" in A Eser, G Heine and B Huber (eds) *Criminal Responsibility of Legal and Collective Entities* (1999) p 21.

[51] Although this latter uses 'senior officer' rather than 'high managerial agent', Criminal Code S 22.

[52] S 12.3 (2) (c)

(4)   iv. 'proving that the body corporate failed to create and maintain a corporate culture that required compliance with the relevant provision'.[53]

C.69   'Corporate culture' means an attitude, policy, rule, course of conduct or practice.[54] The factors relevant to the application of corporate culture include:

(a) whether authority to commit an offence of the same or a similar character had been given by a high managerial agent of the body corporate; and

(b) whether the employee, agent or officer of the body corporate who committed the offence believed on reasonable grounds, or entertained a reasonable expectation, that a high managerial agent of the body corporate would have authorised or permitted the commission of the offence.[55]

C.70   Where route ii) (proof of fault in a high managerial agent) is relied upon there is a reverse burden defence of due diligence.[56]

NEGLIGENCE OFFENCES:

C.71   These are dealt with in section 12. (4). If no individual employee, agent or officer can be shown to have been negligent it is possible to look to the conduct of the company as a whole by aggregating conduct. And negligence may be evidenced by the fact that the prohibited conduct was substantially attributable to:

inadequate corporate management, control or supervision or failure to provide adequate systems for conveying relevant information to relevant persons.[57]

Definitions

C.72   'Board of directors' means the body exercising executive authority; 'high managerial agent' means an employee, agent or officer with duties of such responsibility that their conduct may fairly be assumed to represent the body corporate's policy.[58]

---

[53]   S 12.3 (2) (d)

[54]   S 12.3.(6).

[55]   S 12.(3) 4.

[56]   S 12.3.(3)

[57]   Paraphrase taken from J Clough and C Mulhern, *The Prosecution of Corporations* (2002) p 147.

[58]   S. 12.3.(6). The definition of corporate culture is found here also.

Summary

C.73 The Australian Criminal Code Act is thus comprehensive in its scope. It recognises the organisational and structural variety in corporations and the range of circumstances in which wrongdoing might arise. It does not reject the traditional routes of attribution but reconceptualises them through the over-arching concept of authorisation and permission and then provides additional routes (including corporate culture) to proving such authorisation.

Variants

C.74 The previous section outlined the three main models available for a general route to corporate liability. The three need not be mutually exclusive as the Australian Criminal Code Act demonstrates. There are several variants within the main models.

Canada

C.75 The Canadian Criminal Code for example deploys a wider version of the identification principle than in the UK. It defines two layers within the company: representatives and senior officers. Representatives include directors, partners, employees and agents. Senior officers, a sub-set of representatives, are those who play 'an important role in the establishment of an organization's policies or are responsible for managing an important aspect of its activities, and include directors, the chief executive officer and the chief financial officer.[59]

C.76 For offences requiring proof of fault (other than negligence), corporate liability arises when a senior officer:

(1) is party to the offence, or

(2) has the mental state to be party and directs representatives to act or omit as required by the offence or

(3) knowing a representative is about to commit the offence, fails to take all reasonable measure to stop them.[60]

C.77 For negligence offences, liability is a qualified vicarious model. The organisation is party to the offence if one or more representatives have engaged in the relevant conduct and the senior officers responsible have departed markedly from the standard of care that could be reasonably expected to prevent the offence.[61] This bears some similarity to the liability regime in the Corporate Manslaughter and Corporate Homicide Act 2007.

---

[59] Criminal Code, s. 2

[60] S. 22. 2

[61] S. 22.1

UK -Corporate Manslaughter and Corporate Homicide Act 2007

C.78 The CMCH builds on but adapts in important respects the Law Commission's recommendations in its 1996 Report on Involuntary Manslaughter.[62] That Report recognised the need to develop an organisational route to liability and proposed 'management failure' as a model. The CMCH Act however qualifies this by restricting it to '*senior* management' and, possibly more significantly, links that back to individual managers.[63]

(1) Senior management are the 'persons who play significant roles' in decision making in relation to or actually manage the whole or a substantial part of the organisation's activities.[64]

(2) In addition, the way that senior management organises or manages its activities has to play a substantial element in the breach of duty leading to the death.

C.79 In considering whether there has been a gross breach of that duty the jury may consider "the extent to which the evidence shows that there were attitudes, policies, systems or accepted practices within the organisation that were likely to have encouraged any such failure [to comply with health and safety legislation] … or to have produced tolerance of it."[65] Because it only comes into play as a possible source of evidence for the jury in relation to one factor in the offence, it is clear that this provision, while its language is similar to that in the Australian Criminal Code's definition of corporate culture, is not a trigger for liability in the same way.

C.80 The CMCH Act is a complex specific offence provision. Although it began with the Law Commission's 'organisational' notion of management failure, it has transformed into something much closer to an expanded identification model. The mooring to an organisational concept was slipped when 'senior managers' were introduced in the Bill as initially presented to Parliament. The later amendment to 'senior management' did not overcome the problem. Not only does the definition of senior management refer to *persons*, but the word 'management' here plays a quite different grammatical role. When it is linked with 'failure' it qualifies failure, it describes a collective activity. When the word itself is qualified by 'senior' it is used as a collective noun.

C.81 In a somewhat paradoxical shift, the CMCH Act is also unusual in removing the possibility of secondary individual liability.[66]

---

[62] Involuntary Manslaughter (1996) Law Commission No 237.

[63] J Clough, "Bridging the Theoretical Gap: The Search for a Realist Model of Corporate Criminal Liability" (2007) 18 *Criminal Law Forum* 267, 293 to 298; C Wells, "Corporate Manslaughter: Why Does Reform Matter?" (2006) *South African Law Journal* 646; C Wells and D Thomas 'Deaths in the Dental Surgery: Individual and Organisational Criminal Liability' (2008) 204 *British Dental Journal* 497.

[64] S 1(4) (c).

[65] S 8 (3) (a)

[66] S 18

The Law Commission Bribery Proposal[67]

C.82 The Report proposes a stand alone offence of negligently failing to prevent bribery. The three elements of the offence would be:

    (1) A person performing services on the corporation's (the Report uses the term 'organisation') behalf commits an 'active' bribery offence, and

    (2) Another person connected with or employed by the corporation with responsibility for preventing bribery negligently fails to prevent the bribery, and

    (3) except where the negligent failure to prevent was on the part of a director or equivalent, the corporation would have a defence if it showed it had adequate procedures designed to prevent bribery being committed.

C.83 Were this to be adopted as the only route to corporate liability for these, or any other offences, it would considerably constrict liability. It does not relate easily to any of the three main recognised models for corporate liability. Not only must there be an identified person who has failed to prevent, but it would have to be proved that the failure was negligent. On top of that the corporation could show that it had procedures in place designed to prevent bribery.

Non common Law Jurisdictions

C.84 Amongst non common law jurisdictions there is also a wide variety of models. There are inherent dangers in merely reciting translated provisions from the Criminal Codes of unfamiliar jurisdictions, not least because differences in prosecutorial and sentencing procedures significantly affect all liability regimes.[68]

C.85 Finland for example deems any offence by management and employees on behalf of or for the benefit of the corporation as committed 'in the operations of a corporation'. The prerequisites for corporate liability for such offences are that a director or person with decision-making authority has allowed the offence, or if the care and diligence necessary to prevent the offence has not been observed in the operations of the corporation.[69]

---

[67] Reforming Bribery (2008) Law Com No 313, Part 6.

[68] The following sources include discussions of different countries' provisions: A Eser, G Heine and B Huber (eds), *Criminal Responsibility of Legal and Collective Entities* (1999); M Pieth, "Article 2 : The Responsibility of Legal Person" in M Pieth, LA Low and PJ Cullen (eds), *The OECD Convention on Bribery: A Commentary* (2007); Allens Arthur Robinson (for the United Nations Special Representative of the Secretary-General on Human Rights and Business), *'Corporate Culture' as a basis for the criminal liability of corporations* (February 2008); S Adam, N Colette-Basecqz and M Nihoul (eds) *Corporate Criminal Liability in Europe* (2008); and the OECD, *Country Reports on the Implementation of the OECD Anti-Bribery Convention*, http://www.oecd.org/document/24/0,3343,en_2649_34859_1933144_1_1_1_1,00.html (last visited 10 June 2010).

[69] Penal Code of Finland, chapter 9, s. 2, http://www.finlex.fi/pdf/saadkaan/E8890039.PDF, see Allens Arthur Robinson (for the United Nations Special Representative of the Secretary-General on Human Rights and Business), *'Corporate Culture' as a basis for the criminal liability of corporations* (February 2008), Appendix 6,

C.86   Switzerland imputes liability to corporations for offences that 'cannot be imputed to an identified physical Person by reason of the lack of organisation of the corporation.'[70] Some specified offences (including corruption, money laundering and financing terrorism) are attributed to the corporation if it can be said 'to have not taken all reasonable and necessary organisational measures to prevent' them.[71]

Encouraging compliance: Failure to supervise and due diligence

C.87   Vicarious liability, in which the corporations take legal responsibility for the actions of all its employees, is a familiar concept in tort. It was adapted from this to apply to strict liability offences in England and Wales, and to all offences in the federal jurisdiction of the United States. It can be tempered in a number of ways: through prosecutorial and sentencing discretion, through failure to supervise provisions, and through due diligence elements.

Prosecution discretion:

C.88   Health and safety and many other regulatory offences in the UK are prosecuted if not as last resort then generally only after other compliance mechanisms have failed.[72]

Sentencing discretion:

C.89   The US Federal Sentencing Guidelines are designed "so that the sanctions imposed upon organizations and their agents, taken together, will provide just punishment, adequate deterrence, and incentives for organizations to maintain internal mechanisms for preventing, detecting, and reporting criminal conduct."[73]

C.90   The Guidelines include the following principles: First, the court must, whenever practicable, order the organization to remedy any harm caused by the offense; second, the fine range for any other organization should be based on the seriousness of the offense and the culpability of the organization. Culpability generally will be determined by six factors that the sentencing court must consider.

C.91   The four factors that increase the ultimate punishment of an organization are:

(1)   the involvement in or tolerance of criminal activity;

(2)   the prior history of the organization;

(3)   the violation of an order; and

(4)   the obstruction of justice.

---

[70] Swiss Code Penal Art 102.1

[71] Art 102.2

[72] K Hawkins *Law as Last Resort: Prosecution Decision Making in a Regulatory Agency* (2002); N Gunningham and R Johnstone, *Regulating Workplace Safety: systems and sanctions* (1999).

[73] 2007 Federal Sentencing Guideline Manual Sentencing of Organizations, http://www.ussc.gov/2007guid/tabconchapt8.htm, Introductory Comments

C.92   The two factors that mitigate the ultimate punishment of an organization are:

(1)   the existence of an effective compliance and ethics program; and

(2)   self-reporting, cooperation, or acceptance of responsibility.

Failure to prevent/failure to supervise

C.93   The examples below have in the most part been described in more detail in earlier sections of this paper.

C.94   **Canada:** for negligence offences liability has two elements. Either one representative (which includes all employees) is party to the offence,[74] or the conduct of two or more representatives combined and the senior officer responsible departs markedly from the standard of care that could be reasonably expected to prevent a representative from being a party to the offence.[75]

C.95   Liability for all other fault offences requires proof of involvement of a senior officer, as a party to the offence, or directing others, or failing to take all reasonable measures to stop representatives whom they know are about to be a party the offence.[76]

Due diligence:

C.96   Due diligence, as Clough and Mulhern note, "is not a concept susceptible of precise definition and there is much uncertainty concerning requirements necessary to satisfy the defence."[77] It is found in many statutory offence provisions such as the HSAW Act 1974. Failure to exercise due diligence is one route to liability in Finland, see paragraph C.85.[78] It also appears in the Australian Criminal Code Act as a defence to the high managerial route to proving corporate authorisation or permission, see paragraph C.66.

C.97   The requirements for demonstrating due diligence (distilled from Australian and Canadian case law) include:

(1)   A suitable system to ensure compliance (the fact that it has not prevented the breach does not necessarily mean it was unsuitable),

(2)   Adequate supervision and monitoring

(3)   Showing that no reasonable precautions could have been taken'

---

[74] The Criminal Code brings all organisational liability under the umbrella of parties to offences.

[75] S. 22.1.

[76] S. 22.2 (c)

[77] Above n. 57, at p 149. In addition, punishment may be waived if the omission is 'slight'.

[78] Penal Code of Finland, Chapter 9, s. 4

Conformity with industry standards is not necessarily sufficient to show due diligence.[79]

C.98 These examples show that there are numerous ways in which the cross cutting concepts of failure to supervise and lack of due diligence can be expressed. An unusual combination of failure to prevent and due diligence defence is proposed by the Law Commission in relation to bribery offences, see paragraph C.82 above.

Summary

C.99 How can criminal law accommodate the corporation? This question has been taxing lawyers for well over a century. When it was first asked the business corporation was a much less sophisticated instrument than now and played a less central role in national and global economies. Nonetheless the legal adaptation has not kept pace. There remains, in England and Wales, a patchwork of answers, in fact more of a collection of cut out pieces waiting to be sorted before being sewn together to make a coherent structure, than a joined up article.

C.100 Somewhat paradoxically it has been in statutory interpretation rather than in the development of common law principles of attribution, that the courts have been most responsive to the social and economic context of business operations. There is increased recognition that regulatory offences are concerned to prevent harms just as, often more, threatening to health and welfare than many so-called 'real' crimes. An unsafe mine or steelworks can damage employees and the public in ways that bear no comparison with Saturday night pub violence. A corrupt corporation can similarly wreak damage to the economy that place a professional shoplifter in the shade.

C.101 The variety in corporate form, reach and activity take together with the extensive range of criminal laws require a flexible response in terms of corporate liability models. The vicarious model assumes that all employees contribute to the corporate goal. This is a good starting point but a blunt instrument in terms of encouraging or rewarding the development of effective compliance policies. It is better combined with a due diligence defence. The identification model is not appropriate as a single model. On their own neither of these models is a solution. They are better conceived as part of a broader organisational model.

C.102 There are circumstances where the senior officers or managers of a corporation are themselves to blame for illegal corporate behaviour. It is important that any system provides for this. Although individual liability has been outside my remit, it is important to note that corporate liability in such a case should not replace individual liability.

---

[79] J Clough and C Mulhern, *The Prosecution of Corporations* (2002) pp 154 to 155.

Table 1: Liability Models

Model	Jurisdiction	Variants
Vicarious / agency	UK strict liability offences	UK: regulatory reverse burden offences. Reas practicable / other due diligence defences.
		US federal: all offences. Due diligence applies at the sentencing stage.
	South Africa: all offences.	
		Austria: due diligence.
Identification	UK: fault based offences except manslaughter	US: some states.
		US some states (Model Penal Code)
		Canada: senior officers.
		France: organs and representatives.
Organisational	Australia (C'th): 'authorisation or permission'	Due diligence defence relevant where high managerial agent responsible for authorisation/permission.
Failure to prevent	England and Wales proposed for bribery Switzerland – specified offences.	With due diligence defence

FURTHER INFORMATION

Australia Criminal Code Act 1995

Part 2.5 – Corporate Criminal Responsibility

DIVISION 12 GENERAL PRINCIPLES

12.1(1) This Code applies to bodies corporate in the same way as it applies to individuals. It so applies with such modifications as are set out in this Part, and with such other modifications as are made necessary by the fact that criminal liability is being imposed on bodies corporate rather than individuals.

(2) A body corporate may be found guilty of any offence, including one punishable by imprisonment. Note: Section 4B of the Crimes Act 1914 enables a fine to be imposed for offences that only specify imprisonment as a penalty.

Physical elements

12.2 If a physical element of an offence is committed by an employee, agent or officer of a body corporate acting within the actual or apparent scope of his or her employment, or within his or her actual or apparent authority, the physical element must also be attributed to the body corporate.

Fault elements other than negligence

12.3(1) If intention, knowledge or recklessness is a fault element in relation to a physical element of an offence, that fault element must be attributed to a body corporate that expressly, tacitly or impliedly authorised or permitted the commission of the offence.

(2) The means by which such an authorisation or permission may be established include:

> (a) proving that the body corporate's board of directors intentionally, knowingly or recklessly carried out the relevant conduct, or expressly, tacitly or impliedly authorised or permitted the commission of the offence; or

> (b) proving that a high managerial agent of the body corporate intentionally, knowingly or recklessly engaged in the relevant conduct, or expressly, tacitly or impliedly authorised or permitted the commission of the offence; or

> (c) proving that a corporate culture existed within the body corporate that directed, encouraged, tolerated or led to non-compliance with the relevant provision; or

> (d) proving that the body corporate failed to create and maintain a corporate culture that required compliance with the relevant provision.

(3) Paragraph (2)(b) does not apply if the body corporate proves that it exercised due diligence to prevent the conduct, or the authorisation or permission.

(4) Factors relevant to the application of paragraph (2)(c) or (d) include:

(a) whether authority to commit an offence of the same or a similar character had been given by a high managerial agent of the body corporate; and

(b) whether the employee, agent or officer of the body corporate who committed the offence believed on reasonable grounds, or entertained a reasonable expectation, that a high managerial agent of the body corporate would have authorised or permitted the commission of the offence.

(5) If recklessness is not a fault element in relation to a physical element of an offence, subsection (2) does not enable the fault element to be proved by proving that the board of directors, or a high managerial agent, of the body corporate recklessly engaged in the conduct or recklessly authorised or permitted the commission of the offence.

(6) In this section:

"board of directors" means the body (by whatever name called) exercising the executive authority of the body corporate;

"corporate culture" means an attitude, policy, rule, course of conduct or practice existing within the body corporate generally or in the part of the body corporate in which the relevant activities takes place;

"high managerial agent" means an employee, agent or officer of the body corporate with duties of such responsibility that his or her conduct may fairly be assumed to represent the body corporate's policy.

Negligence

12.4(1) The test of negligence for a body corporate is that set out in section 5.5.

(2) If:

(a) negligence is a fault element in relation to a physical element of an offence; and

(b) no individual employee, agent or officer of the body corporate has that fault element; that fault element may exist on the part of the body corporate if the body corporate's conduct is negligent when viewed as a whole (that is, by aggregating the conduct of any number of its employees, agents or officers).

(3) Negligence may be evidenced by the fact that the prohibited conduct was substantially attributable to:

(a) inadequate corporate management, control or supervision of the conduct of one or more of its employees, agents or officers; or

(b) failure to provide adequate systems for conveying relevant information to relevant persons in the body corporate. Mistake of fact (strict liability)

12.5(1) A body corporate can only rely on section 9.2 (mistake of fact (strict liability)) in respect of conduct that would, apart from this section, constitute an offence on its part if:

(a) the employee, agent or officer of the body corporate who carried out the conduct was under a mistaken but reasonable belief about facts that, had they existed, would have meant that the conduct would not have constituted an offence; and

(b) the body corporate proves that it exercised due diligence to prevent the conduct.

(2) A failure to exercise due diligence may be evidenced by the fact that the prohibited conduct was substantially attributable to:

(a inadequate corporate management, control or supervision of the conduct of one or more of its employees, agents or officers; or

(b) failure to provide adequate systems for conveying relevant information to relevant persons in the body corporate. Intervening conduct or event

12.6 A body corporate cannot rely on section 10.1 (intervening conduct or event) in respect of a physical element of an offence brought about by another person if the other person is an employee, agent or officer of the body corporate.

Austria[80]

Section 1 ...

(2) For the purpose of this statute entities shall mean corporations, general and limited commercial partnerships [*Personenhandelsgesellschaften*], registered partnerships [*Eingetragene Erwerbesgesellschaften*] and European Economic Interest Groupings.

(3) For the purpose of this statute the following shall not be entities:

1. a (deceased person's) estate;

2. the federal state, provinces and municipalities and other corporations to the extent they enforce laws;

3. recognised churches, religious societies and religious communities to the extent they are engaged in pastoral care.

DECISION MAKERS AND STAFF

Section 2

(1) For the purpose of this statute decision maker shall mean a person who

1. is a managing director, an executive board member or *Prokurist* [translator's note: compare: authorised officer] or who is authorised in a comparable manner to represent the entity vis-à-vis third parties either according to statutory power of representation or based upon contract,

2. is a member of the supervisory board or board of directors or otherwise exercises controlling powers in a leading position, or

3. otherwise exercises relevant influence on the management of the entity.

(2) For the purpose of this Statute staff shall mean a person who works for the entity

1. on the basis of an employment relationship, apprentice relationship or other training relationship,

2. on the basis of a relationship that is subject to the provisions of the Outwork Act [*Heimarbeitsgesetz*] 1960, BGBl. [Federal Law Gazette] No. 105/1961 or that is of an employee-like status,

---

[80] Translation from German. Adopted by the *Nationalrat* (upper chamber of the Austrian Parliament) on 28 September 2005. In force 1 January 2006.

3. as an employee provided on a temporary basis as defined in Section 3 para 4 of the Act on Temporary Provision of Employees [*Arbeitskräfteüberlassungsgesetz – AÜG*], BGBl. No. 196/1988, or

4. on the basis of a service relationship or other special public-law relationship.

Chapter 2

RESPONSIBILITY OF ENTITIES – PROVISIONS RELATING TO SUBSTANTIVE LAW

RESPONSIBILITY

Section 3

(1) Subject to the additional conditions defined in paragraphs 2 or 3 an entity shall be responsible for a criminal offence if

1. the offence was committed for the benefit of the entity or

2. duties of the entity have been neglected by such offence.

(2) The entity shall be responsible for offences committed by a decision maker if the decision maker acted illegally and culpably.

(3) The entity shall be responsible for criminal offences of staff if

1. the facts and circumstances which correspond to the statutory definition of an offence have been realised in an illegal manner; the entity shall be responsible for an offence that requires wilful action only if a staff has acted with wilful intent, and for a criminal offence that requires negligent action only if a staff has failed to apply the due care required in the respective circumstances; and

2. commission of the offence was made possible or considerably easier due to the fact that decision makers failed to apply the due and reasonable care required in the respective circumstances, in particular by omitting to take material technical, organisational or staff-related measures to prevent such offences.

(4) Responsibility of an entity for an offence and criminal liability of decision makers or staff on grounds of the same offence shall not exclude each other.

...

LEGAL SUCCESSION

Section 10

(1) If the rights and obligations of the entity are transferred to another entity by way of universal succession, the legal consequences provided for in this Federal Statute shall apply to the legal successor. Legal consequences imposed on the legal predecessor shall also apply to the legal successor.

(2) Individual succession shall be deemed equivalent to universal succession if more or less the same ownership structure of the entity exists and the operation or activity is more or less continued.

(3) If there is more than one legal successor, a fine imposed on the legal predecessor may be enforced vis-à-vis any legal successor. Other legal consequences may be attributed to individual legal successors to the extent this is in line with their area of activities.

APPLICABILITY OF GENERAL CRIMINAL LAWS

Section 12

(1) For the rest, the general criminal laws shall also apply to entities unless they exclusively apply to natural persons.

Canada Criminal Code

PARTIES TO OFFENCES

21. (1) Every one is a party to an offence who

(*a*) actually commits it;

(*b*) does or omits to do anything for the purpose of aiding any person to commit it; or

(*c*) abets any person in committing it.

...

OFFENCES OF NEGLIGENCE — ORGANIZATIONS

22.1 In respect of an offence that requires the prosecution to prove negligence, an organization is a party to the offence if

(a) acting within the scope of their authority

(i) one of its representatives is a party to the offence, or

(ii) two or more of its representatives engage in conduct, whether by act or omission, such that, if it had been the conduct of only one representative, that representative would have been a party to the offence; and

(b) the senior officer who is responsible for the aspect of the organization's activities that is relevant to the offence departs — or the senior officers, collectively, depart — markedly from the standard of care that, in the circumstances, could reasonably be expected to prevent a representative of the organization from being a party to the offence.

OTHER OFFENCES — ORGANIZATIONS

22.2 In respect of an offence that requires the prosecution to prove fault — other than negligence — an organization is a party to the offence if, with the intent at least in part to benefit the organization, one of its senior officers

(a) acting within the scope of their authority, is a party to the offence;

(b) having the mental state required to be a party to the offence and acting within the scope of their authority, directs the work of other representatives of the organization so that they do the act or make the omission specified in the offence; or

(c) knowing that a representative of the organization is or is about to be a party to the offence, does not take all reasonable measures to stop them from being a party to the offence.

236 A 'representative' is defined in s2 to include directors, partners, employees, members, agents and contractors.

237 A 'senior officer' is defined in s2 as 'a representative who plays an important role in the establishment of an organization's

policies or is responsible for managing an important aspect of the organization's activities and, in the case of a body corporate, includes a director, its chief executive officer and its chief financial officer'.

...

732 (3.1) The court may prescribe, as additional conditions of a probation order made in respect of an organization, that the offender do one or more of the following:

(a) make restitution to a person for any loss or damage that they suffered as a result of the offence;

225

(b) establish policies, standards and procedures to reduce the likelihood of the organization committing a subsequent offence;

(c) communicate those policies, standards and procedures to its representatives;

(d) report to the court on the implementation of those policies, standards and procedures;

(e) identify the senior officer who is responsible for compliance with those policies, standards and procedures;

(f) provide, in the manner specified by the court, the following information to the public, namely,

> (i) the offence of which the organization was convicted,
>
> (ii) the sentence imposed by the court, and
>
> (iii) any measures that the organization is taking — including any policies, standards and procedures established under paragraph (*b*) — to reduce the likelihood of it committing a subsequent offence; and

(g) comply with any other reasonable conditions that the court considers desirable to prevent the organization from committing subsequent offences or to remedy the harm caused by the offence.

CONSIDERATION — ORGANIZATIONS

(3.2) Before making an order under paragraph (3.1)(*b*), a court shall consider whether it would be more appropriate for another regulatory body to supervise the development or implementation of the policies, standards and procedures referred to in that paragraph.

France Penal Code[81]

Article 121-2

ACT NO. 2000-647 OF 10 JULY ART 8 OFFICIAL JOURNAL OF 11 JULY 2000

Juridical persons, with the exception of the State, are criminally liable for the offences committed on their account by their organs or representatives, according to the distinctions set out in articles 121-4 and 121-7 and in the cases provided for by statute or regulations.

---

[81] http://www.legifrance.gouv.fr/html/codes_traduits/code_penal_textan.htm.

However, local public authorities and their associations incur criminal liability only for offences committed in the course of their activities which may be exercised through public service delegation conventions.

The criminal liability of legal persons does not exclude that of the natural persons who are perpetrators or accomplices to the same act, subject to the provisions of the fourth paragraph of article 121-3.

Article 121-3

ACT NO. 1996-393 OF 13 MAY 1996 ARTICLE 1 OFFICIAL JOURNAL OF 14 MAY 1996; ACT NO. 2000-647 OF 10 JULY ARTICLE 1 OFFICIAL JOURNAL OF 11 JULY 2000

There is no felony or misdemeanour in the absence of an intent to commit it.

However, the deliberate endangering of others is a misdemeanour where the law so provides.

A misdemeanour also exists, where the law so provides, in cases of recklessness, negligence, or failure to observe an obligation of due care or precaution imposed by any statute or regulation, where it is established that the offender has failed to show normal diligence, taking into consideration where appropriate the nature of his role or functions, of his capacities and powers and of the means then available to him.

In the case as referred to in the above paragraph, natural persons who have not directly contributed to causing the damage, but who have created or contributed to create the situation which allowed the damage to happen who failed to take steps enabling it to be avoided, are criminally liable where it is shown that they have broken a duty of care or precaution laid down by statute or regulation in a manifestly deliberate manner, or have committed a specified piece of misconduct which exposed another person to a particularly serious risk of which they must have been aware.

There is no petty offence in the event of *force majeure*.

UK Corporate Manslaughter and Corporate Homicide Act 2007

1 The offence

(1) An organisation to which this section applies is guilty of an offence if the way in which its activities are managed or organised—

> (a) causes a person's death, and

> (b) amounts to a gross breach of a relevant duty of care owed by the organisation to the deceased.

(2) The organisations to which this section applies are—

(a) a corporation;

(b) a department or other body listed in Schedule 1;

(c) a police force;

(d) a partnership, or a trade union or employers' association, that is an employer.

(3) An organisation is guilty of an offence under this section only if the way in which its activities are managed or organised by its senior management is a substantial element in the breach referred to in subsection (1).

(4) For the purposes of this Act—

(a) "relevant duty of care" has the meaning given by section 2, read with sections 3 to 7;

(b) a breach of a duty of care by an organisation is a "gross" breach if the conduct alleged to amount to a breach of that duty falls far below what can reasonably be expected of the organisation in the circumstances;

(c) "senior management", in relation to an organisation, means the persons who play significant roles in—

(i) the making of decisions about how the whole or a substantial part of its activities are to be managed or organised, or

(ii) the actual managing or organising of the whole or a substantial part of those activities.

...

8 Factors for jury

(1) This section applies where—

(a) it is established that an organisation owed a relevant duty of care to a person, and

(b) it falls to the jury to decide whether there was a gross breach of that duty.

(2) The jury must consider whether the evidence shows that the organisation failed to comply with any health and safety legislation that relates to the alleged breach, and if so—

(a) how serious that failure was;

(b) how much of a risk of death it posed.

(3) The jury may also—

(a) consider the extent to which the evidence shows that there were attitudes, policies, systems or accepted practices within the organisation that were likely to have encouraged any such failure as is mentioned in subsection (2), or to have produced tolerance of it;

(b) have regard to any health and safety guidance that relates to the alleged breach.

(4) This section does not prevent the jury from having regard to any other matters they consider relevant.

(5) In this section "health and safety guidance" means any code, guidance, manual or similar publication that is concerned with health and safety matters and is made or issued (under a statutory provision or otherwise) by an authority responsible for the enforcement of any health and safety legislation.

Switzerland

Art 102 Swiss Code Penal

1. A crime or a misdemeanour that is committed in a corporation in the exercise of commercial activities conforming to its objects is imputed to the corporation if it cannot be imputed to an identified physical person by reason of the lack of organisation of the corporation. In such a case, the corporation shall be punished with a maximum fine of five million francs.

2. In the case of a breach referred to in articles [money laundering, financing terrorism, corruption] the corporation is punished independently of the culpability of physical persons if the corporation can be said to have not taken all reasonable and necessary organisational measures to prevent such a breach.

3. The judge shall fix the fine, in particular, according to the gravity of the breach, the lack of the organisation and the damage caused, and in accordance with the economic capacity of the corporation.

APPENDIX D
IMPACT ASSESSMENT

INTRODUCTION

Background to the problem

D.1 Since 1997, more than 3000 criminal offences have come on to the statute book. Putting that in context, and taking a longer perspective, Halsbury's Statutes of England and Wales has four volumes devoted to criminal law. Volume 1 covers the offences created in the 637 years between 1351 and 1988. Volume 1 is 1382 pages long. Volumes 2 to 4 cover the offences created in the 19 years between 1989 and 2008. Volumes 2 to 4 are 3746 pages long. So, more than two and a half times as many pages were needed in Halsbury's Statutes to cover offences created in the 19 years between 1989 and 2008 than were needed to cover the offences created in the 637 years prior to that. Moreover, it is unlikely that the Halsbury volumes devoted to 'criminal law' capture all offences. These figures must be set alongside ways in which it has become easier for criminal offences to be created. It is now common for a statute to provide that criminal offences can be created by regulation, at the suggestion of regulatory authorities, rather than setting out that offence itself. As secondary legislation is easier to create than primary legislation, it has become correspondingly easier to create ever more criminal offences.

D.2 The project stems from a request made to the Law Commission jointly by the Ministry of Justice (MoJ) and the department for Business, Innovation and Skills in 2009. The primary focus is the use of the criminal law in regulatory contexts. Very broadly speaking, regulatory contexts are contexts in which a measure of central or local government control is sought over methods or outcomes of, for example, waste disposal, farming, retail sales, transport or the maintenance of animal welfare. The paper suggests ways of reducing dependence on the criminal law in supporting the regulatory process.

The problem

D.3 The criminal process is commonly long drawn-out, relatively costly and may be ineffective. There are likely to be many instances in which non-criminal measures, such as fixed civil penalties or 'stop now' notices, will be a quicker, cheaper, more predictable and also a fairer response to wrongdoing in regulatory contexts than the use of the criminal process. It is suggested that criminal liability should be restricted in regulatory contexts mainly to cases where wrongdoing was intentional, reckless or dishonest.

Rationale

D.4 The conventional economic approach to government intervention to resolve a problem is based on efficiency or equity arguments. The Government may consider intervening if there are strong enough failures in the way markets operate (eg monopolies overcharging consumers) or if there are strong enough failures in existing government interventions (eg waste generated by misdirected rules). In both cases the proposed new intervention itself should avoid creating a further set of disproportionate costs and distortions. The Government may also intervene for equity (fairness) and redistributional reasons (eg to reallocate goods and services to the more needy groups in society).

D.5   It is failures in existing government intervention that are the subject of the current project. In other words, Government has in the past too frequently intervened through the use of the criminal law in regulatory contexts, generating a waste of resources on employing the criminal process. Achieving the goals set by the Consultation Paper's proposals could be achieved to a minimal degree without legislation, if Government departments simply undertake to use the criminal law in future only as suggested in the Consultation Paper, or if departments simply suspend the use of nominated criminal offences. However, reduction of the number of criminal offences currently in force would involve legislation.

Objectives

D.6   A negative cycle has developed in which criminal offences are continually created to help regulatory objectives to be achieved, but many of those offences are then rarely, if ever, prosecuted. This is in part because when the offences are used they may often involve a waste of time and resources and the penalty imposed by the courts may be small compared with the cost of bringing the prosecution. The Government response is often then simply to create 'improved' versions of these criminal offences. Our objectives are to break this negative cycle.

(1)   To modernise law enforcement, by replacing criminal offences in regulatory contexts with civil measures.

(2)   To reduce the role of the courts at the front line of regulatory enforcement.

(3)   To make the law fairer to those subject to regulation, especially smaller businesses.

(4)   To remove or replace outmoded doctrines of criminal liability applicable to businesses, especially when they are unduly harsh on small businesses.

Scale and context

D.7   A substantial proportion of the new offences mentioned above underpin regulatory contexts that did not exist in the same form or on the same scale many years ago, such as environmental care or animal welfare. Yet, these offences are rarely prosecuted. For example, section 8 of the Asylum and Immigration Act 1996, which prohibited the employment of illegal migrant workers, saw on average only one prosecution a year between 1998 and 2004.

D.8   Consequently the steep increase in numbers of criminal offences since 1997 has not led to a corresponding increase in prosecutions and convictions. In 1997, 2 million defendants were proceeded against in magistrates' courts, but in 2008, only 1.64 million faced prosecution (Criminal Statistics: England and Wales 2008). In the Crown Court there was some increase from 80,000 defendants facing prosecution in 1997, to 89,000 in 2008, but that increase may in large measure simply reflect a greater number of cases being transferred from the magistrates' court.

D.9 The total of those found guilty in both kinds of courts put together was 1.49 million in 1997, but only 1.36 million in 2008. If a very large number of offences is being created, but these offences are not being used, resources put into creating them may be being wasted. Further, ordinary people are being subjected to an ever increasing numbers of what in all probability will turn out to be illusory or empty threats of criminal prosecution.

D.10 A rough estimate, (based on an analysis of categories of offences dealt with in the criminal courts in 2008) is that only 1.5 to 2.0% of defendants tried in the Crown Court, and about 10% of defendants tried in the magistrates' courts, are tried for offences arising out of regulatory contexts (excluding motoring offences).

D.11 In recent years there have been a number of initiatives encouraging regulators to move away from reliance on criminal prosecution as a means of securing regulatory compliance. For example the Macrory report (*Regulatory Justice: Making Sanctions Effective*, November 2006) recommended that greater use should be made of administrative sanctions and Part 3 of the Regulatory Enforcement and Sanctions Act 2008 provides for a minister to confer on a regulator the power to impose a range of civil sanctions.

D.12 It is anticipated that as a result of these initiatives the number of prosecutions of regulatory offences in the magistrates' court is likely to fall further. The impact assessment for the Regulatory Enforcement and Sanctions Bill anticipated that as a result of its introduction the number of criminal prosecutions brought by "a regulator" would be reduced from 900 a year to 360. Our proposals would provide another piece of the jigsaw in reducing reliance upon the criminal law in regulatory contexts and consequently contribute to the trend of diminishing reliance upon prosecutions to secure regulatory compliance.

Policy options and option appraisal

Option 0: do nothing

D.13 This option would avoid the costs involved in abolishing offences that do not make a significant contribution to underpinning regulatory enforcement. However, in respect of the creation of future regulatory offences there would be no significant saving in maintaining current practice, since it is assumed that there is no significant additional cost involved in providing for civil sanctions in legislation as opposed to criminal offences.

D.14 However there are costs associated with leaving unnecessary and inappropriate offences on the statute book: the statute book would continue to be cluttered with unused offences and would be unnecessarily unwieldy, making searches of legislation slow and difficult. It would also make the risks of non-compliance more difficult to assess.

D.15 By continuing to rely on the criminal law for the enforcement of relatively minor regulatory breaches, regulators will incur unnecessary cost in an often ineffective enforcement mechanism. In the light of changes in practice following Macrory and the provisions of the Regulatory Enforcement and Sanctions Act 2008, it is anticipated that such reliance on criminal prosecution will diminish but that the removal of existing unnecessary and inappropriate regulatory criminal offences from the statute book, and avoiding their creation in future, will further contribute to this.

***Option 1: replacement of low-level criminal offences by non-criminal
measures***

D.16   Under our proposals, criminal offences would have to be created by primary
legislation (statute). It would no longer be possible for regulatory authorities to
create criminal offences under powers delegated to them, even with the approval
of MoJ. However, under our proposals, criminal offences would involve only
serious wrongdoing of a kind appropriately dealt with in primary legislation; that
is, wrongdoing which is intentional, knowing, reckless or dishonest. As regards
existing low-level criminal offences, we propose that where the introduction of a
civil penalty would do as much to secure appropriate levels of punishment and
deterrence they should be repealed. The effect of these proposals would be
increased reliance by departments on non-criminal civil measures, such as civil
penalties, formal warnings, and prohibition or 'stop now' notices, to achieve their
enforcement goals, as envisaged by the Macrory report in 2006. We believe this
would lead to a fairer, more efficient and more cost-effective system of regulatory
enforcement across departments.

D.17   Beyond this, we have some additional proposals. Since the effect of these would
be to limit the scope of criminal liability and/or reflect current best-practice, while
reducing uncertainty, the cost of these proposals is believed to be negligible

D.18   The first additional proposal is that individual directors should not be criminally
liable personally for offences committed by their companies unless they
'consented or connived' at the commission of those offences. Mere negligence on
an individual director's part should not be enough to establish personal criminal
liability for the company's offence. Implementing this proposal would require
legislation. A further consideration is whether there is sufficient justification for the
creation of a separate offence of 'failing to prevent' the offence committed by the
company, an option that would also require legislation.

D.19   Secondly, the criminal law doctrine of 'delegation' is criticised. This doctrine
makes it possible to find someone liable for an offence committed by someone to
whom they have delegated the running of their business. Liability will arise even if
the business owner expressly instructed the person to whom the business was
delegated not to commit the offence in question. The paper asks whether it would
be fairer to establish liability on the basis that the business owner failed to
prevent the commission of the offence by the person to whom the running of the
business was delegated. Implementing this option would require legislation.

D.20   Thirdly the 'identification' doctrine is considered as a basis for making companies
liable for criminal offences involving proof of fault. The doctrine requires someone
at directorial level to have possessed the fault in question, if the company is to be
criminally liable. The doctrine can operate unduly harshly in cases where small
firms are charged with criminal offences. This is because it is always more likely
that directors (or equivalent persons) in such firms will have personal knowledge
of all the companies' activities, unlike the directors of large firms. The paper
encourages the courts not to apply the identification doctrine unless the statutory
context shows that it was Parliament's intention that it should govern the
imposition of criminal liability. This proposal does not require legislation.

D.21 Fourthly and finally, it is suggested that the courts be given a power to apply a 'due diligence' defence to criminal offences created by statute that would otherwise permit, in whole or in part, criminal liability to be established without proof of fault on the defendant's part. In appropriate cases, the courts would permit someone to be acquitted if that person could show that he or she had exercised due diligence in all the circumstances to avoid committing the offence. This new defence would in effect replace the so-called 'presumption of fault' that is currently applied by the courts – with no degree of consistency – to some offences that would otherwise impose liability without proven fault. We believe that the due diligence defence would prove to be much more effective in securing that, where appropriate, people are only convicted when they were at fault, whilst avoiding the imposition of undue burdens on the prosecution. This option would require legislation.

Option 2: a general administrative offence

D.22 This option is an ambitious one with the potential to have effects well beyond regulatory contexts. It involves the creation of a new 'middle tier' type of offence, falling between criminal offences and private civil actions. Such offences are not uncommon in mainland European jurisdictions. As an administrative offence is not a criminal offence, the burden of proof on the prosecuting authority would not be as onerous. In effect, it would be a generalised version of the civil penalties currently used only in specific contexts in England and Wales, as in the case of parking fines. Departments would be obliged to consider whether a proposed offence should fall within the administrative offence regime, or should be a criminal offence. It would be possible to say that any offence punishable only by a specified maximum fine must be an administrative offence.

D.23 We believe that the cost of creating a whole new category of offences, including establishing rules of procedure, evidence and possibly specialist tribunals would represent a disproportionate cost as compared with the benefit anticipated.

COST AND BENEFIT ANALYSIS

D.24 This impact assessment identifies both monetised and non-monetised impacts on individuals, groups and businesses in the UK, with the aim of understanding what the overall impact to society might be from implementing these options. The costs and benefits of each option are compared to the do nothing option. Impact assessments place a strong emphasis on valuing the costs and benefits in monetary terms (including estimating the value of goods and services that are not traded). However there are important aspects that cannot sensibly be monetised. These might include how the proposal impacts differently on particular groups of society or changes in equity and fairness, either positive or negative.

Option 0: do nothing

Costs

D.25 Each time an offence is taken to court there is the risk that the substantial investment of time and money will produce an inadequate return, even if – and this can by no means be guaranteed – a conviction is obtained. The court may impose a fine that does not fully reflect the damage done or the seriousness of the wrong, because the court is insufficiently familiar with the context in which these matters fall to be measured.

D.26 This option is inconsistent with Government acceptance of the Macrory report, which recommended reduced reliance on criminal procedures in regulatory enforcement.

D.27 Because the do nothing option is compared against itself its costs and benefits are necessarily zero, as is its Net Present Value (NPV). The NPV shows the total net value of a project over a specific time period. The value of the costs and benefits in an NPV are adjusted to account for inflation and the fact that we generally value benefits that are provided now more than we value the same benefits provided in the future.

Option 1: replacement of low level criminal offences by non-criminal measures

D.28 We have calculated the costs and benefits of the main proposal of option one, as discussed in paragraph D.11.

Costs

TRANSITIONAL COSTS

Departmental drafting and procedure

D.29 Departments would have to identify offences that should be replaced by civil measures, and ensure that those civil measures were in place. Legislation might be necessary in some cases (although not all) to introduce the civil measures. It is unlikely that the criminal offences could be abolished before the civil measures were introduced. There is a cost associated with the repeal of existing unnecessary and inappropriate criminal offences. Although it is always possible simply to leave the offences on the statute book and let them fall into disuse, to do so would mean that the benefits of de-cluttering the statute book would be lost and the risk of their inappropriate use as a means of securing regulatory compliance would remain.

Setting up tribunals

D.30 There would not be a need for new tribunals, or for increased use of existing tribunals, unless these are introduced as an extra safeguard against inappropriate use of a civil measure, although we anticipate that existing tribunals could be used for this purpose.

Training

D.31 Enforcement officers in some departments may need training in the use of civil measures, as opposed to taking criminal prosecutions, in so far as they do not already have such training.

Legal Uncertainty

D.32 If new offences are introduced, such as a failure to prevent an offence being committed by someone to whom the running of a business has been delegated, there may be cases taken to the higher courts to determine the scope of the offence. However, after this possible non-recurring spike in litigation it is anticipated that our proposals will result in greater certainty and consequently fewer appeals.

ON-GOING COSTS

Increased enforcement cost to regulatory bodies

D.33　A large proportion of the costs of regulatory enforcement will transfer from the courts to the regulatory bodies. However, the courts will retain jurisdiction for the more severe cases and also for repeat offenders. There will still be recourse to the courts on appeal, but we assume that the rate of appeals will remain low. The impact assessment on the Regulatory Enforcement and Sanctions Bill assesses appeals to regulatory prosecutions at 2%.

D.34　The estimated costs for regulatory bodies following the repeal of low-level criminal offences and the replacement of prosecutions with non-criminal measures is based on the number of prosecutions within the magistrates' court and Crown Court in 2008 (See Table 1). In 2008, 89,000 defendants faced prosecution in the Crown Court, of which 1.5% are estimated to have been regulatory cases. During this period 1.64 million faced prosecution in the magistrates' courts, of which an estimated 10% related to regulatory matters. The estimate provided in Table 1 is based on the following assumptions

(1)　The magistrates' courts represent a lower cost option and mainly hear the less serious regulatory cases.

(2)　1% to 5% of cases relating to regulatory matters currently dealt with by way of prosecution in the magistrates' courts would instead be dealt with by way of civil sanctions administered by regulators.　2% is the best estimate. This is relatively low because it is assumed that a large proportion of cases that would otherwise be caught by our proposals will be dealt with by way of civil sanctions by virtue of Macrory's recommendations and the alternatives to prosecution available under the Regulatory Enforcement and Sanctions Act 2008.

(3)　0% to 5% of cases relating to regulatory matters currently dealt with by way of prosecution in the Crown Court would instead be dealt with by.way of civil sanctions administered by regulators.　1% is the best estimate. This lower percentage reflects the greater seriousness of cases heard in the Crown Court including those relating to serial offenders which would make many of them less suitable to be dealt with by way of civil sanction.

(4)　There is a 10% increase in the number of cases dealt with by way of civil sanctions as compared with the number dealt with by way of prosecution because these are more straight-forward and more cost-effective.

(5)　The administrative cost of issuing a low level civil sanction, such as a fixed penalty notice, is £600. This corresponds to the estimated cost associated with a warning letter. A more severe civil sanction, such as a stop notice, costs the regulator £2,200. In line with current trends we have assumed that 90% of the sanctions will be low level and 10% will be more severe (the average cost of each sanction would therefore be £760). See *DEFRA's impact assessment of the fairer and better environmental enforcement proposals* (Table A, p 12).

D.35   Using £760 as the estimated cost of pursuing civil penalties in cases that would currently be dealt with in the courts, a best estimate of annual enforcement costs to departments is £2,753,000.

Table 1: Estimated annual enforcement cost to regulators

	Low	Best	High
Magistrates' Court	1%	2%	5%
Annual Cases	1,804	3,608	9,020
Annual Cost @ £760	£1,371,040	£2,742,080	£6,855,200
Crown Court	0%	1%	5%
Annual Cases	0	15	73
Annual Cost @ £760	£0	£11,161	£55,803
Total			
Annual Cases	1,804	3,623	9,093
Annual Cost	**£1,371,040**	**£2,753,241**	**£6,911,003**

Challenges to court interpretation

D.36   Uncertainty is associated with: (i) change to the way in which the doctrine of identification is to be used by the courts; and (ii) the introduction of a defence of due diligence. It is possible that the changes will generate an increased number of challenges to trial courts' interpretations of the basis of corporate liability, and to the decision to apply, or not to apply, a due diligence defence. At present the number of cases in which such issues are litigated in the higher courts is very small. There are up to five cases reported in the Law Reports annually.

Continued training

D.37   There will be a continuing need to train enforcement officers in the use of civil measures, as opposed to undertaking prosecutions, in so far as this is not being done already.

Increased compliance costs

D.38   We have assumed that it is mostly businesses, rather than individuals, who are affected by regulatory offences. They might face higher and more frequent fines in the form of fixed penalty notices than if criminal prosecution were relied on as the sole or main enforcement tool, which could reflect in increased insurance costs. Conversely, the risk of prosecution and consequently of stigma associated with criminal conviction would be reduced.

D.39   In 2008, 99.2% of all businesses in the UK were small businesses (under 50 employees) (BERR). There is a concern that small businesses carry a disproportionately large share of the regulatory burden (Macrory report, p 6). If compliance costs increase there might be a further burden on small businesses.

The cost of regulatory awareness is fixed, and if compliance costs have a fixed cost component (as they often do), then awareness and compliance becomes relatively more expensive for smaller companies.

D.40 Small businesses could also be disproportionally affected by an increase in penalties. They may already be more compliant with regulation, as even the (typically relatively low) fines under the existing prosecution regime are a bigger deterrent to them. Additionally, as they are smaller, they are less able to budget for and absorb irregular costs. Macrory acknowledges that small businesses are disproportionally affected by fines as *"each type of business can have significantly different abilities to pay and absorb financial penalties"*. There are concerns in industry that smaller businesses might not have the resources to challenge a penalty, which could be problematic if the business cannot absorb the penalty

Benefits

ON-GOING BENEFITS

Savings to Her Majesty's Court Service and prosecuting authorities

D.41 In general, civil procedures are less expensive to enforce and are more efficient as measured through the reduced use of court resources. The savings to Her Majesty's Court Service (HMCS) and prosecuting authorities from not carrying out criminal prosecutions of regulatory offences are estimated using data from MoJ estimates and DEFRA's *impact assessment of the fairer and better environmental enforcement proposals* (Table A, p 12).

D.42 The estimated cost savings to regulators in Table 2 are based on the following assumptions:

(1) The reduction in the number of prosecutions is calculated using the same assumptions as were used for Table 1, but there is no 10% adjustment for increased usage.

(2) The best estimate for the cost savings to the regulators of a prosecution in the magistrates' court is £2,888. This is the mid-point of the range between £175, the estimated cost to the Crown Prosecution Service (CPS) and £5,600, the average cost to the regulator of an investigation and prosecution.

The CPS estimate is used as the smallest potential saving. This is because the CPS has systems in place for high volume prosecutions which may mean that there are economies of scale that may not be available to smaller regulatory prosecuting bodies. It does not take into account the costs of investigation and is therefore an underestimate.

The figure for the highest potential saving, £5,600, comes from DEFRA. It is an average of the cost for a prosecution in the magistrate's court and in the Crown Court, so is an overestimation of the cost of a prosecution in the magistrates' court. It includes the cost of investigating the offence.

(3) For the cost savings to regulators in avoiding a prosecution in the Crown Court we have used a range of £2,435, estimate cost to the CPS (which

again does not include the cost of investigation), to £5,600, the average legal cost to a regulator of a prosecution and investigation. Since this figure from DEFRA represents the average cost of a prosecution brought whether in the Crown Court or magistrates' courts, it is also an underestimate. The best estimate is the mid-point of £4,018.

Table 2: Estimated annual cost savings to regulators

	Low	*Best*	*High*
Magistrates' Court	1%	2%	5%
Annual Cases	1,640	3,280	8,200
Saving per Case	£175	£2,888	£5,600
Annual Saving	£287,000	£9,471,000	£45,920,000
Crown Court	0%	1%	5%
Annual Cases	0	13	67
Saving per Case	£2,435	£4,018	£5,600
Annual Saving	£0	£53,634	£373,800
Total			
Annual Cases	1640	3293	8267
Annual Saving	**£287,000**	**£9,524,634**	**£46,293,800**

D.43   The best estimate of the annual gross savings to regulators is £9,525,000.

D.44   The estimated cost savings to the criminal justice system in Table 3 are based on the following assumptions:

(1)   The estimated reduction in prosecutions is the same as in Table 2.

(2)   In some cases the costs may fall on the defendant, not the Legal Services Commission (LSC). However we have assumed that the costs are the same.

(3)   Costs to HMCS depend on whether a plea is an early guilty plea (EGP) or another type of plea. Based on current trends we have used a range of 30% to 70% for EGPs in the magistrates' court and Crown Court. Our best estimate is that half of all pleas are EGPs.

(4)   The cost of a prosecution is comprised of the estimated costs to the LSC and HMCS. We have assumed that 40% of cases in the magistrates' court are indictable offences and 60% are summary offences.

(5)   We do not have information of the costs to the LSC of summary offences, so we have used costs of shoplifting cases as a proxy. This is a suitable proxy because it is a simple indictable case. The average cost to the LSC

for a prosecution in the magistrates' court is estimated at £333.

(6)   The best estimate of the cost to the HMCS of a prosecution in the magistrates' court is £922, taking account of the split between summary and indictable offences, and between EGP and other pleas. The range is £638 to £1,206.

(7)   Cost to LSC per defendant of the prosecution of an indictable offence in the Crown Court is estimated at £4,579.

(8)   The best estimate of the cost to the HMCS of a prosecution in the Crown Court, taking into account the split between EGP and other pleas, is £6,319. The range is £4,404 to £8234.

Table 3: Estimated annual cost savings to the criminal justice system

	Low	*Best*	*High*
Magistrates' Court	1%	2%	5%
Annual Cases	1,640	3,280	8,200
Saving Per Case	£971	£1,255	£1,539
Annual Saving	£1,591,686	£4,116,072	£12,621,932
Crown Court	0%	1%	5%
Annual Cases	0	13	67
Saving Per Case	£8,983	£10,898	£12,813
Annual Saving	£0	£145,488	£855,254
Total			
Annual Cases	1,640	3,293	8,267
Annual Saving	**£1,591,686**	**£4,261,560**	**£13,477,186**

D.45   The best estimate of the annual gross savings to the criminal justice system is £4,262,000.

Enhanced deterrence effect

D.46   There may be a general deterrence effect from civil penalties, which will be easier to enforce and will probably attract higher fines than current criminal penalties. The deterrent effect of sanctions is determined by the severity of the sanction and the probability of it being applied. There is the potential that both of these will increase under our proposals.

D.47   MoJ suggests that for non-custodial sentences a minor level of general deterrence, 0% to 2% should be assumed for significant alterations in sentence.

Avoidance of the cost of creating criminal offences

D.48   The creation of criminal offences involves a cost. Government departments are required to consult with each other, as well as, in many instances, consulting with businesses and others who may be affected by any proposed offence. Any new offence must, of course, comply with Article 6 of the European Convention on Human Rights (as well as with the other Articles), and so the time and effort of Parliament's Joint Select Committee on Human Rights may be involved.

Avoidance of delay and uncertainty as regards sentencing

D.49   Once created, even relatively low-level criminal offences may not be cheap to enforce, and preparation for trial may involve considerable delay. The standard of proof that must be met means that convictions may not be easy to obtain even in simple cases, and the discretion the courts have over sentence means that the consequences of a conviction cannot easily be predicted. In the case of the aforementioned section 8 of the Asylum and Immigration Act 1996, the cost of staff time involved in a prosecution was estimated at between £1,000 and £2,000, but fines obtained upon conviction tended to be less than £1,000.

Favourable perception compliance effect

D.50   The perception of law is more likely to be influential in affecting compliance for crimes that are morally and socially ambiguous, easier to commit and that carry less severe punishment. The type of illegal behaviour that this 'perception effect' would apply to low-level fraud and tax evasion, copyright infringement, non-severe traffic violations, littering, petty theft and general anti-social behaviour. This was supported by a study by Nadler (See J Nadler, "Flouting the Law", (2005) 83 *Texas Law Review* 1399).

D.51   Such crimes are generally considered as less immoral when compared with violent crime, for example, and are more difficult to detect. Even if the perception effect could only be applied to these types of crime, there would still be a significant economic and social benefit from an improvement in the perception of the law governing regulatory offences. If an improvement led to a greater willingness to comply, that outcome would impact favourably where the law is used to try to achieve a reduction in greenhouse gas and an improvement of wider environmental issues.

Greater predictability and consistency in outcome

D.52   In general, civil measures are less expensive to enforce. In the case of section 8 of the Asylum and Immigration Act 1996, enforcement of the civil measure is about £500, which is roughly half that of taking a criminal case. Moreover, where civil measures take the form of fixed penalties, the outcomes are clearly more predictable than when the amount of any fine falls to be determined by the courts at their discretion.

Net impact

D.53   Option 1 is intended to provide a cheaper and more predictable alternative to the creation of and reliance on criminal offences. The capacity of option 1 to generate savings depends in part on how vigorously departments are prepared to implement this option, in so far as they can. From a business point of view, the outcome should be that businesses will have a greater degree of certainty about the likely outcome of wrongdoing, in, for example, the case of fixed penalties. Procedures should also prove to be faster than they are in the criminal courts.

Table 4: Estimated net impact of option 1

	Low	Best	High
Savings to Regulators	£287,000	£9,524,634	£46,293,800
Savings to Criminal Justice System	£1,591,686	£4,261,560	£13,477,186
Total Savings	*£1,878,686*	*£13,786,194*	*£59,770,986*
Total Costs	*£1,371,040*	*£2,753,241*	*£6,911,003*
Total Annual Savings	**£507,646**	**£11,032,953**	**£52,859,983**

Risks

(1)   There is a moderate risk that fewer offences than anticipated will turn out to be appropriately dealt with by non-criminal penalties, and thus that there will be fewer savings than might otherwise have been the case.

(2)   There is a risk that wider use of a due diligence defence, that puts the burden on the defendant to prove that due diligence was exercised, will increase business costs in the relevant sector. However it is anticipated that few cases will be affected.

(3)   There is a small risk that there may be a larger increase in appeals than has been assumed, especially if the system is not transparent. LSC and HMCS would bear some of this cost.

Option 2: a general administrative offence

Costs

TRANSITIONAL COSTS

Departmental drafting and procedure

D.54   A new category of offences, in the form of administrative offences, would have to be created, and the nature and limits of these offences determined. A procedural framework and rules would also have to be devised for prosecuting and defending with respect to the new offences.

Setting up tribunals

D.55   It is possible that a new network of tribunals would be required to handle administrative offences, if the use of the magistrates' court is thought to make these offences too close to the criminal offences they are meant to be replacing.

Training

D.56   Those operating the system of administrative offences would need to be trained in the new procedures, whether they were prosecutors, judges or defence advocates. Some training for court staff might also be necessary. As an administrative offence scheme would be a nation-wide scheme, these training costs would be incurred at all court centres.

Legal Uncertainty

D.57   As with any new scheme, it is difficult to predict the extent to which an administrative offence scheme would be faced by legal challenges to its procedures, either in general, or in relation to decisions taken in particular cases. To some extent such uncertainties can be reduced by limiting in law the opportunities that exist to challenge the procedure, but such limitations may themselves be open to challenge, for example, under human rights legislation.

ON-GOING COSTS

D.58   A system of administrative penalties would create an entirely new problem for debate within departments and in Parliament: how should a prospective offence be categorised, or re-categorised (criminal, or administrative)? Adding in this way to the questions that must be considered before offences are created will slow down the process of legislation.

Benefits

CONSISTENCY IN APPROACH

D.59   This option has the potential to bring some consistency of approach across departments. In theory, each department would be dealing with the same unit of account in tackling wrongful behaviour other than through the criminal law or civil measures, namely the administrative offence. This might send a clearer, less ambiguous message to the public about what is at stake than other kinds of non-criminal enforcement mechanism.

Risks

(1)   Simply categorising an offence as administrative will not prevent it being challenged in the European Court of Human Rights as essentially criminal in nature. It therefore cannot be assumed that the creation of an administrative offence regime will produce the certainty and clarity of distinction from criminal offences that is desired. Although a scheme of administrative offences may introduce consistency of approach across departments, the downside of such consistency is inflexibility. The range of contexts subject to regulation is now very diverse. Forcing departments to choose between criminal penalties or administrative penalties may fail to accommodate the need for diversity in enforcement policy in different areas.

(2)   There is a risk that administrative offences will be liked by neither departments nor those subject to them. They may be perceived as falling between two stools, being neither criminal nor civil in nature, and thus might come to be regarded as lacking legitimacy. There is a risk that they will simply replicate the task currently done in some areas by civil

penalties, causing confusion that introduces ambiguity into the message received by the public about the function of administrative offences.

Summary of options

D.60 Option 0 involves continuing with the current policy of using low-level criminal offences to deal with less serious wrongdoing, an option that involves higher costs and greater delay when it comes to enforcement. Option 1 involves replacing low-level criminal offences with a flexible range of civil measures for departments to tackle less serious wrongdoing, measures that should prove cheaper and faster to put into effect. Option 1 is preferred because it would free departments to devise measures in such a way as to meet the demands of the particular context. Criminal offences would be reserved for intentional, reckless or dishonest wrongdoing of a kind that could warrant a prison sentence or unlimited fine. Option 2 involves creating a new 'administrative offence' regime for low-level offending. This option involves less flexibility, although it may create a clearer message about how wrongdoing is regarded and categorised for the general public. However, there is a risk that it will prove too difficult to distinguish administrative offences from civil penalties or other non-criminal measures. It is believed that option 2 would be extremely costly to implement and unlikely to deliver benefits in proportion to this cost.

Questions

(1)　We think that, after taking into account a reduction in prosecutions for regulatory breaches post Macrory, about 1% of remaining regulatory cases from the Crown Court could reasonably be dealt with by way of civil sanction instead under our proposals. Do you agree?

(2)　We think that, after taking into account a reduction in prosecutions for regulatory breaches post Macrory, about 2% of remaining regulatory cases currently heard within magistrates' courts could reasonably be dealt with by way of civil sanction instead under our proposals. Do you agree?

(3)　We think that there will be a net benefit from option 1 for small businesses. Do you agree?

(4)　It is assumed that the monetised impact of the proposed changes to aspects of the basis corporate liability is likely to be minimal. Do you agree?